Secrecy

Secrecy

A Cross-Cultural Perspective

Edited by
Stanton K. Tefft, Ph.D.
Wake Forest University
Winston-Salem, N.C.

HUMAN SCIENCES PRESS
72 Fifth Avenue   3 Henrietta Street
NEW YORK, NY 10011 ● LONDON, WC2E 8LU

Copyright © 1980 by Human Sciences Press, Inc.
72 Fifth Avenue, New York, New York 10011

All rights reserved. No part of this work may be reproduced or utilized in any form or by any means, electronic or mechanical, including photocopying, microfilm and recording, or by any information storage and retrieval system without permission in writing from the publisher.

Printed in the United States of America
0123456789 987654321

Library of Congress Cataloging in Publication Data

Main entry under title:

Secrecy, a cross-cultural perspective.

  Bibliography
  Includes index.
  1. Secrecy (Psychology) 2. Privacy, Right of.
3. Official secrets. I. Tefft, Stanton K.
HM291.S392   322.44'8   LC 79-25454
ISBN 0-87705-442-8
ISBN 0-87705-443-6 pbk.

Contents

Editor's Preface	7
General Introduction	13
Acknowledgments	19

UNIT 1. THE DIMENSIONS OF SECRECY
Introduction — 23
1. Privacy and Secrecy: A Conceptual Comparison
   Carol Warren and Barbara Laslett — 25
2. Secrecy, Disclosure and Social Theory
   Stanton K. Tefft — 35

UNIT 2. ASPECTS OF PRIVACY
Introduction — 77
3. Exposure and Seclusion: A Study of Institutionalized Isolation Among the Mehinaku Indians of Brazil
   Thomas Gregor — 81
4. Privacy, Intimacy and Shame in a French Community
   Jeffrey S. Victor — 100

UNIT 3. THE POLITICS OF SECRECY
Introduction — 119
5. On Secrecy and the Control of Knowledge: Taos Pueblo
   Elizabeth Brandt — 123

6. Bizango: A Voodoo Secret Society in Haiti
   Michel S. Laguerre 147
7. The Management of Secrecy: The Ku Klux Klan's Successful Secret
   Richard T. Schaefer 161
8. The Dynamics of Military Conspiracy
   Kenneth Fidel 178

UNIT 4. SECRECY IN BUSINESS
Introduction 201
9. Hunt and Conceal: Information Management in Newfoundland Deep-Sea Trawler Fishing
   Raoul Andersen 205
10. Secrecy in Business: A Sociological View
    Brian J. O'Connell 229

UNIT 5. BUREAUCRATIC SECRECY
Introduction 247
11. Secrecy as an Organizational Control Strategy: Police Planning for a National Political Convention
    Patricia E. Erickson and James Flynn 251
12. Secrecy, Intelligence and Community: The U.S. Intelligence Community
    Fred Kaiser 273
13. Toward a Sociology of Secrecy and Security Systems
    Ritchie P. Lowry 297

UNIT 6. A COMPARATIVE PERSPECTIVE
14. Secrecy as a Social and Political Process
    Stanton K. Tefft 319

INDEX 347

Editor's Preface

Within the last decade we have seen government secrecy employed not in the interests of rational and efficient administration but to circumvent existing laws and to subvert democratic values either in the interests of political ambition or in the guise of "protecting national security." Increasingly such political secrecy has enabled government agencies to operate as semiautonomous bodies, less and less responsible to the people and their governmental representatives.

Recent revelations also suggest that giant corporations have not just concealed "trade secrets" from competitors but have hidden violations of the law that such corporations have perpetrated to increase their profits. And if it suits their purposes these giant businesses have concealed vital economic information from their own government, thereby making it more difficult for government economic planners to control corporation activities detrimental to the national economy. More startling is the fact that both the government and private business have, on many occasions, been secret collaborators in political intrigue aimed at overthrowing foreign governments considered hostile to their common interests.

These events have precipitated a passionate debate by scholars as well as politicians over the following secrecy issues: What constitutes the necessary balance between government secrecy and openness in democratic society? What is the appropriate role of intelligence agencies in national and international affairs? Are the dangers to personal privacy growing? Is the growth of such dangers inevitable? Is secrecy an inherent part of private and governmental bureaucracy in both democratic and totalitarian systems? Does it constitute a dysfunctional element only in democratic systems? Or does secrecy within any political system promote maladaptation?

Our preoccupation with these disclosures involving political secrecy makes us unaware of the role secrecy plays in the day-to-day social life of all human communities. To understand the social function of secrecy we must not only concern ourselves with political secrecy but also with privacy and the relations between the two. To what extent does privacy operate as a defense against the state's increasing intrusion on private life activities? Is such privacy vital to the well-being of the community and its members? Compared to the small peasant or tribal community, do the citizens of modern states have more or less privacy? If privacy has diminished within modern political communities, why is this the case?

On these and other secrecy issues social scientists can give us new perspectives. Their research enables us to not only view such problems of secrecy and privacy in the perspective of history but also cross-culturally. To understand the functions and dysfunctions of secrecy in modern society, we must also study its past and present role in different Western and non-Western societies.

Unfortunately, students have no ready source available if they are interested in such a cross-cultural analysis of secrecy. Much of the recent research on the topic is unpublished. Published research has often appeared in various obscure journals; to some of these the student has little access. Of course, there have been a few collections or readers published on secrecy but they are confined to a narrow aspect of the problem (e.g., *Secret Societies,* Norman MacKenzie (editor) Collier Books, 1971; *Secret Societies in Ireland,* T. Desmond Morris (editor) Barnes and Noble, 1973; *None of Your Business,* Norman Dorsen and Stephen Gillers (editors) Viking Press, 1974; *The Lawless State,* Morton Halperin, et al., Penguin, 1976; *Secrecy and Foreign Policy,* Thomas M. Franck and Edward Weisband (editors) Oxford, 1974; *Government Secrecy in Democracies,* Itzhak Galnoor (editor) Harper, 1977; *Freedom vs. National Security,* Morton Halperin and Daniel Hoffman (editors) Chelsea, 1977; *The Right to Privacy,* Grant McClellan (editor) H. W. Wilson, 1976; *Privacy,* John B. Young (editor) John Wiley, 1978). None of these collections presents a historical and cross-cultural analysis of secrecy.

The collection of papers published here, taken as a whole, present students with a broader analysis of secrecy issues than has previously been given them in other edited volumes. Included in the collection are papers written by scholars from various social science disciplines on a wide range of topics. These selections include an analysis of the secrecy process in both Western and non-Western cultures and within industrial, peasant, and tribal societies. Included also are several comparative papers showing the similar adaptive or maladaptive operations of secrecy in modern and premodern society.

The secrecy process operates on all levels of sociopolitical organization (e.g., interpersonal, interfamily, interorganizational, interstate). It involves the interaction of various social mechanisms that prevent disclosure of secrets or that go into operation when unauthorized disclosure occurs. The articles in this book are organized so that the student can study the operation of the secrecy process at the various levels of socio-political complexity, not only in modern society, but in tribal and peasant society also.

Papers in Unit I give the student an introduction and overview to secrecy issues or topics discussed in later units. Distinctions are made between different types of secrecy. After a critical review of the social science contributions to a theoretical understanding of the secrecy process, Unit I discusses the advantages a conflict model can give students in their analysis of secrecy.

Unit II is concerned with the issue of privacy. The papers provide a contrast between a Western and non-Western society in regard to the motives for protecting personal secrets and the means for achieving privacy. Through privacy the French maintain their highly valued individual freedom while the South American Mehinaku Indians employ secrecy to avoid disruption of community relationships. In both these communities there are established procedures for maintaining privacy.

In contrast to Unit II where secrecy was employed to achieve largely personal goals, Unit III deals with groups whose secrets are vital to the perpetuation of the association or organization. For most secret associations secrecy is either an end in itself or an inherent element in the organizational structure without which the group would not or could not exist. The goals of secret orders, associations, or conspiratorial organizations discussed in Unit III differ. They may be conformative secret societies whose leaders maintain or defend the traditional basis of power or alienative secret organizations whose goals are to subvert the political status quo or resist established authority. In all cases, however, secrecy is crucial to the fulfillment of the organization's goal and to its continued existence.

Secrecy is also an important strategy employed by business organizations in economic competition with each other. The role that secrecy performs in economic affairs is discussed in Unit IV. Even in small-scale economic enterprises, economic competition can generate deceptive practices. One example is presented in the article on Newfoundland deep-sea trawler fishing. However, secrecy employed by giant business corporations in capitalist societies has a more significant impact on the well-being and livelihood of the citizens. In this unit the role of secrecy in the internal and external operations of U.S. business corporations is discussed. The economic consequences of such secrecy for the nation are analyzed and a program for reform is presented.

The secrecy dynamics of governmental bureaucracy at both the local and national level is discussed in Unit V. As the papers in this unit demonstrate, there are clear parallels between the objectives of national intelligence agencies and a local police intelligence unit in Kansas City, Missouri; all these intelligence units operate to predict, control, and manipulate their environments. Moreover, all such intelligence organizations must deal with similar problems of internal and external security. The papers in this unit discuss how intelligence agencies maintain such security as well as suggest some of the maladaptive functions of such security systems within intelligence organizations as well as other governmental agencies.

In Unit VI the editor presents a cross-cultural analysis of the secrecy process showing that, regardless of the culture, secrecy is an important aspect of all social relationships. By giving examples from different cultures, both historic and modern, the author shows the recurrent interrelationship between secrecy/security, espionage, persuasion and evaluation processes. While the institutional mechanisms through which these secrecy processes operate may be unique to particular cultures, the processes themselves seem to be universal.

I would like to close this preface by thanking the contributors to this volume for their patience since the project has taken longer than any of us expected or desired. To the authors who have revised their papers in order to make them conform to the requirements of the book I give special thanks.

Stanton K. Tefft

Winston-Salem, North Carolina
Fall 1978

General Introduction

The papers published in *Secrecy: A Cross-Cultural Perspective* focus on various secrecy issues in different historical, cultural, community, political, and organizational contexts. While the central problem dealt with in this collection involves the concealment of information about events, acts, or relationships (secrecy), each author is concerned with a different aspect of secrecy and each employs different concepts and theoretical models to analyze the secrecy phenomenon.

Nonetheless, there are theoretical and conceptual issues that are of common concern to the authors of these papers: Are there different forms of secrecy and do they have different social and political functions? Who collaborates in keeping secrets and why? What are the dangers of disclosure? Under what circumstances do outsiders employ espionage to discover secrets? How is espionage carried out? What security procedures are used to protect secrets? What factors determine the success and failure of security systems? What is the response to security failures? Under what circumstances does secrecy prove to be dysfunctional to an organization or lead to conditions that promote community maladaptation?

What are secrets and how do we classify different types of secrecy? There is less apparent agreement here than one might imagine. Some contributors stress distinctions between privacy and secrecy, with privacy involving voluntary concealment and secrecy involving obligatory concealment. Disputing these distinctions, other authors place their emphasis on the nature of the facts or relationships concealed, that is, whether they are moral-neutral or legal (privacy) or immoral or illegal (secrecy). To claim, as some writers do, that secrecy is goal-oriented while privacy exists for intrinsic satisfaction alone seems an inaccurate way to distinguish the two. Most contributors treat secrecy as a formal, conscious, and deliberate concealment of information.

Thoughts or feelings that people are incapable of communicating to others are not secrets. Secrecy is established to protect information or to conceal knowledge of acts or relationships that outsiders have an interest in, for whatever reasons, and that they are capable of acquiring without the consent of the secret holders by espionage. To understand what secrets are concealed we must find out who conceals them—and from whom and for what purpose.

It is obvious that many secrets concealed by individuals, or shared by kinsmen, friends, or anyone bound by deep emotional ties involve private information or acts whose revelation to outsiders would not subject them to legal punishments. The secret sharers might be embarrassed or shamed by such disclosures (e.g., on inadequate performance of sex roles or economic tasks); or, subject to pressures for social conformity, be required to undertake new obligations that they would have liked to avoid. However, privacy may also hide acts or relationships whose discovery could jeopardize existing social ties as in the case of a husband's or wife's infidelity.

Stigmatized persons keep secrets to protect themselves from economic, legal, and social punishments. Both gays and alcoholics are people with stigma. Outsiders who discover their stigma will punish them in different ways. Some gays conspire together to keep their secret from the straight (heterosexual) members of society. Alcoholics try to hide their condition from fellow workers. On the other hand, the families of either gays or alcoholics may collaborate in the secrecy process to avoid the "disgrace" that the exposure would bring.

While secrecy is a normative requirement of certain intimacy relationships, it also forms the bond that unites the members of secret orders or associations. In such secret societies individuals never have the option of choosing openness or secrecy as individuals do in other social relationships. Vows of secrecy are one of the requirements of membership and these secrecy rules are strictly enforced by the association. The purposes for which secrecy is required vary with the goals of the organization. Two basic types of secret societies exist: those that support the existing political leadership or, at least, are politically neutral, and those that oppose the existing political status quo. The first type of secret association enables political leaders to deny outsiders access to the appropriate religious or mystical knowledge (inside secrets) that legitimizes their power. Included within the first type would be mystery cults, which, though apolitical, protect the exclusiveness of their special knowledge and ritual through secrecy. On the other hand, secret societies of the second type employ secrecy largely to protect their membership from arrest and punishment or to deny their political enemies knowledge of their plans and strategies (strategic secrets).

At all the levels of social organization discussed so far, secrecy enables individuals and groups to manipulate and control their environments by denying outsiders vital information about themselves. In the arena of economic and political conflict this basic function of secrecy becomes even more important.

Business corporations, being in competition with one another, must not only conceal information about new products and technology from competitors but also marketing and commercial strategies. Just as such trade secrets are important to large-scale business enterprises, political secrets are important to rival modern state governments. Here military, political, and economic plans, policies, and capabilities (when considered vital to national security) are kept secret.

But in the course of economic or political rivalry government leaders or economic administrators have often initiated policies or engaged in acts that they fear if revealed would result in public condemnation or legal punishment. These are "dark" secrets that also must be concealed.

As several authors in this collection point out, the very structure of private and governmental bureaucracy generates a great deal of internal secrecy limiting the flow of information both vertically and horizontally within the organization. Such large and complex organizations develop internal interest groups who employ secrecy to protect themselves by covering up mistakes or inefficiency, avoiding punishment for illegal acts, and defending their technical or administrative performance from outside criticism.

Regardless of what is concealed, by whom, from whom, and for whatever purpose, secrets are threatened by outsider espionage. Thus, without security devices secrecy would be impossible. The sophistication of security systems varies with the social and political resources available to the individuals or groups, the magnitude of the perceived security threat, and the importance of the secrets involved. The security devices may be such simple ones as the locks, burglar alarms, and window shades or drapes used by the homeowner; or they may be complex, as those used by intelligence agencies (e.g., security clearances, constant employee surveillance, administration of lie detector tests, secrecy classifications, complex physical security). Many secret societies as well as private and public bureaucracies have developed elaborate security systems, including counterespionage, to thwart enemy espionage.

When we consider the papers in this collection as a totality, it becomes clear that the secrecy process consists of a series of interrelated subprocesses that reinforce each other. Once information is concealed by individuals or groups, they must establish a security system to protect their secrets. This security system, in turn, necessitates the development of espionage operations by outsiders who, if they are to gain access to the secrets, must subvert the security system. To counteract the effects of espionage, the secret holders not only use counterespionage but also persuasive techniques by which they spread false information to delude outsiders about the true nature of their secrets. The secret holders also divulge some secrets to outside parties for strategic or political reasons. In turn the outsiders must develop ways to evaluate the information they gain from espionage as well as regulated disclosures offered by their opponents. Adequate evaluation of existing intelligence data may necessitate further espionage to establish its reliability and validity.

However, all secret holders seem to use certain elementary security procedures. For example, the dissemination of false information is one such tactic. Through lies, propaganda, and other deceptive information the secret sharers attempt to distort the real significance of their hidden activities or future plans. Since secrecy is employed to achieve certain goals and not sought primarily for intrinsic satisfactions, there are occasions when unimportant secrets are deliberately revealed to outsiders to disguise the existence of more damaging information about the group activities. Several papers in this collection show how such regulated disclosure serves as a security device.

Security systems do fail and, thus, unregulated or unauthorized disclosure of secrets does take place. Such breaches of security are the result of betrayal by one or more of the secret sharers or are the consequence of aggressive espionage by outsiders. Neighbors who spy on one another out of curiosity or malevolence are involved in espionage as much as foreign spies, secret police informants, or industrial spies. Of course, small-scale surveillance remains the prevalent form in tribal and peasant society. The mobility of populations in modern nation-status undermines the effectiveness of neighborhood espionage. Large-scale espionage conducted by police and intelligence bureaucracies against foreign governments as well as against citizens of their own countries has become the prevailing one today.

Responses to the failure of security systems vary with the nature of the secrecy unit and the nature of the secrets that have been discovered by outsiders. Commonly, secret holders try to counteract the effects of disclosure of dark secrets (i.e., illegal acts or immoral behavior) by ex post facto security measures including lies, denials of wrongdoings, placing the blame on outsiders, and similar techniques. The purpose is to disguise and distort the true meaning of the information that has leaked to outsiders and to block further discovery.

Thus, secrecy is an adaptive process. It enables individuals and groups to achieve certain goals and objectives. But as several papers in this collection demonstrate, secrecy can prove to be maladaptive to both the political community and its member institutions. Government secrecy may prevent the formulation and execution of effective foreign and domestic policy and limit the degree of citizen support for administration programs. Secret lawlessness by private corporation or governmental agency only contributes to an erosion of public respect for legal institutions. Internal secrecy within private or public bureaucracies can create barriers to effective communication that undermine the effectiveness of such organizations. Secrecy, then, proves to be dysfunctional for the political community and its member organizations and institutions when it prevents community members from making a realistic assessment of policies and strategies by restricting public access to knowledge about the short-term and long-term consequences for their society in continuing or changing existing adaptive strategies. In evaluating some of the suggestions for political reform presented in this book, we should keep this fact in mind.

Acknowledgements

Chapter

1. Carol Warren and Barbara Laslett, "Privacy and Secrecy: A Conceptual Comparison." Reprinted by permission of the Society for Psychological Study of Social Issues from the *Journal of Social Issues,* 1977, 33, 43–51.

3. Thomas Gregor, "Exposure and Seclusion: A Study of Institutionalized Isolation Among the Mehinaku Indians of Brazil." From *Ethnology,* 1970, 9, 234–50. Reprinted by permission.

5. Elizabeth Brandt, "On Secrecy and Control of Knowledge: Taos Pueblo." Reprinted by permission of the Ballena Press, P. O. Box 1366, Socorro, NM 87801, from the book *Flowers of the Wind: Papers on Ritual, Myth, and Symbolism in California and the Southwest,* 1977.

8. Kenneth Fidel, "The Dynamics of Military Secrecy." Published by permission of Transaction, Inc. from *Studies in Comparative International Development,* 6, 2. © 1971 by Comparative International Development.

9. Raoul Andersen, "Hunt and Deceive: Information Management in Newfoundland Deep-Sea Trawler Fishing." From *North Atlantic Fisherman,* 1972, 120–140. Reprinted by permission of the Institute of Social and Economic Research, Memorial University of Newfoundland.

10. Brian J. O'Connell, "Secrecy in Business: A Sociological View." Published by permission of Transaction, Inc. from *Society* 16, 4. © 1979 by Transaction, Inc.

12. Fred Kaiser, "Secrecy, Intelligence and Community: The U.S. Intelligence Community." Published by permission of Transaction, Inc. from *Society* 16, 4. © 1979 by Transaction, Inc.
13. Ritchie P. Lowry, "Toward a Sociology of Secrecy and Security Systems." Reprinted by permission of The Society for the Study of Social Problems from *Social Problems,* 1972, 19, 437–450.

Unit 1

The Dimensions of Secrecy

Introduction

The discussion and debate about the nature of secrecy, its functions, and its dangers or merits have produced much confusion, in part at least, because neither social scientists nor politicians have made clear-cut distinctions between types of secrecy. Such distinctions must be made if we are to understand better the role that secrecy plays in the social and political life of a community. The selection by Carol Warren and Barbara Laslett discusses the differences between privacy and secrecy, a distinction, they argue, based on the moral significance that the community, the public, and the government attribute to certain forms of concealed behavior. According to these authors, the term "privacy" refers to the concealment of intimate acts or personal relationships that community members consider morally neutral, if not perfectly acceptable, at least within a private setting. In contrast, the term "private-life secrecy" describes the concealment of behavior or relationships, in private settings, that outsiders consider undesirable, immoral, or illegal (e.g., homosexuality or child abuse by parents). Private-life secrecy thus conceals behavior that the community considers a threat to the moral order or, in some cases, the existing political institutions. Private-life secrecy protects individuals from social and legal sanctions or even from political persecution. While private-life secrecy is "passive" or "defensive", public-life secrecy, which involves political secrecy by governmental leaders and their agents (e.g., CIA, FBI) is "aggressive," being directed against political opponents or groups that government officials consider a threat to their political control. Thus, in some respects, private-life secrecy is a defense against the secret agents who employ public-life secrecy to maintain social control. Individuals stigmatized by unpopular political beliefs, deviant sexual preferences or poverty use private-life secrecy as a means of concealment.

The second selection by Stanton Tefft evaluates the usefulness of several social science theories or models in regard to their contributions to an analysis of secrecy/security systems and the involvement of the secrecy process in sociocultural adaptation. To be useful such theories must contribute to our understanding of four interrelated processes: espionage, secrecy/security, persuasion, and evaluation. Espionage consists of either overt or covert activities aimed at discovering secrets. The secrecy/security process involves not only procedures for keeping secrets but other political or social devices to protect such secrets from espionage. A corollary process is persuasion, which includes educational devices as well as the dissemination of deceptive information, obviously another means for preserving secrets (e.g., cover stories, propaganda, planted news stories). The evaluation process operates to protect recipients of deceptive information from making decisions on the basis of false "intelligence data."

According to Tefft, symbolic interaction, exchange, functional and complex adaptive system theories provide inadequate explanations for secrecy systems and the secrecy processes that produce them. Tefft suggests that conflict theory provides students with more useful perspectives on the secrecy process since secrecy plays a role in conflict-group formation and in the dynamics of conflict itself, that is the process of interaction between conflict groups. The pattern of secrecy and disclosure reflects the dynamics of the conflict process over time. Tefft presents and analyzes many cross-cultural examples showing how secrecy is both a precipitant as well as a precipitate of social conflict.

1

Privacy and Secrecy: A Conceptual Comparison

Carol Warren and Barbara Laslett
University of Southern California

The purpose of this paper is to analyze and distinguish the concepts of privacy and secrecy. There is a considerable body of sociological and social psychological literature on secrecy (Ponse, 1976, 1977; Shils, 1956, 1975; Simmel, 1950; Warren, 1974, 1976) and on privacy (Kelvin, 1973; Laslett, 1973; Margulis, 1974; Schwartz, 1968; Shils, 1966). Few writers other than Shils (1966), however, have distinguished between the two concepts. Such a distinction is the focus of this analysis. The level of the analysis will be sociological and conceptual rather than psychological and empirical. Illustrations will be drawn from Laslett's (1973) work on privacy in the family and Ponse's (1976, 1977) and Warren's (1974, 1976) work on secrecy in the gay world.[1]

Two settings that provide opportunities for privacy and secrecy respectively are the family and the gay world. The contemporary Western family, it is felt by some observers, provides a setting for:

> meaningful relationships on a micro-level where one can control one's own destiny or at least not be subordinated; a level which provides numerous options and optimal freedom for deep relationships. (Sussman, 1972, p. 167)

---

[1]Grateful thanks to Stephen T. Margulis and Elizabeth A. Thompson for comments on earlier versions of this paper.

Similarly, as a type of secret society the gay world provides:

> intensified seclusion against the outside (which) is associated with intensifications of cohesion internally.... A purpose which occasions an individual to enter into secret association with others, excludes almost always such an overwhelming part of his general social circle from participation that the potential and real participants gain rarity value. (Simmel, 1950, p. 369)

By contrasting these two social settings in which withdrawal from public observability is possible and access by others is restricted, differences between the two concepts can be highlighted.

DIMENSIONS OF PRIVACY AND SECRECY

Access to private or secret activities is more limited than is access to more public activities and there is, consequently, greater control over the audience of potential observers. Thus, both privacy and secrecy involve reduced observability and an increased potential to deny access to others (Kelvin, 1973; Laslett, 1973; Magrulis, 1974; Warren, 1974). Privacy and secrecy are differentiated, however, by the moral dimension of the behaviors to which they refer. Our research on the family and on the gay world has convinced us that behavior within the boundaries of privacy and secrecy is significant to the differentiation of the two phenomena, just as access and boundaries are crucial to their mutual definition. Secrecy implies the concealment of something negatively valued by the excluded audience and in some instances, by the perpetrator as well. As Simmel states, "The secret is ... the sociological expression of moral badness" (1950, p. 331). Secrecy is, therefore, not only a strategy for hiding acts or attributes that others hold in moral disrepute, but it is also a means to escape being stigmatized for them. The secret gay world exists in part to facilitate the members' avoidance of stigma by nongays (Ponse, 1976, 1977; Warren, 1974, 1976).

> Privacy, by contrast, protects behavior that is either morally neutral or valued by society as well as by the perpetrators. In the family, for example, persons may engage privately in socially approved sexual and intimate interaction and in morally neutral, but necessary, lavatory functions.

Privacy has a consensual basis in society, while secrecy does not. There is an agreed-upon "right to privacy" in many areas of contemporary life; however, there is no equivalent, consensual "right to secrecy." Homosexual behavior, for example, is perceived by many nonhomosexuals as morally wrong; many homosexuals, in response, resort to secrecy to conceal such behavior (Ponse, 1976, 1977; Warren, 1974). In contrast, heterosexual behavior within the confines of the marital dyad is perceived by most persons as morally legitimate. Most married couples seek privacy for sexual interaction, but the existence of their sexual relationship is not hidden as it is in the case of the homosexual.

Secrecy, therefore, is an even more extreme form of denial of access to others than is privacy—for not only is access denied when secrecy is maintained, but the most successful secret occurs when knowledge of denial of access (the secret's very existence) is also withheld (Simmel, 1950). Furthermore, privacy implies the legitimate denial of access, while secrecy in general implies that the denial of access is legitimate.

One basis for the legitimacy of privacy is the belief that private behavior does not affect those to whom access is denied or restricted. Although privacy defines areas that are potentially public, private behaviors are not perceived to be matters affecting the interests of those whom the boundaries of privacy exclude. That which is restricted by secrecy, however, is more likely to be regarded as legitimate public property that must be concealed or hidden illegitimately through secrecy.

Since the existence of the private act is known, its privacy can be violated either intentionally, by those who do not honor the norms that limit access, or unintentionally, by those who do not know that they are violating any norms. Such accidental or intentional violations expose private behaviors and provide the opportunity to deterimine whether the behaviors conducted in private are indeed those legitimated by others. A person waking accidentally into an occupied bedroom would not be surprised to find that washing or defecating or perhaps even marital sex is occuring. To interrupt a couple arguing or making love in their own bedroom assures the unwanted observer that behavior that is approved when conducted away from the observability of others is occuring. Thus, violations of privacy provide empirical validation that behaviors that are protected from the scrutiny of others do not directly affect the interests of the excluded.

But private settings can be used for secret purposes. Occasionally a bathroom may be used for illicit sex instead of the expected, private functions. In such instances, the activity is seen to affect the interests of others through violation of the consensual basis of societal norms, and the actors are liable to negative sanctions from any external audience that inadvertently discovers the secret. Activities such as washing or marital sex would not result in such sanctioning.

PRIVACY, SECRECY, AND THE PUBLIC ORDER

The restrictions on access and observability that privacy and secrecy entail reduce the opportunity for behavior control by various audiences. Sanctions, whether their bases are legal or moral, cannot be applied by others when the behavior to which they might be attached is hidden from public view. Thus, privacy and secrecy are not only in opposition to the public realm, but they are also in potential opposition to the public order. In general, however, privacy is nonthreatening to the public order, despite the reduction in social control it involves, since it is legitimated and agreed-upon withdrawal. Berger & Kellner (1964) comment on the relationship of privacy and public order:

> The public institutions have no need to control the individual's adventures in the private sphere, as long as they really stay within the latter's circumscribed limits. The private sphere is perceived, not without justification, as an area of individual choice and even autonomy. (p. 4)

In contrast to privacy, which is simply a withdrawal from the public order, secrecy operates in disregard of or opposition to that order. As Simmel (1950) notes, "The secret group pursues its own purposes with the same inconsiderateness for all purposes outside itself which, in the case of the individual, is precisely called egoism" (p. 367). "The secret society lives in an area to which the norms of society do not extend" (Simmel, 1950, p. 360)—at least the specific norms that prohibit those behaviors, such as homosexuality, upon which the secret society is based (Warren, 1974).

PRIVATE-LIFE AND PUBLIC-LIFE SECRECY: A CRITIQUE OF SHILS

Shils (1966) offers an alternative view of the dimensions of privacy and secrecy. He asserts that:

> In secrecy, disclosure or acquisition beyond the boundary is prohibited, and the prohibition is attended by sanctions in the event of a breach. In privacy, disclosure is at the discretion of the possessor, and such sanctions as law provide are directed only against coercive acquisition by persons outside the boundary. (p. 283fn)

Shil's definitions of privacy and secrecy, like ours, involve boundaries among persons to whom access is or is not permitted. His definitions differ from ours, however, in several respects.

In the first place, Shil's comments imply a particular type of secrecy—what we would call public-life secrecy. There are two distinctive types of secrecy in our society: public-life and private-life. Public-life secrecy is secrecy on the part of those in power and their agents, acting purportedly in the public interest. Such agents include FBI and CIA officers, plainclothes police officers, and government bureaucrats of various types. They may also include human behavior researchers and journalists (Shils, 1975).

Public-life secrecy is secrecy in relation to the institution of politics. Those with public-life secrets are secretive by virtue of their political role. The ideological justification of public-life secrecy is the seeking out and elimination of "undesirable elements" in society—elements that might threaten the control of the powerful. Therefore, the object of public-life secrecy is the discovery of how the ostensibly private roles of others are in fact relevant to public life.

Private-life secrecy refers to secrecy about one's personal life rather than to secrecy in relation to political roles of other persons. Private-life secrecy is the concealment of attributes, actions, or relationships that, if discovered, might bring harm to the individuals or groups engaged in them (Simmel, 1950; Warren, 1974). Its justification is less an independent ideological one than a response to ideology: a desire to avert the full wrath of whatever powerful groups are in control of the definition of "undesirable elements."

Public-life secrecy is active and directed at the lives of others, while private-life secrecy is passive and protective of the self. The secrecy of those empowered to act in the public interest is aimed at actively uncovering persons, groups, and activities that are a threat to those in power. In contrast, private-life secrecy is protective rather than aggressive; indeed, a major aim of private-life secrecy is to protect persons from secret agents of social control.

Because Shils (1956, 1966) focuses on public-life secrecy, his assertion that such secrecy is shared rather than individual is quite correct. However, private-life secrecy may be either shared or individual. The gay world contains persons, for example, who have not shared the secret of their homosexual inclinations with anyone for perhaps 20 years and have thus been unable to express these inclinations in sexual interaction. Similarly, a family may be viewed as a unit with shared and enforced privacy (Berger & Kellner, 1964; Laslett, 1973) whose breach by any one of the family may be attended with sanctions.

Shils (1966) assumes that privacy is discretionary or voluntary and that secrecy is mandatory; therefore only a breach of secrecy will bring forth negative sanctions. We would argue, however, that in the context of the private family, privacy is not necessarily voluntary, either among those sharing the private information or in relation to the external or public audience. That is, often the right to privacy for certain activities is an obligation to privacy—a requirement that access to others be denied. For example, marital dyads do not have a right but an obligation to have sexual relations in private; the individual is obliged to defecate and urinate in private. Parents may attempt to convince children to keep family information private, and punish them if they do not do so.

Similarly, persons who share a secret—such as members of the secret gay world—may attempt to control information outside the bounds of the gay world and punish those who violate secrecy. In the context of the members of that world, secrecy is an obligation. However, in the context of the public order, private-life secrecy entails neither rights nor obligations, since persons have neither the right nor the obligation to engage in behavior generally considered to be immoral.

The public audience often attempts to lay bare the contents of a secret whose existence is known but whose content is unknown. To know that secret recordings of conversations occured in the Oval Office of the White House during the Nixon administration was not enough; the content of the tapes also had to be disclosed. As indicated, society provides specialists in uncovering morally condemned secrets—those public-life secret agents such as the CIA and FBI.

STRUCTURAL DISTRIBUTION OF PRIVACY AND SECRECY

Like most social rights and obligations, privacy and secrecy have structural dimensions. The use of privacy or secrecy as a mode of withdrawal from the public order tends to be more likely for certain types of persons than for others. Specifically, the probability of having privacy varies directly with socioeconomic and morally approved status, while the probability of resorting to secrecy varies inversely.

The use of privacy is most likely for those whose behavior is not suspect and who have financial and other resources sufficient to draw boundaries around their activities. We would thus expect privacy to be available to adults more than to children (Wolfe & Laufer, 1974) or to the institutionalized elderly (Pastalan, 1974), to the healthy more than to the physically or mentally ill (Fox, 1959; Goffman, 1961) and to higher more than to lower class persons (Handler & Rosenheim, 1966; Schwartz, 1968).

Secrecy would be most likely where persons are morally stigmatized or where they have inadequate financial or other resources to provide themselves with privacy. We would thus expect that secrecy would be utilized more by lower than higher status persons, by children and the institutionalized elderly rather than adults, by the mentally and physically ill more than the healthy, and by the morally stigmatized more than the "normal" (Goffman, 1961, Ponse, 1977, Warren, 1974).

The family in Western society typically has been able to create boundaries within which sexual and other domestic activities can take place. Members of the gay world, too, have private homes in which to engage in sexual behavior. But the behavior of the homosexual couple is secret; it is seen as morally stigmatizing and illegitimate, therefore knowledge of its existence cannot be shared with the external audience. In contrast, the behavior of the heterosexual couple is private since it is legitimate and its existence can be acknowledged to the external audience.

Both privacy and secrecy demand the ability to utilize resources. Some persons of lower socioeconomic status or who are stigmatized may lack not only the economic resources to obtain privacy but also the skills to be successfully secretive. Similarly, privacy may be relatively less available to those with extremely high status and public visibility, such as presidents and movie stars. Such persons may find themselves resorting to secrecy (like moving about in public in disguise) in order to carry out everyday activities.

SUMMARY

The behavioral distinction between privacy and secrecy is apparent in the contrast between the heterosexual family and the gay world. The heterosexual family, as a unit, has legitimated access to private settings within which certain behaviors can be enacted. In contrast, members of the gay world—although they also have access to private settings—must keep the morally stigmatized dimensions of their behavior secret. On a larger scale, disadvantaged persons or those who engage in illicit behavior would in general be expected to make greater use of secrecy than those whose behavior or status is socially approved.

Privacy may be either a right or an obligation; in contrast, secrecy is neither granted to nor required of citizens in Western societies. However, the mutual protection of privacy may be required of members of such private societies as the family. Privacy is consensual; the behavior it protects is socially legitimated and seen as nonthreatening to others. Secrecy is nonconsensual; the behaviors it protects are seen as illegitimate and as involving the interests of the excluded.

References

Berger, P., & Kellner, H. Marriage and the construction of reality. *Diogenes,* 1964, 46, 1–24.

Fox, R. *Experiment perilous: Physicians and patients facing death.* New York: Free Press, 1959.

Goffman, E. *Asylums.* Garden City, N.Y.: Doubleday, 1961.

Handler, J. F., & Rosenheim, M. K. Privacy in welfare: Public assistance and juvenile justice. *Law and Comtemporary Problems,* 1966, 31, 377–412.

Kelvin, P. A social-psychological examination of privacy. *British Journal of Social and Clinical Psychology,* 1973, 12, 248–261.

Laslett, B. The family as a public and private institution: An historical perspective. *Journal of Marriage and the Family,* 1973, 35, 480–492.

Margulis, S. T. Privacy as a behavioral phenomenon: Coming of age. In D. H. Carson (Ed.), *Man-environment interactions: Evaluations and applications* (Part II, Vol. 6: S. T. Margulis, Vol. Ed.) Washington, D.C.: Environmental Design Research Association, 1974; and Stroudsburg, Pa.: Dowden, Hutchinson & Ross, 1975.

Pastalan, L. A. Privacy preferences among relocated institutionalized elderly. In D. H. Carson (Ed.), *Man-environment interactions: Evaluations and applications* (Part II, Vol. 6: S. T. Margulis, Vol. Ed.) Washington, D.C.: Environmental Design Research Association, 1974; and Stroudsburg, Pa.: Dowden, Hutchinson & Ross, 1975.

Ponse, B. Secrecy in the lesbian world. *Urban Life,* 1976, 5, 313–338.

Ponse, B. *Identities in the lesbian world.* Westport, Conn.: Greenwood Press, 1977.

Schwartz, B. The social psychology of privacy. *American Journal of Sociology,* 1968, 6, 741–752.

Shils, E. B. *The torment of secrecy: The background and consequences of American security problems.* New York: Free Press, 1956.

Shils, E. B. Privacy: Its constitution and vicissitudes. *Law and Contemporary Problems,* 1966, 31, 281–306.

Shils, E. B. *Center and periphery: Essays in macro-sociology.* Chicago: University of Chicago Press, 1975.

Simmel, G. The secret and the secret society. In K. W. Wolff (Ed. and trans.), *The sociology of Georg Simmel.* New York: Free Press, 1950.

Sussman, M. B. (Ed.) *Non-traditional family forms in the 1970s.* Minneapolis: National Council on Family Relations, 1972.

Warren, C. *Identity and community in the gay world.* New York: Wiley, 1974.

Warren, C. Women among men: Females in the male homosexual community. *Archives of Sexual Behavior,* 1976, 5, 157–169.

Wolfe, M., & Laufer, R. The concept of privacy in childhood and adolescence. In D. H. Carson (Ed.), *Man-environment interactions: Evaluations and applications* (Part II, Vol. 6: S. T. Margulis, Vol. Ed.), Washington, D.C.: Environmental Design Research Association, 1974; and Stroudsburg, Pa.: Dowden, Hutchinson and Ross, 1975.

2

Secrecy, Disclosure and Social Theory

Stanton K. Tefft
Wake Forest University

Secrecy plays an important role in the sociocultural processes involved in the formation, maintenance, modification and dissolution of social structures at all levels of sociocultural complexity. The concealment and disclosure of information constitutes a dynamic aspect of direct personal relationships. The social boundaries between dyadic groups (friends, lovers), families, kin groups (lineages, clans) or even larger organizations (secret associations, cults, guilds, corporations), government agencies and political communities (including nation-states) are also defined and extended or contracted in relationship to the patterns of secrecy or disclosure that take place between such units. Thus, not only does the secrecy process, that is the dynamics of concealment and disclosure, affect individual relationships within organizations, large or small, but also the nature of the relationships between them.

The concept of secrecy has been more often defined than understood (Fowler and Fowler, 1964; Kelvin, 1973; O'Brien, 1977). Social scientists have made efforts to differentiate types of secrecy or to distinguish the concept of secrecy from related ones (Shils, 1966; Bates, 1964; Rule, 1974; Warren and Laslett, Chapter 1 in this book). Secrecy, however varied its manifestations, is simply a social resource (or adaptive strategy) used by individuals, groups, and organizations to attain certain ends in the course of social interaction. From the individual's point of view secrecy may be either mandatory or voluntary. The concealment of "personal" secrets or their disclosure is usually a decision controlled by the person. However, individuals as citizens of a state or as members of various organizations may be required to guard and/or disclose certain secrets. The process is no longer voluntary but mandatory. The norms governing concealment or disclosure may be enforced through both negative or positive sanctions. In any case, secrecy always involves a calculated concealment of information, activities, or relationships. Such secrets may involve legal or illegal, moral or immoral, political or apolitical activities, plans or relationships. Thus, privacy which involves the concealment of lawful, moral activities or relationships, is a form of secrecy (Warren and Laslett, Chapter 1 in this book).[1] Secrecy may protect an image or reputation, strategic information, ritual knowledge, private act and so forth (Derlega and Chaikin, 1975, 1977; Flaherty, 1972). But in all cases secrecy protects individual or collective interests whatever they might be. Whether or not secrecy brings intrinsic satisfactions to the secret sharers or the individual (ego enhancement, sense of superiority over outsiders, self-identity) is incidental to its social significance.

Of course, by concealing knowledge about another's transgressions, you gain power over that individual. Government agents charged with enforcing business laws failed to report bribes by clients. Thereby, they acquired a coercive device by which they could pressure clients into voluntary compliance with other laws. Their knowledge that the client has offered them a bribe gives them some power over the client's behavior (Strauss, 1978).

In all cases secrecy is employed when the interests of the individual, group, or organization are threatened by other individuals, groups, or organizations. Secrecy can be employed as a strategy in aggressive actions against a nation's rivals (e.g., espionage) or as a defensive strategy (e.g., coup plotters). The nature of the disclosure threat depends to a great extent on the nature of the secret or secrets. Individuals may use secrecy to protect themselves against embarrassing disclosures (e.g., girl who hides her diary from an inquisitive younger sister). Such self-secrets may enable individuals to escape punishment or ridicule (e.g., boy who conceals sex magazines from puritanical parents). People with stigmas, such as homosexuals, may conceal such relationships from family or business associates in

[1] I have modified Warren and Laslett's classification slightly by classifying privacy as *intimate secrecy.*

order to avoid job dismissal or legal punishments (Ponse, 1976). The politician with a personal history of psychological problems that forces him to seek psychiatric aid may conceal such information from associates because of the political dangers if such visits became known to a wider audience.

Organizations, both large and small, guard secrets for similar reasons. Families, whose members' actions endanger family reputations, may hide, as best they can, such stigmas from public knowledge. The competitive nature of relationships between many social units such as families, kin groups, corporations, cults, associations, political parties, factions, political communities and similar collectivities make secrecy a vital social resource by which they attain their goals and further their collective interests. More concrete evidence for these observations will be given later in this chapter.

The act of concealment triggers a chain of interactive and reactive actions that I have called the secrecy process. The tensions and/or conflicts between the secret holder (or holders) and outsiders that necessitate concealment are accentuated in turn by such secrecy; for secrets, whatever their nature, give the secret sharers a power over those outsiders who think the secret information is vital to their own interests and, thus, want to discover what it may be. Such outsiders will resort to espionage, hidden methods of information collection (including secret surveillance and other intelligence methods, whether sophisticated or unsophisticated). In turn, the threat of such espionage or its actuality force secret holders to devise methods for security, the means employed to protect the secrets. In order to protect vital secrets, the secrecy group (or the individual) may leak certain information of an innocuous nature, of little strategic value, to outsiders or their agents in order to protect the more vital information. Thus, insiders attempt to persuade outsiders through forms of propaganda that the group's activities constitute no threat. Outsiders, then, must evaluate the veracity or significance of such disclosures as well as their own espionage data. Thus, the secrecy process involves a dynamic interplay between insider and outsider as each tries to pursue his respective goals (Wilsnack, 1978).[2] Secrecy/security, espionage, persuasion, and evaluation are subprocesses that in their totality constitute the secrecy process.

To understand the secrecy process certain key questions must

---

[2] I have modified Wilsnack's original processual analysis but I am indebted to him for many ideas about the secrecy process.

be answered. Under what conditions do individuals conceal information from one another? What types of organizations are more likely to employ secrecy than others and under what conditions? Do patterns of secrecy and disclosure, characteristic of any social unit (or individual), vary over time? Why? Under what conditions do individuals or secret sharers divulge secrets to outsiders? How do security requirements effect the norms governing relationships within and between social units? How does the existence of espionage within and between organizations affect interpersonal and intergroup relations?

Existing theories of social organizations have ignored such questions or have been unsuccessful in explaining the role of secrecy as a social process that is as both a cause and a consequence of conflict. The purpose of this paper is to review briefly some of the prominent sociological theories and to evaluate their potential contribution to our understanding of the secrecy process. I will review the symbolic interaction, exchange, functional and complex adaptive system theories of social organization, demonstrating their inadequacy as explanations for secrecy systems. I then propose to show the usefulness of conflict theory in contributing to our understanding of the secrecy process.

SYMBOLIC INTERACTIONISM

Symbolic interactionism describes the processes that enable individuals to fit their actions together through complex symbolic interaction. Symbolic interactionists consider social orders to be "negotiated orders" although they recognize that coercion, persuasion and manipulation also play their part. Such "negotiations" enable the parties to get things accomplished by enabling the social actors to evolve appropriate norms when they need to deal with each other (Strauss, 1978). Normative rules emerge as each person takes the role of others and through this process individuals learn to predict each other's behavior (self-indication). Over time individuals form a consistent picture of group norms by incorporating a "generalized other" into their self-concepts, that is, through social interaction they develop a "value frame of reference" by which they assess the consequences of specific lines of action (Turner, 1974; Blumer, 1969).

Thus, as a result of this process people interpret and define each other's actions. How they react to each other depends on the meaning they attach to each other's actions (Blumer, 1969). Such an interpretative process can take place within the individual, within the individual members of an organization acting in concert, or within agents acting on behalf of an organization (Blumer, 1969). According to this view, stability in social relationships depends on a fair degree of open communication between social actors.

However, Blumer (1969) notes that actors may fail to interpret situations correctly or fail to note important things vital to the construction of appropriate social acts. But Blumer fails to explain the circumstances under which this failure occurs. The presence of information management or deception in human relationships suggests one explanation; individuals make many false evaluations because people mutually disguise or hide feelings, attitudes or intentions. So do organizations and their agents. Therefore it is often hard for actors to correctly interpret the significance of each other's actions or, for that matter, develop a consistent and secure "generalized other" on which to make self-evaluations. Secrecy, then, is a structural limitation placed on the "negotiating" process (Strauss, 1978).

Societies vary in the degree of emphasis that their value systems place on the importance of separation and protection of the private self from the public self (Bates, 1964; Shils, 1975). However, in no society do individuals treat all others with complete candor. In some cases, people are more open with strangers than with intimates. In some cases people hide negative evaluations of friends to protect their friends' images of self-worth as well as to preserve the relationship itself. However, symbolic interaction theory does not explain the variations in those relationships of openness and concealment nor does it enable us to predict when the social boundaries between individuals or groups will be rigid or more permeable.

Under what conditions are people aware of another's stigma or other "dark" secret pretend that they do not know this secret? Such deception is a form of counterfeit secrecy (Ponse, 1976). For example, kinsmen of gays, knowing their secret, may act as if the "stigma" does not exist thereby facilitating the appearance of amicable relations. In a like fashion, Afikbo Ibo women (Nigeria) know many secrets supposedly restricted to the males of the Poro, the tribal male secret society, but both the men and the women engage in the mutual pretense that the women don't know the male secrets (Ottenberg, 1973). Bascom (1944) also indicates that Yoruba women (Nigeria) know secrets about the men's society but are not punished unless they make this knowledge public. Symbolic interaction theory does not enable us to explain the circumstances under which such counterfeit secrecy will occur.

There are many circumstances in which individuals assume "false" roles or "covers" to avoid punishment or pursue "hidden" objectives. Some gays, for example, find it expedient to hide their sexual deviancy by masquerading as "heterosexuals" at work or in social situations with business acquaintances (Ponse, 1976). In a similar fashion, the regular marijuana-user learns to put on a performance before non-smokers without betraying himself when "high" (Goffman, 1959). The undercover agent provides another example. Here the agent assumes a "false" deviant role in order to trap the criminal or provoke illegal acts among target groups to make arrests; or the agent assumes a legitimate "cover" occupation in order to carry out foreign espionage (Marx, 1974, 1979; Walker, 1932; Deacon, 1969, 1972, 1974). Under what circumstances do actors engage in these forms of symbolic interaction and what are the consequences for individual's self-concept formation and for norm formation and norm maintenance? The symbolic interaction theory gives us few answers.

Thus, while the symbolic interactionists recognize that what they call "objects" (norms, motives, actions) must be reinterpreted and reevaluated constantly and, that sometimes, such evaluations are misconceived, they do not clearly indicate the reasons for such mutual misconceptions nor their consequences. Symbolic interactionists seem to ignore the role of secrecy in social interaction. By ignoring the mutual deception that occurs in social relationships, symbolic interactionists have developed a theory with serious conceptual weaknesses. As Gilsenan (1976, p. 192) states "... uncertainty as to the precise degree of lying or truth on both sides will always be subject to active assessment in problematic situations. For insofar as falseness undermines our actions of legitimate and right behavior ... (and) ... the certainty of our grasp of reality of the common-sense world, it constitutes a threat of serious order to our social reality." And this is, of course, the key problem symbolic interactionists ignore or underplay.

A spin-off from symbolic interactionism has been the dramaturgical model. This theory recognizes the importance of secrecy in social interaction not only between individuals but also between groups ("teams"). In the dramaturgical model the social world is structured in terms of the interactions of individuals, scripts, other players (team members) and various audiences. The player or team members thus derive guides for their behavior from social norms (scripts), demands made by other players and the expectations of the audiences. Individuals as well as the teams to which they belong are in the business of impression management.

According to Goffman (1959, p. 69) most relationships involve performances where the actors engage in "concealed practices which are incompatible with fostered impressions." Each team must guard against outsiders "inopportune intrusion" backstage, whereby outsiders discover "dark secrets" which may destroy the public image which the team is trying to convey. Players not only must protect "dark secrets," those whose disclosure could threaten the group's image or reputation but also "strategic secrets", concealment of hidden goals and objectives and "inside secrets," that is knowledge that team members share as a result of a common initiation or socialization process (Goffman, 1959). Team members themselves, of course, share "entrusted" secrets whether "dark" or "strategic". Players also control so-called "free secrets" which can be transmitted to the audience or outsiders if such disclosure is sanctioned by the team in the interests of impression management.

To maintain team secrets there must be internal discipline to prevent inadvertent disclosure by the actors. There is a moral obligation placed on team members not to betray the secrets of the team for any reason.

Goffman's analysis probes the dynamics of the secrecy process to a greater extent than the more orthodox symbolic interactionism. But Goffman lays great stress on the collaboration between the audience and the team wherein the audience "... helps the performers save their own show (1959, p. 229)." It is less clear why either the audience or other outsiders should deliberately seek knowledge of secret backstage activities according to the model proposed by Goffman.[3] While Goffman suggests various circumstances under which team members may betray the team secrets to outsiders, his analysis is less penetrating when it comes to suggesting reasons why individual members of the team may keep secrets from each other as well as from outsiders. Thus, his model is less useful in understanding the secrecy dynamics within large-scale hierarchical organizations or, for that matter, graded secret soci-

[3]Goffman (1959) recognizes that spies and informers operate "backstage" to discover team secrets but he is unclear about the reasons they have for doing so.

eties wherein members are graded according to the degree of secret knowledge they have acquired.

Moreover, Goffman suggests that team members find that it is in their reciprocal interest to keep secrets from the audience. In reality many members of real-life teams keep secrets out of fear of punishment for such disclosure rather than mutual self-interest alone. Employees of intelligence organizations as well as large business corporations are under more or less constant surveillance, a device whereby their behavior and loyalty is ceaselessly monitored.

On the other hand, Goffman does not make clear why the members of teams, be they large ones or small ones (cliques, dyads, families) betray fellow actors. The idea that disclosure of secrets which damage the image of the team or its leaders can serve a useful purpose for individual members in their struggle for power or status seem absent from Goffman's analysis. It is also difficult to determine from Goffman's theory as to what consequences flow from unauthorized disclosure in regard to both the team and its audiences. How do teams or audiences react? Goffman's model tends to emphasize the success of information management rather than its failures (due to betrayal or successful espionage).

EXCHANGE THEORY

Exchange theorists assume that social relations consist of individuals "offering or not offering things to one another, and demanding accepting or avoiding from one another (Bredemeier, 1978, pp. 452-3)." Thus, exchange is intrinsic to social relations. In adapting to their environment people obtain things from it, dispense things to it, avoid things that are in it, and retain things that might escape (Bredemeier, 1978). However, the theory does not make clear under what specific conditions people decide upon a particular option.

According to Homans (1950, 1961) people in pursuit of their goals, that is, in optimizing their adaptation, will try to minimize the cost but maximize their profits; to do so they direct their activities in such a way as to gain rewards and avoid punishment (keep rewards high and cost low). The more profit a person expects from another individual in pursuit of some activity the more likely the person is to persist in that activity.

Of course to gain maximum reward people calculate alternatives in terms of reward, cost, and profit. Exchange theory assumes that people make rational choices. In circumstances where a riskless choice is involved a person knows his high value preferences, whether or not he has appropriate resources, and the consequences, in terms of reward, or punishment, for a particular line of action. However, often people cannot predict the consequences of actions in terms of reward and punishment. These are risky choices (Bredemeier, 1978). Exchange theory does not explain why individuals must make so many risky choices nor why they do so. As Bok (1978, p. 19) suggests "... estimates of the costs and benefits of any action can be endlessly varied through successful deception." Homans (1974) recognizes the existence of such deception but minimizes its importance even in adversary situations.

It is obvious in a social world in which competition for resources, wealth, power, and prestige exist, retaining knowledge or dispensing it can either help or hinder an individual's or group's adaptation. Secrecy may increase the value of exclusive knowledge and thereby enhance the prestige of those who possess it (Daraul, 1961; Smart, 1967; Roberts, 1972). In turn secrecy can improve one's economic position as well as help other individuals to achieve and retain political power (Gunther, 1927; Koch, 1974; Little, 1947, 1948, 1964, 1965, 1967; Ford, 1941; Murphy, 1976; Brandt, Chapter 5 in this book). On the other hand, exchange of confidential information between groups can work to their mutual economic and political interests. For example, government agencies "market" secrets to various lobbies as a means to enhance their political power (Galnoor, 1975, 1977).

George Homans suggests that people determine whether the costs and investments they have made lead to a fair profit in their exchanges by means of some system of "distributive justice." To determine a fair profit an individual (or group) compares his (their) reward with what another individual (group) gets (Homans, 1974). Such calculations would be difficult when the necessary information to make such determinations is denied the actor or the group. For example, corporation management may encourage corporation officials to conceal information about their salaries from each other in order to prevent jealousy over differential rewards for similar work (Moore, 1962). In this case, as with many others, an individual determination of whether or not his (her) standards of distributive justice have been violated is made impossible by such secrecy. The mere fact that an individual is not aware that his investments are greater than his rewards, does not make the exploitation any less real.

Exchange theory has proved useful in the study of power relationships. Peter Blau has developed this area of analysis. Blau (1963, 1975) suggests that all exchange operates on the principle of reciprocity; normally people who bestow rewards will receive rewards in turn. Such exchanges define superordinate-subordinate relations. If leaders abide by the political norms they give appropriate services in return for subordinate compliance. In such situations superordinate-subordinate relations are stable. However, leaders who fail to provide the expected rewards provoke negative sanctions on the part of subordinates who no longer comply with the leaders' wishes. Blau considers that the source of conflict lies in the unbalanced exchange relations that violate the norms of reciprocity and fairness (Turner, 1974).

Blau, of course, seems to ignore completely the frequency with which political leaders deceive their followers by concealing normative transgressions, trangressions that often violate the rights of such followers but serve the selfish interests of the leaders. Since modern political authority is a rational-legal authority maintained by a system of laws, public knowledge of leaders' violations of law would seriously undermine their claims to rightful leadership (Collins, 1975). By maintaining control over the channels of communication leaders can maintain their authority.

Secret politics seem to encourage deviancy from normative rules. Secrecy provides a cloak behind which forbidden acts, legal violations, evasion of responsibility, inefficiency, and corruption are concealed (Simmel, 1950). The executive branch of modern states often use the requirements for state secrecy as a device to hide such illegality and corruption (Reese, 1977). Closed sessions by legislative bodies, for example, may hide the influence of powerful interest groups on lawmakers' legislative decisions.

In both public and private bureaucracies the forms of secrecy are much the same (Rigney, 1975). Just as the specialized divisions of a corporation fiercely compete for a larger share of corporate resources, so do government agencies compete for more funds. Both corporate unit and government agency keep secret, information which would damage their budget claims (Wilensky, 1967; Rigney, 1975). The hierarchical organization of government bureaucracies prevents the downward flow of damaging information which would threaten the position of agency heads who must maintain the mystique of superior administrative leadership, and the upward flow of information that would subject experts to criticism or reveal the mismanagement and violation of formal and informal rules at the lower levels (Wilensky, 1967; Rigney, 1975).

Thus, secrecy enables government leaders, who profess support for the dominant political values, to ignore or subvert them when required by concerns of political expediency, yet still retain their authority, which they couldn't if their lawless acts became public knowledge. In such situations, it is obvious the reciprocal exchanges have broken down but the powerless party is unaware of it and continues to comply with the wishes of his leaders.

Blau (1977) also argues that individual conformity to group norms rests on the rewards that flow from such conformity while violations bring no reward or social disapproval, thus discouraging deviance. However, as long as norm violations can be concealed from sanctioning agents, and this would be especially likely in large-scale organizations, then individuals may violate some norms at least without suffering ostracism.

FUNCTIONAL THEORY

The functionalists assume that observed cultural forms or patterns of behavior must fit the social system, that it must have a "function". Human social systems, then, consist of differentiated units which are interdependent. Such units may be individuals or various groups or categories of people. Thus, societies and cultures are viewed as social systems made up of units that constitute the systems' subsets (Moore, 1978).

The most sophisticated presentation of functional theory has been made by Talcott Parsons (1951, 1968, 1971). Unlike the symbolic interactionists and exchange theories, Parsonian functionalism assumes that men's decision-making options are under considerable restraint. Parsonian functionalism suggests that each actor makes subjective judgments about the means to achieve goals but all actors are constrained by the ideas, values, and social structural requirements of the system. Thus, men play roles according to the specifications laid down by the social systems to which they belong. To survive each social system or subsystem must adapt: that is secure from the environment sufficient resources and distribute these resources; attain goals by establishing goal priorities and mobilizing the system's resources; maintain system integration by coordinating relationships between the system's units as well as motivating actors to play appropriate roles (pattern maintenance) and by tension or conflict management (Turner, 1974). Actors must behave in such a way to enable the system to achieve these basic requirements of adaptation. For them to do otherwise would destroy the system. Thus, certain common orientations or "modes of evaluation" are required if the system is to accomplish its goals and make successful adaptations. Norms emerge as a way of adjusting the orientations of the actors to each other but such norms are obviously circumscribed by the general cultural patterns.

The widespread presence of secrecy norms within various social systems suggest that this behavioral attribute of social systems must have a "function," contribute to system maintenance and adaptation. However, the fact that secrecy often contributes to deviances at all levels of sociocultural organization indicates that it promotes "dysfunctions" by helping reinforce the barrier between approved procedures and an avowed purposes of the subsystems or system. Thus, functional perspectives give us no indication as to the circumstances under which secrecy contributes to order or disorder, equilibrium or disequilibrium.

Merton's (1968) modification of the functional model provides a more useful framework than orthodox functionalism for analyzing the secrecy process. Merton makes a distinction between latent and manifest function; manifest functions are the overt or stated purposes of individual or group while latent functions are additional but unintended consequences for social structural arrangements or systems (or subsystems) of certain overt actions. Some cults or organizations state quite openly that one of their goals (manifest function) is to protect the secrecy of their ceremonies and rites. On the other hand, secrecy may serve to cover up unintended actions by an individual or organization which could bring potential negative sanctions from outsiders. A boy in the course of building a tree-house may break his father's saw and hide this fact from his father; business executives by setting their corporation profit goals so high, may encourage subordinates to seek illegal means to cut costs; executives cover up such activities once they discover them to protect the business from potential lawsuits.

Merton's functional model enables us to specify certain circumstances under which secrecy occurs as a manifest function or as a consequence of some latent function. However, it is still unclear how even Merton's model can enable us to determine the conditions under which secrecy proves to be functional or dysfunctional to the system or subsystem nor the varied circumstances under which secrecy operates in social systems.

COMPLEX ADAPTIVE SYSTEM THEORY

Unlike Parsonian functionalism, complex adaptive system theory does not assume that the sociocultural system is a preprogrammed machine. Such a dynamic system model suggests that norms and values do not specify concrete behavior, only general rules or guides. Such values do not give actors enough information to successfully "map" their external or internal environments. The units of the system at all levels of complexity are generated, maintained, elaborated and exchanged as successful or unsuccessful adaptations are attempted (Buckley, 1967, 1968).

The basic assumption of general system theory is that sociocultural systems are goal-oriented, adaptive systems generating internal and external information exchanges. So-called "organizing centers" receive environmental feedback. Such feedback may be negative, indicating unsuccessful goal attainment or positive, indicating successful goal attainment. In this way the "organizing centers" determine whether or not the system is attaining its goals, thus adapting successfully. In this way the systems (or in reality their "organizing centers") are constantly involved in "mapping" their environments, that is, discriminating, acting upon, and responding to aspects of the environmental variety or its constraints according to "criterion variables" (goals, values). According to complex system theory a sociocultural system is self-regulative, maintaining stable structures but is also self-directive, changing and elaborating structures when necessary. A "pool of adaptive variability" is necessary if the sociocultural system is to make successful adaptations. Thus, systems must maintain a necessary range of deviancy from existing norms, values, and strategies, from which new solutions to adaptive problems may be formulated.

It is obvious that the complex system theory assumes that feedback to the "organizing centers" operate effectively enough to enable such centers to determine a mismatch between current environmental adaptation or internal relationships and the system's goals. Adequate information of this sort is needed if successful remapping and reorganization is to keep the sociocultural system adapted (Buckley, 1967, 1968). For it is assumed by complex system theory that a system's adaptations must always fail, at least to some extent, because the social structure fails to define, specify or provide adequately for some eventualities or unstructured events in the environment. Moreover, the system itself will generate internal conflicts, tensions, failures, discrepancies. Communication networks and information flows within the system operate to disseminate information about such conflicts and tensions, thus exerting such social pressure on interpersonal relation that new selective responses are evolved to maintain or change the system.

Buckley (1967, p. 174) mentions "complicating factors" that may prevent "organizing centers" from making effective corrective actions to "negative feedback flows." Thus "... stabilizing or adaptive control mechanisms will not automatically come into play when 'disturbances' occur in the system.... Social systems may generate and maintain deviant and disorganizing forces....... (Buckley, 1967, p. 163)." However, Buckley does not clearly formulate the circumstances under which these adaptive control mechanisms fail to operate. An assumption of complex system theory is that feedback from the environment and within the system itself (whether positive or negative) takes place through information flows and communications that operate effectively. The secrecy that characterizes interpersonal and intergroup relationships suggests that this assumption is incorrect. It is often the case that sociocultural systems do not correctly map their environments because they are denied adequate information about these environments; nor do the administrative centers have adequate information concerning goal-related deviancy within the system itself.

For example, intelligence agencies help the system "map" its environment. In some instances intelligence agencies place such secrecy on their past and present operations that they deny the executive branch as well as other government bodies or officials vital information. Secret operations of the Central Intelligence Agency (CIA) may serve as examples. The CIA did not tell the Kennedy administration that it was involved in a plot to assassinate Fidel Castro. Nor did the CIA provide the Commission investigating Kennedy's assassination this information even though it had a bearing on the President's assassination (Schorr, 1977). In fact the CIA has concealed both their successful and unsuccessful attempts to assassinate foreign leaders from several United States presidents (Wise, 1976). In the Bay of Pigs affair the CIA consulted few knowledgeable officials about the operation; thus Cuban experts were unable to warn President Kennedy of the dangers of the CIA organized invasion of Cuba (Halperin, 1975). Even more astounding are the CIA activities in China during the mid-1960's. While high government officials had decided not to intervene in China during the "Cultural Revolution," the CIA, unknown to these officials, was mounting covert operations designed to increase the turmoil in China during this period. These operations subverted the agreed upon policy of senior Chinese officials in the State Department (Halperin, 1975).

The CIA's preoccupation with clandestine operations (political disruption, paramilitary operations, subversion) have undermined its information gathering functions. Such covert tactics have eroded the agency's ability to provide useful information for purposes of decision-making. Covert intelligence is often obtained from informants of dubious reliability; moreover, information obtained in covert ways can be more easily distorted by analysts for personal or political reasons than overt intelligence subject to review of more experts (Lowry, 1975).

These illustrations of "intelligence failures" are a few among many other examples that suggest that complex system theory makes certain assumptions that are not consistent with the social or political reality of sociocultural systems. Let me emphasize again that contrary to the assertion by complex system theorists information flow to a social system from the environment as well as through the social system or its subsystems is often blocked, distorted, or diverted as a consequence of certain secrecy subprocesses. It is for this reason that social systems often fail to "map" their environments correctly.

CONFLICT THEORY

Our review of symbolic interaction, exchange, functional and complex adaptive system theories has suggested some of their inadequacies in explaining the importance of secrecy as a social process. Our review so far has indicated that secrecy, at all levels of sociopolitical complexity, serves as a social resource by which both individuals and groups whose interests are in conflict, pursue and defend such interests. Conflict theory provides us with a model whose assumptions are more consistent with the social world in which secrecy is a vital element in social relations. Turner (1974, p. 123) lists the following assumptions made by Cohen about conflict theory:

Interests are the basic elements of social life
Social life involves inducement and coercion
Social life is necessarily divisive
Social life generates opposition, exclusion, and hostility
Social life generates structural conflict
Social differentiation involves power
Social systems are malintegrated and beset by contradictions
Social systems tend to change.[4]

Divisive interests which are manifest in the incompatibility of individual or group goals, objectives or values have a structural basis. Inequalities in wealth, status, and/or power generate such divisive interests. Groups or individuals subject to coercion or manipulation by more powerful groups or individuals make efforts to equalize this power differential. Limited supplies of desired objects or conditions (resource scarcity) or limited access to desired political or social positions (position srcity) also generate incompatible interests or objectives (Mack and Snyder, 1957).

Such divisive interests are often the direct consequence of structural contradictions: established activities or objectives pursued by social actors, classes or groups that interfere, undermine and/or jeopardize the position or interests of other social actors, classes or groups. Such incompatible structural arrangements produce social experiences through which social actors, groups or classes develop antagonistic interests, goals or ideologies. The clash of these counterposed viewpoints may eventually lead to structural change (Benson, 1973). In work organizations, for example, professionals, whose dominance is the result of their previous successful mastery of a particular technical process, and organized labor, which is opposed to job-threatening innovations, will both resist management's efforts to introduce new, innovative labor-saving techniques which will increase the growth of the productive forces but endanger the power position of the professionals and the jobs of the workers (Heydebrand, 1977). Here the structural contradiction is manifest as a class contradiction.

However, for structural contradictions to precipitate social

[4]From Percy Cohen, *Modern Social Theory* (New York, 1968), p. 167, by permission of Basic Books.

conflict, parties such as the managers, workers and professionals in the above example, must be aware that they have incompatible goals, interests, or values. In consensual conflict the parties each want the same thing but success of one means the failure of the other (zero-sum-game). In dissensual conflicts the parties want different things (Kriesberg, 1973). In either case the actions by one party to gain scarce resources or positions, to change policies, and so forth, is opposed by the other party. The parties to the conflict attempt to "destroy, injure, thwart or otherwise control" each other (Mack and Snyder, 1957, p. 218).

Whatever the structural sources of conflict, and they may be many and varied, secrecy plays a role in conflict-group formation and the dynamics of conflict itself, that is the processes of interaction between conflict groups and the forms of conflict (Oberschall, 1978). The pattern of secrecy and disclosure reflects the dynamics of the conflict process over time. The more intense the conflict the greater efforts to conceal information from antagonists, information that might give them an advantage. Conflict also leads to in-group cohesion by setting group boundaries and strengthening group cohesiveness. Often in-group secrecy norms help maintain such social boundaries and contribute to group cohesiveness.

The interrelations between social conflict and secrecy takes place at all levels of sociopolitical organization. Space limitations force me to defer an analysis of the role of secrecy in interpersonal conflicts to a future paper. Therefore I will begin my analysis at the intergroup level.

For example, intense interfamily, interclan or interlineage conflicts are characteristic of the social relations within many tribal or peasant societies. Such conflicts are usual consensual ones. Families strive to attain the same goals but one family's success must be based on another's failure. To protect kinsmen's interests families and clans operate as secrecy units. In the Greek Community of Sarakatsan family rivalry fosters malicious gossip by which families attempt to destroy each others' reputations. Family secrecy operates as a defense against the diffusion of potentially damaging information to rivals (Campbell, 1964). There are similar conflicts between lower class families of Aughnaboy (Northern Ireland). As a result of such conflicts families require that their adult male members restrict contacts with youthful companions and confine most of their contacts with family and kin; these early life friendships, which involve exchanges of intimacies, constitute a potential threat to the family which must guard secret transgressions by its members to avoid the leakage of this compromising information to its rivals (Leyton, 1974).

Within political communities (tribes, chiefdoms, states) people organize groups or associations to pursue special interests. The pursuit of these special interests may put them in conflict with each other or with the government. Secret societies may be contrasted with so-called "open" associations. Even secret societies differ in the type and nature of the secrets they conceal. But more generally secret societies are organizations that maintain both internal and external secrecy, not only concealing the objectives and activities of the association but often the location and membership as well (Gross, 1974; Hazelrigg, 1969; Gist, 1940; Wedgwood, 1930; Bhuntani, 1952). Even some "open" organizations maintain forms of internal secrecy by concealing inner activities and relationships but they do make the existence, membership and objectives of the association known to outsiders (Gross, 1974).

Some secret associations pursue goals that are hostile to the central values and institutions of the political community. Such secret associations are alienative ones. Other secret organizations support or at least are in close accord with the dominant values of the community. These are conformative secret orders (Lyman, 1964, 1970). In many instances such conformative secret orders have provided political leaders with an organization capable of not only reinforcing the legitimacy of their political status but enabling them to expand and consolidate their power.

In situations where political leaders find that their authority is subject to potential challenge or is actually being challenged, conformative secret orders provide a means through which such leadership can control access to adult rank, status, and political power by using their dominant position in the secret association to defend their privileged positions. Without secret society membership, adult men and women cannot marry, acquire property or assume normal sex roles. By regulating social mobility in this way, the leaders of the secret society make certain that individuals, before attaining adult status, have been properly socialized to political and social values of the tribe (Webster, 1908; Little, 1948). In fact, in many of these tribal communities, the elders perpetuate their authority over the junior members by controlling the access of junior tribesmen to social, political, economic, magical, and religious knowledge. The Kpelle of Liberia, West Africa, provide one example of such elder control. Kpelle elders use their position of leadership in the secret societies and the special control over access to important information which this position gives them to assert and maintain their dominance over the youth (Murphy, 1976). In a like fashion, Taos Pueblo leaders ("the Old People") use their leadership in the Kiva groups and the secret knowledge this position gives them to deny members of opposing political factions access to political authority in the Pueblo. The political position of the "Old People" rests on their monopoly and control of certain esoteric information concerning the meaning and symbolism of ritual equipment, the sequencing and timing of rituals, and the ritual activities of the participants. Acquisition of such knowledge of outsiders might be diffused back into the community and utilized by political rivals in their attempt to wrest political control from the traditional leadership. So these traditional leaders restrict the flow of these secrets to outsiders as well (Brandt, Chapter 5 in this book).

Secret organizations often function to maintain or extend political and economic control. A secret society of the Banks Island, the *Tamate Livoa,* was employed by the chiefs to enforce peace among villages (Bradfield, 1973, I) and, among the Mende of Sierra Leone, the local lodges of the Poro, the secret society of tribal males, were used by paramount chiefs to police the territories (Little, 1965). The high chief of one lodge would place subordinate chiefs under a Poro oath who, in turn, would bind their members under the same oath. Through this process the whole chiefdom was made ready to respond to the paramount chief's directions (Bozeman, 1976). These secret associations exercise such complete authority because members' loyalty to the lodge supercedes responsibility to any other group.

Powerful secret orders in the employ of governments provide political leaders with an organizational weapon for punishing, repressing, or destroying political enemies. The *Tamate Livoa* of the Banks Islands, mentioned above, imposed economic sanctions against its enemies by closing off certain garden lands from common access and then robbing the fields of people it wanted to punish (Bradfield, 1973, vol. I). In 13th century Westphalia a secret order called Holy Vehm (*Fehm-Gerichte*) dispensed its justice against violators of the Christian faith in both secret and public tribunals. Initiated members denounced "evil-doers", served citations for court appearances, and dispensed immediate punishment on people caught in acts of wrongdoing (Keightley, 1864; Daraul, 1961).

And in early Spain the Garduna was an unofficial weapon of the Holy Inquisition for about 140 years (1520 to 1667). The priests and officers of the Spanish Inquisition commissioned about one-fifth of all the Garduna crimes such as murder, assassination, and robbery (Daraul, 1961). The Camorra, a direct offshoot of the Garduna, ruled Naples during the period of the Spanish Bourbons (1738-1860), by gaining control over every aspect of economic enterprise. Not only did the Camorra commit crimes on commission for high government officials, but also they gained much revenue from control of illegal enterprises (brothels, gambling, and lotteries) as well as other economic ventures (Chandler, 1975).

Alienative secret orders may organize political rebellions or provide the secret leadership for revolutionary organizations. In either case, the existence of such secret associations is both a consequence and a cause of political conflict.

Within tribal society or traditional states secret revolutionary organizations are absent. However, there are numerous instances of tribal secret societies being formed as a defense against the abuse of power by the chiefs, as was the case of the Nkpe among the Yako of Africa. The Nkpe was organized to defend its members against the abuse of power by village leaders and priests who dominated village affairs (Forde, 1961, 1967). In a like fashion, North American Iroquois religious brotherhoods, and Potawatomie Indian medicine groups operated in secret to avoid persecution by the leaders of new religious movements (Parker, 1909; Landes, 1970). And among the modern-day Sabo Hausa Muslims of Ibadan (Nigeria) the bori cult, a group that attributes most illnesses to certain spirits, must practice secret curing rituals because members are under attack by the dominant Tijaniyya Muslim brotherhood (Cohn, 1968).

Some modern secret societies have been involved in a more violent defense of their political interests. Modern Mende Poro lodges, after a considerable period of secret preparation, staged riots and battles in Sierra Leone during 1955-56, protesting against the policies of some of the tribal chiefs (Bozeman, 1968); and in Liberia the secret Baboon Society was implicated in a plot to overthrow the government (Liebenow, 1964).

Revolutionary or subversive organizations are more well-known examples of groups which must employ forms of secrecy as a means of survival against the police forces of the governments which they hope to overthrow. History provides many examples. The Arab Karmathians and their successors, the Assassins aimed at overthrowing the Sunni Caliphs (Keightley, 1864; Annan, 1967b, Daraul, 1961). In early China secret societies, originating either from religious sects or mutual aid associations, defended peasant interests against rapacious soldiers, bandits and government tax collectors as well as provided leadership in the struggle against the Mongols and the Manchus (Comber, 1959; Chesneaux, 1971, 1972, 1973; Davis, 1971).

And down to present-day. Irish Catholic secret orders or terrorist organizations have resisted alien rule, in this case Protestant domination. The eighteenth and nineteenth century Irish agrarian secret orders were organized to fight the economic oppression of Protestant landowners; later the Defenders were established to defend the Catholics against Protestant terrorist organizations; and in more recent times the nationalistic revolutionary groups such as the United Irishmen and its successor, the Irish Republican Army, serve as examples (Senior, 1966, 1973; Nowland, 1973).

In colonial situations, secret societies often oppose the spread of foreign groups who compete with them for potential "converts". In these instances loyalty to the secret order serves to insulate the membership and prevent them from making contact with foreigners who might undermine their loyalty to the traditional associations (Moore and Tumin, 1949). In Asia such nativistic or nationalistic secret organizations may have at one time operated as money-lending societies, protectionistic organizations, mutual aid or mortuary societies, and gambling groups (Deacon, 1974; Coulet, 1926). Yet in colonial societies they have also fostered anti-foreign feeling and organized opposition to the government. In Malaya, for example, secret societies in 1825 plotted insurrection; and in 1851 and 1854 these societies led anti-Christian riots in Singapore to counter Roman Catholic influence (Purcell, 1948).

The presence of alienative secret associations along with more open organizations critical of government policies may, under certain circumstances, give impetus to the inherent tendency of most governments to expand surveillance over the various sectors of the population. In state systems ruling class dominance does not permit the simultaneous presence of competing ideologies. Secret associations help perpetuate anti-ruling class ideologies. To protect the dominant power interests such associations must be controlled or destroyed. Thus, state governments must keep constant check on groups with actual or potential competing ideologies. Such surveillance tasks are usually assigned to those agencies responsible for foreign espionage, the intelligence agencies or security organs.

While the conflict of interests between rulers (government) and alienative secret or semi-secret associations provokes further secrecy as well as counterespionage, economic conflicts between business organizations does likewise. Economic competition has always provided a rationale for secrecy especially when certain exclusive knowledge possessed by one competitor gives him a power advantage over his economic rivals.

In both tribal and modern society secrecy and deception is a part of the economic relationship between small-scale competitors. The 17th century West African middleman tribes, in order to maintain their monopoly on European trade to the interior, spread horror stories to the Europeans about interior nations, thus keeping the whites on the coast and preventing them from making direct trading contact with the interior groups (Sunström, 1974). In like fashion the fierce competition between modern Newfoundland deep-sea trawler fishing captains for large catches necessitates each keeping economic secrets from the other. Secrecy enables a captain to retain a temporary monopoly on a successful fishing site and thus bring more profits to his crew and himself; by so doing he retains the valuable loyalty of a highly trained crew (Andersen, Chapter 9 in this book).

Corporations keep secrets from competitors to maintain a competitive advantage. By so doing, they can realize the corporation goal of profit maximization as well as stability. Secrecy, moreover, enables such private economic bureaucracies to shield illegal acts such a bribes, price fixing, and political gifts from both the government and the public. Disclosure of such "dark" secrets might damage the corporate image.

Successful modern industrial espionage produces all sorts of useful information that a rival company may use to advantage: the know-how and details of secret processes and formulas, plans and drawings, specimens, prototypes of machines or apparatus, as well as commercial information involving marketing and sales plans, promotional designs, and so forth (Smith, 1970). Such knowledge is necessary if companies are to avoid unprofitable ventures. The corporation management, as Smith suggests, must learn "not only what the competition is doing but also what it is planning to do (Smith, 1970, p. 4)." Without such knowledge corporation investments in business ventures might result in profit losses rather than gains.

Large corporations have a somewhat different relationship with certain government agencies than with their economic competitors. Governmental bureaucracy forms alliances with many corporations not only as a means to facilitate effective administration but also to gain partisan political support. The executive branches of government disclose sensitive information to business interests who reciprocate with some vital secrets of their own. Such large businesses get advance information vital to their economic or political interests while the executive branches receive vital information and political support in turn (Galnoor, 1975). However, this secrets' reciprocity between big government and big business does give the powerful corporations a distinct advantage over smaller businesses since the information big business receives from the government is vital for profitable business investment of capital (Nadel, 1975). Further, these special ties with government give the managers of such large corporations highly profitable knowledge about stocks and taxes not available to outsiders (Nadel, 1975). Nonetheless, there is a constant tension between government and the business "insiders" for each party has the potential power to use their "marketable" information as a means of coercion; in fact, they often do so (Galnoor, 1975).

The political community, whatever its size or complexity, being self-governing and autonomous, conducts its political transactions with similar political units in terms of its own self-interests. The usual mistrust and rivalry that marks such intertribal or international relationships makes secrecy an inevitable factor in such intercommunity affairs. The major concern of the government, in this instance, is with the protection of military, political, or economic information useful to the rival or enemy community. Such "state secrets" must be protected from the espionage of enemy states.

While most of us are aware that modern governments do engage in espionage, we may not be aware that political communities have been engaged in such enterprises for quite a long period of human history. Before setting out on cattle raids, the Kikuya (East Africa) employed military spies disguised as members of the enemy tribe. The Meru (East Africa) employed ex-members of the tribes they raided as spies (Kenyatta, 1966; Fadiman, 1973). Yoruba (Nigeria) military leaders used an association of hunters for espionage (Fadipe, 1970). The Aztecs employed agents disguised as traders and speaking the language of the region to which they journeyed to collect vital military information for the Aztec rulers (Soustelle, 1962; Berdan, 1975). Members of the West African Dahomean army called *agbadjibeto* served as spies in enemy territory and were given the "inducement of substantial reward in the event of Dahomean victory (Katz, 1967, p. 79)." The Tausug of the Philippines deliberately sent women who had kinship ties with people living in enemy territory on visits to such relatives in order to obtain military intelligence (Kiefer, 1968). And Asian Mogul emperors employed members of the scavenger caste as spies because they had access to the enemy houses. The use of professional merchants as spies was also a quite common practice of government in the civilizations of the Middle East, Southern Europe, and Southeast Asia.

Beginning with the Prussians under Frederick the Great and Bismarck and continuing down to modern-day, Western governments have used espionage on a vast scale in order to better predict and control the complex political and military events taking place in the international community (Cookridge, 1971; Friedrich, 1972; Deacon, 1969, 1972; Ransom, 1959, 1968, 1970). The espionage and counterespionage networks of such modern states serve some of the same functions as they did for premodern states. Now, however, most modern intelligence services, at one time or another, appear to have intervened in the political affairs of foreign states by giving various forms of covert support to opponents of these unfriendly governments, or in some cases, directing paramilitary operations against disfavored governments. This is a radical departure from the traditional role of foreign intelligence, that of information collection and analysis.

Modern state intelligence operations gives further support to Simmel's view that secrecy tends to breed more secrecy. Espionage provokes greater concern for security by foreign governments or domestic groups. Aside from developing more effective security systems to guard their own secrets, including counterespionage, they also try to deceive their enemies by planting false information with known agents or subverting the enemy agent for their own counterespionage purposes. Intelligence gained due to deceptions may be of dubious value, requiring further espionage and evaluation. Many agents share the same age, face, class or cultural characteristics of people upon whom they spy, and therefore may develop strong sympathy for their cause. Because of this they may betray their employer (Marx, 1974, 1979). Thus, intelligence bureaucrats must conduct surveillance over their own employees as well as the enemy.

The security systems of state intelligence serve the function of not only advancing their own aggressive foreign espionage networks, but also protecting their own internal operational secrets from foreign counterespionage. Moreover, the intelligence community also must investigate possible foreign espionage against any branch of government.

Counterintelligence agencies are responsible for investigating foreign espionage. The work of counterintelligence or counterespionage agents involves a wide variety of tasks, including checking on reported disaffection cases (employees with grudges against a government organization or personnel with big financial problems), suspected leaks, routine surveillance of embassies or diplomatic residences, and suspicious incidents such as missing documents that might indicate espionage (Copeland, 1974).

The great concern for state security within totalitarian systems obliterates the distinction between internal and external intelligence. Foreign intelligence is combined with domestic counterespionage. But such distinctions between internal and external intelligence operations become hazy in democratic societies during periods of major international crisis, war, or periods of political paranoia generated by hyperpatriotism and xenophobia. During these periods, intelligence agencies are quite capable of utilizing the same espionage techniques employed in foreign espionage against their own citizens.

As recent events have demonstrated modern democratic governments have increased secret surveillance of their citizens, using the techniques of foreign espionage. Of great concern to such governments is the possible use of dissident political organizations by foreign agents for "subversive" ends. It is understandable why secret orders still provoke such suspicion. Secrecy, indeed, breeds the suspicion by outsiders that activities which must be hidden are likely illegal, immoral, or subversive. Moreover, the secret society being a power separate and independent of state government is often considered a threat by political leaders unless they can establish control over it or discover its true plans and have knowledge of its activities. Thus, modern secret associations are subject to much government espionage.

But even many "open" associations, ones whose goals and membership are not concealed, have become the object of state surveillance. Indeed, in some cases intelligence agents, after joining such groups, act as agent provocateurs, encouraging violent acts to bring discredit on such organizations, thus enabling the authorities to arrest and put in jail the group leaders or its other members for illegal acts. Such agents may also provoke dissension and conflict within the organization to weaken it. In the United States, for example, agents have used such tactics not only against such secret associations as the Ku Klux Klan and the Weathermen, but also against the Students for Democratic Action, the Vietnam Veterans Against the War, the Black Panthers and other campus radical organizations (Marx, 1974).[5]

Historical evidence seems to support the view that intelligence services, whatever their nature, are usually coopted by political leaders for internal surveillance in addition to their role in foreign espionage. Dahomean kings also used internal espionage to maintain their authority. These monarchs employed a large body of part-time spies to keep subordinate chiefs under observation, largely to prevent the chiefs from subverting their authority or plotting against them. These spies reported to one of the Dahomean ministers who, in turn, reported their observations to the King (Katz, 1967). Both Hawaiian chiefs and Zulu rulers used their intelligence agents for internal and external espionage (Hommon, 1976; Walter, 1969).

The internal politics of both public and private bureaucracies also generate a climate of competition and strife, conflict which fosters various patterns of deception and secrecy. However, social science has little interest in the secrecy systems related to the internal politics of complex organizations (Sjoberg and Miller, 1973). Their disregard of the role of information control within such bureaucracies is in marked contrast to their fascination with the secrecy process within small-scale organizations such as secret orders or associations. This lack of interest in bureaucratic secrecy is a consequence, in part, of the social scientists' use of theoretical models or perspectives that exclude from analysis the internal conflict of interests within complex organizations, conflict which results in much mutual secrecy by the antagonistic parties. For example, the Weberian

[5]In the United States Presidents, beginning with Franklin Roosevelt, have authorized such agencies as the Federal Bureau of Investigation (F.B.I.) to conduct surveillance of their political enemies (Bernstein, 1976). Planting or recruiting agents within terrorist groups may prove difficult since such terrorist organizations either operate from secure geographic bases (like the Palestine Liberation Organization) or have no fixed headquarters or visible ties with society (e.g., the Japanese "Red Army") (Rositzke, 1977).

model focuses attention on the legally prescribed structures and the mechanisms by which they are maintained; the classical management theorists attribute conflict to a failure of adequate control and planning while human relations theorists attribute it to a failure of leadership or adequate management (Haas and Drabek, 1973).

In reality within bureaucracies there is a continuing struggle by each group (unit, department, division, agency) for autonomy, security and prestige (Haas and Drabek, 1973). Through bargaining struggles such groups attempt to preserve or enlarge the domains over which they have some discretion by limiting their dependence on other groups within the organization; they also strive to maintain or increase their share of scarce organizational resources in order to enhance their security and they also attempt to increase their prestige by presenting management with a picture of their activities that puts their units in the most favored position possible. Such divisional competition, needless to say, promotes divisional secrecy and deception. Departments may keep two records, one to be viewed by supervisors that minimizes or hides poor performance and one for internal consumption that gives a more realistic assessment of department activities. Of course, such secrecy strategies are employed by government bureaucracies as well as industrial organizations. For example, while J. Edgar Hoover was Director of the Federal Bureau of Investigation, bureau officials were required to keep separate files, one which was serialized and, thus, subject to court order, and another, containing unrecorded information potentially damaging to the Bureau; under the appropriate circumstances such secret files could be destroyed without outsiders even knowing of their existence (Theoharis, 1978).

At the management or directorate level of complex organizations competition for prestigeful positions in the organization promotes both secrecy as well as disclosure. The heads of both public and private bureaucracies try to maintain control over strategic information that, if revealed, might enable lower-ranking managers to challenge their authority and leadership (Collins, 1975). It is for this reason that managers frequently withhold information about the reasons for certain executive decisions, thereby minimizing threats to their autonomy (Haas and Drabek, 1973). However, given the nature of the bureaucratic system some individuals must breach internal security if they are to get power within the organization (Lowry, 1972; Wilensky, 1967; Nadel, 1975; Galnoor, 1975). Certain management or technical employees may also find it expedient to leak secrets to rival companies as a means of increasing their job chances with a company competitor (Rourke, 1961).[6]

The internal secrecy within large-scale business organizations is also one manifestation of the conflict of interests between workers and managers. Often workers who have a more practical grasp of production techniques than either the managers or technicians fail to inform the management that managerial orders require them to perform operations that are technical mistakes. On the other hand, management control over financial and production data prevents unions from using such secret information in challenging decisions (Goldman and Van Houten, 1977). Such political, economic and social antagonisms between workers and managers merely reflect the more basic class contradictions that dominate such business organizations (Heydebrand, 1977).

These class contradictions within complex organizations are also manifest in the managements' use of internal surveillance to assure stability and predictability of the work force in order that organizational production and efficiency is achieved. As Rule (1974) suggests, modern corporations accumulate as much detailed documentation as possible on their employees to better control and regulate their behavior. Many businesses maintain constant surveillance of their employees, even after they are hired, to assure loyalty, honesty, and adequate work performance (Creech, 1966).

Government bureaucracies, and most particularly intelligence agencies, use much the same security techniques as many private organizations. These include secrecy classifications, screening and security clearances for potential employees, indoctrination, oaths of loyalty (sometimes), severe penalties for unauthorized disclosure, and continued surveillance of employees once hired ("aftercare"). Within the executive leadership only the most trusted officials may be privy to the totality of some secret plans or activities, while others know only small details rather than the whole picture. Still others gain access to certain details on a need-to-know basis. Advisory committees simply hold closed meetings, not open to the public or press.

The social order of most complex organizations is politically negotiated rather than merely enforced by administrative de-

---

[6]Perrow (1972) is correct when he criticizes Wilensky (1967) for placing too much emphasis on the failure of internal intelligence as a reason for the abuse of power and bureaucratic pathologies. As Perrow points out, in many instances, bureaucrats have enough information about alternative course of action, but they choose to ignore certain information or to suppress it for their own purposes.

cree (Benson, 1973). Intelligence organizations constitute exceptions since within such organizations order is imposed rather than negotiated. The rigid secrecy requirements imposed on departments as well as on individuals within intelligence agencies and the intensive nature of the internal surveillance makes normal political negotiation impossible. In such cases, then, the bureaucratic organizations are "inflexible" ones; most members have a high sense of identity, purpose and commitment (Perrow, 1972; Kaiser, Chapter 12 in this book).[7]

However, within most bureaucracies the structural contradictions that generate departmental or class conflict necessitate the same sort of political bargaining that takes place in the wider society. Bureaucratic politics is no different than state politics for it breeds secrecy and deception. The bargaining parties hide their weaknesses, stress their virtues, and keep secret any information that is harmful to their cause.

CONCLUSIONS

Conflicts of interests between individuals and groups over values, prestige, power, wealth, control of resources, or political goals initiate processes of social interaction which include information control (secrecy). The actions and reactions of individuals, organizations, and political communities to each other depends not only how they define their own interests but also on how they perceive these to be threatened by outsiders. Individuals and the organizations to which they belong determine the rewards or costs of secrecy or disclosure in terms of their own self-interest as the conflict with outsiders intensifies or dissipates.

Secrecy is a social resource which opponents can use defensively or offensively during social conflicts. Antagonists who keep secrets from one another, must employ security devices to protect such secrets. The nature as well as the effectiveness of such security systems are determined by social structural, cultural, economic, ecological and political factors.

Information control, then, defines the social boundaries be-

---

[7]However, even in highly authoritarian organizations there can be secret resistance to leadership. In "total institutions" such as prisons, concentration camps, and mental hospitals, informal secrecy groups emerge in response to the coercive environment of such organizations. For example, in the Nazi State Security (SS) concentration camps prisoner groups smuggled healthy prisoners in danger of being killed or shipped to death camps, onto the sick list to put them beyond control of the SS (Strauss, 1978).

tween individuals and also between organizations. During the conflict process such social boundaries can be extended or contracted. But at the present time our knowledge is insufficient to determine the exact nature of this process at all levels of social organization.

As we have seen small social systems such as the family, may impose secrecy norms on its members when information control protects the interests of the group in conflict with outsiders. In peasant communities, where family rivalries may be intense, such information control serves to hide "dark secrets" that could damage the family's social or economic position.

Where the family or kinship unit constitutes a corporate group engaged in criminal activities that put it in conflict with the government, family secrecy is even more vital. Criminal gangs such as the Chauffers of Italy and the Thugs of India initiated their own children or adopted children (Annan, 1967a; Heckethorn, 1965, I). In a like fashion the I-Kuan-Tao society of China recruited entire families (Deliusin, 1972).

Elected or appointed officials must also establish a network of secret keepers if they are to use their public office for financial gain. Those who profit from the "corruption" of such officials are likely to conceal such transgressions. For example, corrupt judges, who take or force financial bribes, build-up of a "working team" that has a vested interest in concealing the judges' illegal acts. So too do the politicians or others who gain economic advantages from corrupt political machines such as the Tweed Ring in New York City between 1866-1871 (Strauss, 1978). Of course outsiders may suspect that graft is occurring but the details of the operation as well as its major participants are not known except to the insiders to particular deals. However, "team" loyalty probably is less assured in this case compared to the "team" loyalty characteristic of the Thugs.

Membership in alienative or conformative secret associations restricts an individual's decision-making role in the secrecy process even further. Through their control of conformative secret associations tribal leaders reinforce the mystic characteristic of their offices as well as have available to them an organizational weapon for controlling their political enemies. These secret societies also put on public rituals which dramatize the power of their leaders and reinforce the traditions that serve as charters for chiefly power (Collins, 1975). On the other hand alienative secret associations employ secrecy to further their anti-establishment political goals in face of government espionage and repression. In both these cases such associations place a high value on security. Strict secrecy norms are enforced. Secret organizations have devised ways to test the reliability of initiates (Simmel, 1906; Butt-Thompson, 1969; Harley, 1941, 1950; Ruel, 1969; Daraul, 1961; Heckethorn, 1965, II; Meek, 1950). Unreliable initiates will never advance to the stage where "dark secrets" will be transmitted to them (Simmel, 1950). Once initiated, association members are required to observe strict security procedures. Breaches of security are harshly punished. The extent to which a secret association can successfully appropriate the complete devotion and loyalty of members, to that extent its secrets are safe.

In modern nation-states, as we have demonstrated, it is not an individual's membership in secret associations but his (her) membership in large-scale organizations (bureaucracies) as well as citizenship itself that determines what the person will be required to reveal or keep secret. To fulfill his legal obligations to the government, to get credit or loans, to even obtain jobs the citizen must reveal to both private and government organizations or agencies considerable personal information. In this regard there is often a clash between a citizen's self-interest and that of the state or private employer. While citizens may attempt to deceive both government and employers their options in these matters are more restricted than they are in the concealment or disclosure of information during interpersonal encounters.

Once hired by the government or private corporation the individual employee will be under various degrees of surveillance depending on the nature of his job. Through such surveillance systems managers hope to maximize the efficiency and productivity of their organizations by preventing employee disloyalty or subversion of corporate goals. Here again the concern for security by both public and private bureaucracies stems from economic and political rivalry inside as well as outside such large-scale organizations. The rivalries between nation-states merely transfer these secrecy processes from the national to the international levels.

If secrecy, security, deception, espionage and counterespionage contributed to system maintenance or system adaptation by helping a system maintain a value consensus or improving the "mapping" propensities of the system or subsystem, we could rightly attribute a functional significance to the secrecy process. But the evidence which we have summarized in this paper suggests that secrecy does not make these contributions.

The secrecy process within bureaucracies intensifies internal political rivalries and class contradictions, subverts the flow of vital information up and down the hierarchy, hides as well as creates inefficiency and, at the policy making levels of government, secrecy prevents useful criticism and evaluations by those excluded from the "inner circles". The informational feedback system which is supposed to generate changes and new direction in social systems simply does not operate in the way system theories suggest it does. And instead of reinforcing consensual values, patterns of espionage and surveillance provoke alienation, sometimes even anti-establishment ideologies.

The increasing employment of undercover agents by police forces further illustrates these social consequences of secrecy. Such secret agents are used against political dissenters or members of criminal subcultures. Rather than discourage criminal activity such undercover agents encourage criminal acts in order to make arrests and under some circumstances in their "cover" role as gamblers and narcotic dealers, they eventually embrace criminal values, thus becoming converted to the criminal subculture. In a like fashion, such agents often encourage terrorist acts by political radicals rather than suppress them (Marx, 1974, 1979).

Social systems also lack reliable information to successfully "map" their external environments, thereby adjusting or changing structures to achieve goals in more realistic ways. Our discussion of modern foreign espionage has served as one illustration. There is some question as to whether, in the long run, espionage really contributes to national security. Many policy makers "grossly exaggerate its importance and reliability (Scoville, 1976, pp. 3–6)." Much of the information collected by secret agents or informants is unreliable. The enemy may give false information to known agents. Agents themselves may lie, exaggerate, misperceive, or improperly evaluate the facts they collect (Marx, 1974; Lowry, 1979). In effect, then, secrecy prevents what systems theories call the "pool of adaptive variability" from being effectively employed by systems in working out creative adaptations to their environments.

The concern for state secrecy which modern nationalism has in part generated may, in the long run, work against the interest of modern states rather than for them. For example, military secrecy is supposed to result in ambiguity about the measures of relative strength of rival nations. But this situation merely increases the likelihood of violence. The deception employed by adversary states regarding their power and military capability may convince one state that it has more power than a rival and therefore should exercise it before other states reach a parity with it. Under these conditions no state really knows for sure whether it is more powerful until it goes to war (Coser, 1963). If adversaries could measure each other's strength prior to a confrontation, their antagonistic interests might be adjusted without conflict (Mack and Snyder, 1957). This is further indication that secrecy prevents adequate "system mapping."

Thus, social divisiveness which is generated by conflicting interests creates the social conditions under which secrecy thrives. To the extent that secrecy denies social actors information which might reveal that they are exploited, or manipulated by others, to that extent then secrecy promotes order. For the most part, however, secrecy furthers social antagonisms and tensions. Outsiders, whose goal ambitions are denied by the secrecy of their antagonists, seek to penetrate the security barriers of their enemies. This espionage and, in turn counterespionage, exaccerbates conflict which leads in turn to further deception.

People are not exclusively "secret leakers" or "secret keepers." They are both. Each of us, by choice or by the requirements of certain group memberships, pursue our interests through both concealing information and disclosing it. The social roles which each of us play involve us in the structural contradictions that characterize all social systems and which generate structural conflict. Such conflict leads to the social divisiveness, the clash of interests, that make secrecy so important an element in all social relationships. Secrecy enables the powerful to escape accountability for their exploitation and manipulation of the weak and enables the weak to escape coercion by the powerful and to oppose them.

References

Annan, D. Thuggee. In *Secret Societies* (edited by N. McKenzie) New York: Collier Books, 1967(a).

———. The Assassins and the Knights Templar. In *Secret Societies* (edited by N. MacKenzie) New York: Collier Books, 1969(b).

Bascom, W. R. *The Sociological Role of the Yoruba Cult Groups.* American Anthropologist Memoir No. 63, 1944.

Bates, A. P. Privacy—A Useful Concept? *Social Forces,* 1964, *42,* 429–434.

Benson, J. K. The Analysis of Bureaucratic Professional Conflict: Functional Versus Dialectical Approaches. *The Sociological Quarterly,* 1973, *14,* 291–308.

Berdan, F. M. J. *Trade, Tribute and Market in the Aztec Empire.* Ph. D. dissertation. University of Texas: Austin, 1975.

Bernstein, B. J. Road to Watergate and Beyond: The Growth and Abuse of Executive Authority since 1940. *Law and Contemporary Problems,* 1976, *40,* 58–86.

Bhuntani, S. *Secret Society System Among the American Indians and the Africans.* Master of Arts thesis, Chapel Hill: University of North Carolina, 1962.

Blau, M. *The Dynamics of Bureaucracy.* Chicago: University of Chicago Press, 2nd ed., 1962.

———. Parameters of Social Structure. In *Approaches to the Study of Social Structure* (edited by P. M. Blau) New York: Free Press, 1975.

———. *Inequality and Heterogeneity.* New York: Free Press, 1977.

Blumer, H. *Symbolic Interactionism.* Englewood Cliffs, N.J.: Prentice-Hall, Inc., 1969.

Bok, S. *Lying.* New York: Pantheon Books, 1978.

Bozeman, A. A. *Conflict in Africa.* Princeton, N.J.: Princeton University Press, 1976.

Bradfield, R. M. *A Natural History of Associations.* Vol. I, II. London: Duckworth, 1973.

Bredemeier, H. C. Exchange Theory. In *A History of Sociological Analysis* (edited by T. Bottomore and R. Nisbet) New York: Basic Books, 1978.

Buckley, W. *Sociology and Modern Systems Theory.* Englewood Cliffs, N.J.: Prentice-Hall, Inc., 1967.

———. Society as a Complex Adaptive System, In *Modern System Research for the Behavioral Scientist* (edited by W. Buckley) Chicago: Aldine, 1968.

Butt-Thompson, F. W. *West African Secret Societies.* New York: Argosy-Antiquarian, Ltd., 1969.

Campbell, J. K. *Honour, Family and Patronage.* Oxford: Clarendon Press, 1964.

Chandler, D. L. *Brothers in Blood.* New York: E. P. Dutton and Co. Inc., 1975.

Chesneaux, J. *Secret Societies in China.* London: Heinemann Educational Books, 1971.

———. Secret Societies in China's Historical Evolution. In *Popular Movements and Secret Societies in China 1840–1950* (edited by J. Chesneaux) Stanford, Cal.: Stanford University Press, 1972.

———. *Peasant Revolts in China, 1840–1949.* New York: W. W. Norton and Co., 1973.

Cohen, A. The Politics of Mysticism in Some Local Communities of Newly Independent African States. In *Local Level Politics* (edited by M. J. Swartz), Chicago: Aldine, 1968.

Collins, R. *Conflict Sociology.* New York: Academic Press, 1975.

Comber, L. F. *Chinese Secret Societies of Malaya.* Monographs of the Association for Asian Studies No. 6. Locust Valley, New York: J. J. Augustin, Inc., 1959.

Cookridge, E. S. *Gehlen: Spy of the Century.* New York: Random House, 1971.

Copeland, M. *Without Cloak or Dagger.* New York: Simon and Schuster, 1974.

Coser, L. A. The Dysfunctions of Military Secrecy. Social Problems, 1963, *11,* 12–33.

Coulet, G. *Secret Societies in the Country of Annam.* Saigon: Imprimerie Commercial D. Ardin, Translated by Human Relations Area Files (1957), 1926.

Creech, W. A. The Privacy of Government Employees. Law and Contemporary Problems, 1966, *31,* 413–433.

Curzon, D. The Generic Secrets of Government Decision Making. In *Government Secrecy in Democracies* (edited by I. Galnoor), New York: Harper and Row, 1977.

Daraul, A. *A History of Secret Societies.* New York: Citadel Press, 1961.

Davis, F. *Primitive Revolutionaries of China.* Honolulu: University Press of Hawaii, 1971.

Deacon. R. *A History of the British Secret Service.* New York: Taplinger, 1969.

———. *A History of the Russian Secret Service.* New York: Taplinger, 1972.

———. *The Chinese Secret Service.* New York: Ballantine Books, 1974.

Deliusin, L. The I-Kuan-Tao Society. In *Popular Movements and Secret Societies in China, 1840–1950* (edited by J. Chesneaux), Standord: Stanford University Press, 1972.

Derlega, V. I. and Chaikin, A. L. *Sharing Intimacy: What We Reveal to Others and Why.* Englewood Cliffs, N.J.: Prentice-Hall Inc., 1975.

———. Privacy and Self-Disclosure in Social Relationships. *Journal of Social Issues,* 1977, *33,* 102–113.

Fadiman, J. A. *Traditional Warfare Among the Meru of Mt. Kenya.* Ph.D. dissertation. Madison, Wisc,: University of Wisconsin, 1973.

Fadipe, N. A. *The Sociology of the Yoruba.* Ibadan: University of Ibadan Press, 1970.

Flaherty, D. H. *Privacy in Colonial New England.* Charlottesville: University Press of Virginia, 1972.

Ford, C. *Smoke from Their Fires.* New Haven: Yale University Press, 1941.

Forde, D. The Government Roles of Associations Among the Yako. *Africa,* 1961, *31,* 309–323.

———. The Government Roles of Associations Among the Yako. In *Comparative Political Systems* (edited by R. Cohen and J. Middleton) Garden City, N.Y.: Natural History Press, 1967.

Fowler, H. W. and Fowler, F. G. (eds.) *The Concise Oxford Dictionary, 5th ed.* Oxford: Clarendon Press, 1964.

Friedrich, C. L. *The Pathology of Politics.* New York: Harper and Row, 1972.

Galnoor, I. The Information Marketplace, In *Government Secrecy in Democracies* (edited by I. Galnoor), New York: Harper and Row, 1977.

———. Government Secrecy: Exchanges, Intermediaries, and Middleman. *Public Administration Review,* 1975, *35,* 32–42.

Gilsenan, M. Lying, Honor and Contradiction. In *Transaction and Meaning* (edited by B. Kepferer) Philadelphia: ISHI, 1976.

Gist, N. P. *Secret Societies: A Cultural Study of Fraternalism in the United States.* The University of Missouri Studies, *15,* 1940.

Goffman, I. *The Presentation of Self in Everyday Life.* Garden City, N.Y.: Doubleday and Co., 1959.

Goldman, P. and Van Houten, D. R. Managerial Strategies and The Worker: a Marxist Analysis of Bureaucracy. *The Sociological Quarterly,* 1977, *18,* 108–125.

Gross, F. *The Revolutionary Party.* Westport, Conn.: Greenwood Press, 1974.

Gunther, E. *Klallam Ethnography.* University of Washington Publications in Anthropology, 1927, I, 171–314.

Haas, J. E. and Drabek, T. E. *Complex Organizations: A Sociological Perspective.* New York: Macmillan, 1973.

Halperin, M. H. Decision-Making for Covert Operations, *Society,* 1975, *12,* 45–51.

Harley, G. W. *Notes on the Poro in Liberia.* Papers of the Peabody Museum of American Archaeology and Ethnology, 1941, *19,* Cambridge, Mass.: Harvard University.

———. *Masks as Agents of Social Control in Northeast Liberia.* Papers of the Peabody Museum of American Archaeology and Ethnology, 1950, *32,* Cambridge, Mass.: Harvard University.

Hazelrigg, L. E. Reexamination of Simmel's the Secret and the Secret Society: Nine Propositions. *Social Forces,* 1969, *47,* 323.

Heckethorn, C. *The Secret Societies of All Ages and Countries.* Vols. I, II. New Hyde Park, N.Y.: Universal Books, 1965.

Herskovits, M. J. *Dahomey: An Ancient West African Kingdom.* Locust Valley, N.Y.: Augustin, 1938.

Heydebrand, W. Organizational Contradictions in Public Bureaucracies: Toward a Marxian Theory of Organizations. *The Sociological Quarterly,* 1977, *18,* 83–107.

Homans, G. C. *The Human Group.* New York: Harcourt, Brace and World, 1950.

———. *Social Behavior: Its Elementary Forms.* New York: Harcourt, Brace, Javanovich Inc., 1974.

Hommon, R. J. *The Formation of Primitive States in Pre-Contact Hawaii.* Ph.D. dissertation. University of Arizona, 1976.

Katz, N. The Kingdom of Dahomey: *Political Organization and Ecological Relations in a Slave Trading State.* Ph.D. dissertation, Los Angeles: University of California, 1967.

Keightley, T. *Secret Societies of the Middle Ages.* London: M. A. Nattali, 1864.

Kelvin, P. A Socio-Psychological Examination of Privacy. *Journal of Social and Clinical Psychology,* 1973, *12,* 248–261.

Kenyatta, H. E. M. *My People of the Kikuya.* Nairobi: Oxford University Press, 1966.

Kiefer, T. M. Institutionalized Friendship and Warfare Among the Tausug of Jolo. *Ethnology,* 1968, *7,* 225–245.

Koch, K. F. Sociogenic and Psychogenic Models in Anthropology: the Function of Jale' Initiation. *Man,* 1974, *9,* 367–382.

Kriesberg, L. *The Sociology of Social Conflict.* Englewood Cliffs, N.J.: Prentice Hall, Inc., 1973.

Landes, R. *The Prairie Potawatomi.* Madison, Wisc.: University of Winconsin Press, 1970.

Leyton, E. Irish Friends and "Friends": The Nexus of Friendship, Kinship and Class in Aughnaboy. In *The Compact* (edited by E. Leyton), Newfoundland Social and Economic Papers No. 3. Institute of Social and Economic Research. Memorial University of Newfoundland, 1974.

Liebenow, J. G. Liberia. In *Political Parties and National Integration in Tropical Africa* (edited by J. S. Coleman and C. G. Rosberg), Berkeley: University of California Press, 1964.

Little, K. L. Mende Political Institutions in Transition. *Africa,* 1947, *17,*

———. The Poro Society as an Arbiter of Culture. *African Studies,* 1948, *7,* 2–15.

———. Secret Society. In *A Dictionary of the Social Sciences* (edited by J. Gould and W. L. Kolb), New York: Free Press, 1964.

———. The Political Function of the Poro. *Africa,* 1965, *35,* 350–353; 1966, *36,* 62–71.

———. Voluntary Associations in Urban Life: A Case Study of Differential Adaptation. In *Social Organization* (edited by M. Freedman) Chicago: Aldine Publishing Co., 1967.

Lowry, P. *The Case Against the C.I.A.: A Functional Critique of Covert and Political Intelligence* (Unpublished Manuscript), 1978.

Lyman, S. M. Chinese Secret Societies in the Occident: Notes and Suggestions for Research in the Sociology of Secrecy. *The Canadian Review of Sociology and Anthropology*, 1964, *1*, 79–102.

———. *The Asian in the West* (Social Science and Humanities Publication No. 4), Western Studies Center. Desert Research Institute. University of Nevada, Reno and Las Vegas, Nevada, 1970.

Mack, R. W. and Snyder, R. C. The Analysis of Social Conflict: Toward an Overview and Synthesis. *Journal of Conflict Resolution*, 1957, *1*, 212–248.

Marx, G. Thoughts on a Neglected Category of Social Movement Participant: The Agent Provocateur and The Informant. *American Journal of Sociology*, 1974, *80*, 302–420.

———. The New Police Undercover Work. *Urban Life*, 1979 (In press).

Mass-Dionisopoulas, R. The Evil Eye and Bewitchment in a Peasant Village. In *The Evil Eye* (edited by C. Maloney) New York: Columbia, 1976.

Meek, C. K. *Law and Authority in a Nigerian Tribe.* New York: Oxford University Press, 1950.

Merton, R. K. Manifest and Latent Functions. In *Social Theory and Social Structure* (edited by R. Merton). New York: Free Press, 1968.

Moore, W. E. *The Conduct of the Corporation.* New York: Random House, 1962.

———. Functionalism. In *A History of Sociological Analysis* (edited by T. Bottomore and R. Nisbet). New York: Basic Books, 1978.

——— and Tumin, M. Some Social Functions of Ignorance. *American Sociological Review*, 1949, *14*, 787–795.

Murphy, W. P. *A Semantic and Logical Analysis of Kpelle Proverb Metaphors of Secrecy.* Ph.D. dissertation. Stanford University, 1976.

Nadal, M. V. Corporate Secrecy and Political Accountability. *Public Administration Review*, 1975, *35*, 14–23.

Nowland, K. B. Conclusion. In *Secret Societies in Ireland* (edited by D. Williams). New York: Barnes and Noble, 1973.

Obershall, A. Theories of Social Conflict. *Annual Review of Sociology*, 1978, *4*, 291–315.

O'Brien, D. M. *Privacy: Purposes and Paradoxes*, 1977, (In press)

Ottenberg, S. *Secrecy and Secret Society Initiation Rites.* Mimeo. University of Washington, 1973.

Parker, A. C. Secret Medicine Societies of the Seneca. *American Anthropologist* 1909, *11*, 161–185.

Parsons, T. *The Social System.* New York: Free Press, 1951.

———. *The Structure of Social Action.* New York: Free Press, 1968.

———. *The System of Modern Societies.* Englewood Cliffs, N.J.: Prentice-Hall, Inc., 1971.

Passin, H. Tarahumara Prevarication: A Problem in Field Method. *American Anthropologist,* 1942, *44,* 235–247.
Perrow, C. *Complex Organizations.* Glenview, Ill.: Scott, Foresman & Co., 1972.
Ponse, B. Secrecy in the Lesbian World. *Urban Life,* 1976, *5,* 313–342.
Purcell, V. *The Chinese in Malaya.* London: Oxford University Press, 1948.
Ransom, H. H. *Central Intelligence and National Security.* Cambridge, Mass.: Harvard University Press, 1959.
———. Intelligence, Political and Military. In *International Encyclopaedia of the Social Sciences* (edited by D. L. Sills), vol. 7. New York: Free Press-MacMillan, 1968.
———. *The Intelligence Establishment.* Cambridge, Mass.: Harvard University Press, 1970.
Reese, J. The Federal Republic of Germany. In *Government Secrecy in Democracies* (edited by I. Galnoor), New York: Harper and Row, 1977.
Rigney, D. C. *Organizational Secrecy. An Investigation of Hidden Realities.* Ph.D. dissertation. The University of Texas at Austin, 1975.
Roberts, J. M. *The Mythology of the Secret Societies.* New York: Charles Scribners Sons, 1972.
Rositzke, H. *The C.I.A.'s Secret Operations.* New York: Readers' Digest Press, 1977.
Rourke, F. E. *Secrecy and Publicity.* Baltimore: Johns Hopkins Press, 1961.
———. The United States. In *Government Secrecy in Democracies* (edited by I. Galnoor), New York: Harper and Row, 1977.
Ruel, M. *Leopards and Leaders.* London: Tavistock Publ., 1967.
Rule, J. B. *Private Lives and Public Serveillance.* New York: Shocken Books, 1974.
Schorr, D. The Assassins. *The New York Review of Books,* 1977, *24,* 14–22.
Scoville, Jr., H. Is Espionage a Necessary Instrument for Intelligence Gathering. *Center Report,* 1976, *9,* 3–5.
Senior, H. *Orangeism in Ireland and Britain: 1795–1836.* London: Routledge and Kegan Paul, 1966.
———. The Early Orange Order 1795–1870. In *Secret Societies in Ireland* (edited by T. D. Williams), New York: Barnes and Noble, 1973.
Shils, E. Privacy: Its Constitution and Vicissitudes. *Law and Contemporary Problems,* 1966, *31,* 281–306.
———. *Center and Periphery: Essays in Macrosociology.* Chicago: University of Chicago Press, 1975.
Simmel, G. The Society of Secrecy and the Secret Society (translated by Albion W. Small). *American Journal of Sociology,* 1906, *11,* 441–498.
———. *The Sociology of George Simmel* (edited and translated by K. H. Wolff). Glencoe, Ill.: Free Press, 1950.

Sjoberg, G. and Miller, P. J. Social Research on Bureaucracy: Limitations and Opportunities. *Social Problems,* 1973, *21,* 129–143.

Smart, N. The Mysteries. In *Secret Societies* (edited by N. MacKenzie), New York: Collier Books, 1967.

Smith, P. I. S. *Industrial Intelligence and Espionage.* London: Business Books Ltd., 1970.

Soustelle, J. *The Daily Life of the Aztecs,* New York: MacMillan, 1962.

Strauss, A. *Negotiations.* San Francisco: Jossey-Bass, 1978.

Sundström, L. *The Exchange Economy of Pre-Colonial Tropical Africa.* New York: St. Martin's Press, 1974.

Theoharis, A. *Spying on Americans.* Philadelphia: Temple University Press, 1978.

Turner, J. H. *The Structure of Sociological Theory.* Homewood, Ill.: Dorsey Press, 1974.

Walker, J. The Secret Service Under Charles II and James II. *Transactions of the Royal Historical Society,* 1932, *115,* 211–235.

Walker, E. V. *Terror and Resistance.* London: Oxford University Press, 1969.

Webster, H. *Primitive Secret Societies: A Study of Early Politics and Religion.* New York: MacMillan, 1908.

Wedgwood, C. H. The Nature and Functions of Secret Societies. *Oceania,* 1930, *1,* 124–141.

Wilensky, H. L. *Organizational Intelligence.* New York: Basic Books, Inc., 1967.

Wilsnack, R. Information Control: A Conceptual Framework for Sociological Analysis. *Urban Life,* 1979 (In Press).

Wise, D. *The American Police State.* New York: Vintage Books, 1976.

Unit 2

Aspects of Privacy

Introduction

Privacy, as we learned in Unit I, involves the seclusion or withdrawal of individuals from public scrutiny in order that they may engage in intimate acts or relationships considered to be no threat to the social order by outsiders. By contrast private-life secrecy involves concealment of deviant or illegal acts or relationships. In either case, successful concealment cannot be taken for granted. Community surveillance (espionage) may necessitate some form of security system, which may or may not succeed in providing protection. In part, the relative ease or difficulty in preserving privacy or private-life secrecy will depend on the size of the community and the nature of its structure.

In small communities, where individuals are subject to a high level of neighborhood surveillance, protection of secrets is difficult. Thomas Gregor conducted a study of information control in such a small community. His paper is based on his fieldwork among the Mehinaku Indians of Central Brazil. Within the Mehinaku Indian village there was a high level of intense, personal interaction. As a consequence of the small size of the village and as a result of its layout and the design of its houses, village members were highly vulnerable to community observation. Information on individual behavior was, then, quickly disseminated throughout the community by gossip. Much of this gossip circulated information detrimental to various social relationships. To prevent the disruption of such social ties, the Mehinaku must conceal misconduct, such as adultery, or theft, or inadequacies of sexual or economic performance.

Village members reduce the level of community surveillance and preserve their privacy by carrying out clandestine activities, such as adultery, in secluded forest clearings or by taking advantage of the institutionalized seclusion required of adolescents. Also by distorting information about their own activities, they try to persuade the village that the gossip about them, no matter how accurate in reality, is quite misleading. In this way miscreants, by manipulating village opinion, can undermine village confidence in the accuracy of the gossip about them.

However, too much secrecy can prove disruptive. Lack of village information about individuals and their whereabouts or activities may generate village fear that they are "up to no good," possibly even conducting witchcraft against someone in the community. To maintain village cohesion then, the Mehinaku must maintain a balance between exposure and seclusion.

People's desire for privacy is as much influenced by community values as by their wish to avoid the social consequences of misconduct. The selection by Jeffrey Victor, based on his research in the French working-class village of Rival, located in Normandy, suggests that the French employ privacy as a social device through which they maintain individualism, the components of which involve French suspiciousness, stubbornness, and a desire for independence. Privacy enables the French to actualize these values.

The French working class employ various strategies to maintain the social distance necessary for privacy. These include physical barriers, like high walls around their houses, exclusion of co-workers from their intimacy group, as well as formalism and ritualism in social relations with outsiders.

Privacy also enables the French to resist pressures to conform. With their intimates, kinsmen and close friends, the Frenchman can engage in unguarded and unrestrained interaction. Intimates freely express feelings, evaluations, and emotional reactions.

While such close associates are sources of psychological satisfaction, outsiders constitute a threat to the Frenchman's individualism because they are a potential source of ridicule, criticism, and jealousy. Thus, the Frenchmen in this community have a strong need for privacy to protect themselves and their circle of intimates from outside social control.

A conclusion one must reach after reading the papers in this unit is that the "right" to privacy, whether sanctioned by law or custom, varies in significance from society to society. Nowhere can individuals dictate where, when, and under what conditions these rights can be exercised. Such rights are not absolute or unqualified. Moreover, in all societies, individuals must devise strategies, sometimes quite elaborate, to protect their privacy or secrets.

3

Exposure and Seclusion: A Study of Institutionalized Isolation Among the Mehinaku Indians of Brazil[1]

Thomas Gregor
Vanderbilt University

Among the Mehinaku Indians, a small tropical forest tribe in Central Brazil, there is an ethnographically unusual elaboration of seclusion practices. During a Mehinaku's lifetime he may spend as many as eight years in relative isolation, cut off from his fellows by real and symbolic barriers. The purpose of this paper is to make this practice intelligible and at the same time to provide a useful perspective for examining social relationships in a small primitive society.

The Mehinaku are a small tribe of 77 Arawakan-speaking Indians occupying one village near the headwaters of the Xingu River in Central Brazil. They and their culturally similar though linguistically distinct neighbors[2] have developed a peaceful system of relationships based primarily on intertribal trade, ceremonies, and marriage.

Subsistence among the Mehinaku and the surrounding tribes

---

[1] This paper is based on ten months' field research among the Mehinaku in 1967 under the sponsorship of the Public Health Service, (Pre-doctoral Fellowship 1-F1-MH-30), the National Science Foundation (G.S. 1393), the Museu Paraense "Emilio Goeldi" in Belem, and the Museu Nacional in Rio de Janeiro. A fuller description of the topic may be found in Gregor (1969). I am grateful and indebted to Robert F. Murphy for his valuable suggestions and many aspects of the theoretical approach, although the responsibility is of course my own. I also wish to thank Roberto Cardoso de Oliveira and Claudio and Orlando Villas Boas for their assistance in the field, and Arthur Gregor and Nicholas Tavuchis for their helpful editorial and critical comments.

[2] These neighbors include tribes speaking Arawakan, Cariban, Tupian, and Trumaí. Statements of the general culture pattern of the area may be found in Galvao (1953) and Levi-Strauss (1948).

depends on fishing and slash-and-burn horticulture. These activities are performed individually, or by small groups of kinsmen. Fish and garden produce, however, are shared equally within the household, which consists of ten to 15 closely related consanguines and their spouses. There are five such households within the Mehinaku village, whose membership is flexibly constituted by ambilocal postmarital residence. Kinship among residence mates and their relatives in other houses is reckoned bilaterally. Marriage is preferably village endogamous to a classificatory cross-cousin living in a different residence.

The small size of the tribe, the bilaterality of kinship, and the essentially endogamous pattern of marriage have important effects on the structure of Mehinaku society, the most significant of which is that any two Mehinaku are associated by a multiplicity of possible relationships. They may be simultaneously consanguineal kinsmen through both the paternal and maternal lines, and at the same time affinal relatives by marriage. Since they may also share nonkin relationships such as those of chief and commoner, or shaman and client, any two individuals may be associated together in a wide range of relationships that include domestic, political, religious, and kinship activities.[3] This wide range of association and diffuseness of social ties mean that the Mehinaku are known and socially available to each other in many capacities. Consequently, they are unusually open to social engagement and interested in learning about one another as total social persons. Accessibility and curiosity lead to high rates of interaction and a widespread awareness of each individual's whereabouts and activities. Such interaction and availability of information constitute what I call "exposure." Since the sources and effects of exposure are critical to the argument, they must be examined in some detail.

EXPOSURE: OBSERVABILITY, AUDIBILITY, AND GOSSIP

An important source of exposure in the Mehinaku community is that social life is highly observable. In large part this observability exists because the layout of the village drastically

---

[3]This overlapping quality of relationships is probably inevitable in a small role system (Gluckman, 1962).

limits back regions and private areas. Most of the regions on this map are public and highly observable. It is nearly impossible to walk across the central plaza without being seen by at least a few people. Someone is almost always sitting in the front door of one of the houses or staring outside just to see what is going on.

The main paths around the village are also highly visible public regions. Nominally owned by the Mehinaku chiefs, they are maintained by all the men of the tribe. The Mehinaku take pride in these paths, building them long, wide, and straight. The trail to the port, for example, is so ample that it could accommodate two small cars side by side. It extends two miles through the forest so that villagers can identify someone walking along it ten to 15 minutes before he or she arrives in the community. The trail to the bathing area is also a very public region. All the Mehinaku go bathe and fetch water several times a day, and frequently meet along the way. Even when no one is immediately present an observer may unexpectedly come paddling around a bend in the river.

Finally, Mehinaku houses and gardens also lack privacy. The buildings around the plaza are never permanently partitioned, and the doors are left open all day. Admission for residents is unannounced and unrestricted. The gardens are public areas once they have been burned over. Since most of the fields are contiguous, it is possible to see from one end to the other until the new crop of manioc and corn ripens and obscures visibility.

Village social life is highly observable partly because the Mehinaku are masters of indirect observation. Everyone's footprint is known to all his or her fellow tribesmen. Since the soil on the plaza and on most of the main paths is sandy and loose, the barefoot Mehinaku leave visual records that the rest of the tribe are astonishingly adept at reading. The print of heels or buttocks on the ground may be enough to show that a couple stopped and had sexual relations alongside the path.

Many other telltales help the Mehinaku keep tabs on their fellow tribe members. Most personal property is so distinctively made that the owner can be identified. Arrows, for example, are wound along the haft with decorative patterns that amount to the signatures of their makers. A lost arrow caught in branches by the side of a river may give away the place where its owner has been fishing—information the Mehinaku sometimes want to keep secret.

If social life in the Mehinaku community seems highly observable it is even more audible. Nothing can be said without considerable risk that it will be overheard. In part this is true because the houses are not soundproof. A couple alone in their house cannot be sure that they are not being overheard through the thatch walls. If they speak in raised voices, they may even be heard in an adjoining residence. Conversations in front of the men's house can also be detected if listening conditions are right. Within a house the Mehinaku must whisper to obtain privacy, since normal speech can carry from one end of the building to the other. Even then care must be taken to make sure that another person is not eavesdropping close by, wrapped unseen in a hammock.

Speech is not the only sound that conveys information about the Mehinaku and their activities. At dawn the boys and younger men of the tribe whistle through their hands as they walk to the river. The whistling is a kind of alarm clock that tells the Mehinaku who are still sleeping that their fellow tribesmen are already up. After returning from the river some of the men go to their gardens playing small flutes. Since everyone who plays these flutes has his own distinctive style, the melodies may announce to the community who is on the way to the fields.

Within the windowless, dimly lit houses nonverbal sounds furnish important clues to the activities of others. At night, it becomes pitch dark after the doors have been closed and the fires have died down. At these hours thieves, lovers, and, the Mehinaku say, witches prowl about in the darkness. Sometimes the prowlers can be detected by the sounds they make with other people's possessions and female kinsmen.[4]

The permeability of the community to sound allows the Mehinaku to signal to each other with high pitched whoops. These calls are an important method of nonverbal communication; they keep the tribe well informed about the activities of its members. Whenever food is brought into the village, for example, the men whoop, using distinctive calls for fish or monkey. The hunter or fisherman always remains silent for he

---

[4]The following ceremonial song of the cricket illustrates the Mehinaku's awareness of some of the sounds of night:

I, the cricket, have a song:
I hear the hammock pole and the cords creaking
I hear my mother having sexual relations
Pilaw! Kulei! Pilaw, Pilaw, Pilaw!

(The last line consists of Mehinaku onomatopoetic words for the sounds of intercourse.)

may not be happy about the attention he is receiving. Once he has been seen it will be very difficult for him to withhold the food from the other members of the tribe. There are many other such whooping signals, indicating agreement among the older men of the tribe on an important course of action, the trading of personal property, or the approach of a stranger to the village.

The seen, the overheard, and the system of signals provide the Mehinaku with a great deal of information about their fellow tribesmen. An equally important source of information is the gossip network. Mehinaku gossip includes discussion of marital and extramartial relationships, detailed descriptions of sexual misadventure, and allegations of theft and witchcraft. Stories of witchcraft are usually accompanied by lurid descriptions of the witch's methods of casting spells. Although it is unlikely that any of the Mehinaku actually practice witchcraft, the stories are widely credited and invariably increase the level of hostility and tension in the village. A rough measure of their importance in stimulating overt hostility is that each of the last three witch killings in the Mehinaku community was justified on the basis of such gossip.

Stories of sexual escapades usually have greater basis in fact than tales about witchcraft. Although they are greeted with uproarious laughter, such accounts are not a laughing matter for those who are most affected by them. Descriptions of adultery and inadequate sexual performances are especially compromising. The women often gossip when one of their lovers is impotent or ejaculates prematurely. The men talk about the women's behavior during coitus, and the size, color, and odor of their genitals. These intimate reports quickly spread through the gossip network much to the embarrassment of the persons concerned.

It would be difficult to underestimate the efficiency of the gossip network. The Mehinaku are a face-to-face community, involved with and curious about one another. Stories of misconduct, of sexual misadventures, and of allegations of witchcraft can circulate throughout the entire tribe in a matter of hours. Such tales are usually accompanied by a warning to "keep this story in your belly," that is, not to pass it along; but such injunctions seem to be honored more in the breach than the observance. As a result the community is usually alive with compromising gossip and scandal.

It is apparent that privacy is a scarce commodity among the

Mehinaku. Wherever a person goes in the village he or she can be seen or heard. When two people speak there is a chance that a third person is listening, and that in a short time everyone else will know what has been said. Even the most intimate details of one's sex life often become a matter of public knowledge. The pressures of living in this kind of situation are high, for although knowledge of others is a prerequisite for social action it can also be an embarrassment that jeopardizes social relationships (Simmel, 1950). Necessarily, the Mehinaku must conceal such frequent activities as theft, adultery, and accusations of witchcraft. If the villagers were fully aware of the covetousness and hostility of their fellows, as well as the whereabouts of their possessions and spouses, the tranquility of village social life would be seriously compromised.

Misconduct is not the only kind of activity that must be kept out of the public eye. A Mehinaku's self-image and reputation depend on adequate role performances. A man, for example, is expected to be an effective fisherman and sexual partner. Even if he is highly skilled in both areas, inevitably there will be poor performances that he would prefer to conceal. The fisherman who often comes home with nothing and the impotent lover are understandably ashamed about having their failures become common knowledge. Performances more complex than that of the fisherman or the lover are under even greater pressure from the public character of Mehinaku social life. Team relationships, for example, are especially difficult to manage without privacy and back regions (Goffman, 1959). Thus husbands and wives are hard pressed to present their relationship to the community as that of a cooperating team. Problems that they would prefer to work through privately all too often become public knowledge.

Fortunately for the Mehinaku a number of ways are available to them for controlling the spread of compromising information. They can, for example, take advantage of the natural back regions offered by the forest surrounding the village. The maze of small paths around the periphery of the community is largely hidden from sight by bushes and forest and enables a man to enter the back of a house unseen. Small cleared areas within the forest allow the villagers to carry on clandestine activities, such as extramarital affairs, in relative privacy. Within the houses symbolic restrictions such as affinal avoidances and a code of etiquette that prevents a Mehinaku from casually entering any dwelling but his own helps to establish semiprivate areas for the residents.

The effectiveness of gossip as a source of information is in part limited by a prohibition on the free discussion of such socially explosive topics as witchcraft, theft, and extramarital sex. An even more significant limitation on the gossip network is a widespread skepticism about the tales that are bandied around the village. The Mehinaku routinely fabricate information about themselves in an effort to conceal their sexual affairs, their involvement in theft, and the extent of their possessions. Such distortions partially discredit all the stories passed along whether true or not. The truth is as open to question as an out-and-out lie, and gossip is thereby partly compromised as a reliable source of information.

Despite such strategic use of back regions, and limitations on communication, the Mehinaku live very much in the public eye. They are frankly curious and suspicious about their fellow villagers' whereabouts and activities, and on occasion they even secretly spy on one another. Thus because the Mehinaku consider it very shameful to be seen having sexual intercourse, they limit their sexual activities to hidden areas in the forest. Nevertheless, most of the men can relate with considerable enthusiasm how they have observed their fellow tribesmen copulating. This interest in voyeurism is representative of the Mehinaku's social curiosity. Wherever one is, whatever one is doing, it is possible that a Mehinaku is nearby, surreptitiously listening and watching. Opportunities for privacy must be consciously sought after and manipulated before an individual can really gain control over what others know about him.

EXPOSURE: ACCESSIBILITY TO SOCIAL ENGAGEMENT

The exposed nature of Mehinaku social life renders the individual highly visible within his society and makes compromising information about his or her attitudes and activities readily Available. Still another component of exposure is an abrasive rate of interaction and accessibility to social engagement.

The Mehinaku are frequently interacting with one another. Within their houses they live at very close quarters. Hammocks are tied just a few feet from each other, and family hearths and personal possessions are often adjacent. Access to these living areas requires that householders duck under the tangle of their neighbors' hammock cords, and thread their way through the cluster of bowls and benches at their feet, often accompanying these movements with greetings, laughing apologies, and when appropriate, displays of affinal respect. In addition to such polite interaction, residence mates are usually open to each other's conversational gambits and requests for domestic assistance. Even a man asleep in his hammock may not be free from this kind of involvement. He is awakened routinely if food is being passed around, and he is expected to answer such questions as "Are you sleeping?" with good humor.

If persons are open to social involvement within their own houses, they are still more exposed outside. Mehinaku etiquette dictates that no one should be passed in most public places without a polite exchange or a show of affinal respect. If two people meet on the path to the river, for example, they may say:

"Where are you going?"
"I'm going to the river."
"To the river?"
"Yes."
"Then go."

There are other set dialogues for similar encounters that occur many times during the course of the day.

Although polite social engagement provides Mehinaku social life with a veneer of courteousness and good fellowship, frequent interaction is in and of itself abrasive. In part this is because all social action is deselfing and a threat to the ego (Simmel, 1950). High rates of such action seem to breed feelings of ambivalence and irritation (Schwartz, 1968). Among the Mehinaku these reactions are incorporated in the notion that polite social contact is often burdensome. Displays of affinal respect, for example, are said to be especially onerous. A Mehinaku must continually on guard against close approaches by his or her parents-in-law and children-in-law, taking care to evade them on the public paths, in doorways, and in all ordinary activities.

Brothers-in-law and sisters-in-law honor less rigidly defined codes of respect, but they too are expected to be formal and constrained in each other's presence. One way this constraint is demonstrated is by honoring a taboo on mentioning the in-law's name. To utter the name constitutes a gross violation of proper conduct. It is difficult to avoid violating the taboo, however, because each Mehinaku has many in-laws, and each of them may have as many as ten names. Since these names are often the terms for animals and commonly used objects, a person is apt to mention a forbidden name unless he or she is vigilant. The need for vigilance and constraint generates considerable resistance to the formation of affinal ties.[5] Many of the Mehinaku feel they already have too many in-laws. Keeping track of still more names that cannot be spoken and people who must be avoided is said to require more exertion that is considered worthwhile.

Ordinary contacts with consanguineal kinsmen may also be unwanted. From time to time people simply do not want to be socially engaged with their fellows. On such occasions they may irritably fail to hold up their end of the numerous polite performances they enact with kinsmen. A Mehinaku who behaves in this fashion regularly is called by a derisive term that means "sullen." A sullen man is one who never smiles or tells jokes, who sits apart from the other Mehinaku in the men's house, who seldom participates in group labor, and who never speaks politely on the path to the river. There is only one Mehinaku who is sullen consistently, but many of the others are sullen from time to time. Although they may attempt to evade interaction by the strategic use of the village's back regions, they cannot avoid coming into contact with their fellows because of the small size and openness of the community. At such times their bad temper and rudeness will generate considerable ill-feeling and hostility.

Mutual hostility is often reason enough for avoiding social contact. There are many sources of antagonism within the community, including sexual jealousy, theft, and widespread fear of witchcraft. Mehinaku who fear their fellows as gossips, thieves, adulterers, and witches must nonetheless act out polite social encounters with them. The villagers do not enjoy these encounters and are very much aware that they are frequently a fradulent presentation of their true feelings. Nevertheless, the spatial ecology of the community is such that these contacts are often unavoidable. The only way a Mehinaku can completely evade unwanted social engagement is to leave the village.

This strategy is frequently employed. When the men feel most pressured by their in-laws, their wives, and their fellow tribesmen whom they fear as adulterers or witches, they are most likely to go on a trip. It may be a solitary overnight fishing expedition, or an extended visit to another tribe. Some of the Mehinaku have even established houses and gardens several miles from the village to which they retreat with their families

---

[5]There is a remarkable degree of flexibility in the formation of many affinal and consanguineal relationships.

and close kinsmen for several months each year. The motivation is not economic, since abundant land and excellent fishing resources exist close to the village, and the Mehinaku themselves often explain their fellow tribesmen's extended absences in terms of fear of witchcraft, or inability to restrain a promiscuous wife.

Despite these trips, the Mehinaku spend most of their time within the village. During much of the six-month rainy season they prefer to stay indoors, and even in fine weather they are often obliged to remain in the village because of commitments to participate in festivals and ceremonies. At such times the Mehinaku are usually open to abrasive social engagement.

We see then that within the arena of the Mehinaku community there are few sanctuaries against unwanted interaction, privacy is scarce, and socially damaging gossip and scandal circulate continually throughout the village. It is in terms of this pattern of exposure that we will interpret the Mehinaku practice of seclusion.

SECLUSION

Seclusion among the Mehinaku is a highly institutionalized set of customs that surround the individual, and often his family, with physical and symbolic barriers to interaction and communication. These barriers may virtually terminate his participation in the public aspects of Mehinaku society for as long as three years at a time. He is so much out of sight during this period that it is as if he did not exist. In fact, it is said that the closer a person comes to seeming not to exist, the more closely he honors the rules and restrictions associated with seclusion.

A Mehinaku first enters seclusion together with his parents at the time of his birth. A palm wood partition is placed around their hammocks so that they cannot be seen by the other Indians in the house. The duration and completeness of their isolation depend on whether the parents have had any other children. If they have, the father never enters seclusion and the mother remains formally isolated for only a few weeks until the postpartal bleeding has stopped. If the child is their first, however, the mother remains secluded for several months. Her husband accompanies her behind the partition and remains there for as long as a year.

These lengthy periods of isolation are considered essential to the health of the parents and their new child. Both father and mother honor numerous food taboos and drink root broths designed to increase their vitality. Ideally, they never leave the house during daylight hours if there is a chance that they will be seen by another villager. When the sun sets, however, the father may go on solitary fishing trips, taking care to return before dawn.

After the parents' isolation is over and the partition is taken down, the child remains symbolically secluded. His mother seldom takes him outside for she fears he will become sick if he is seen by Mehinaku who have recently had sexual relations. Since she is never far from her child during these early months, she participates in his isolation and seldom goes to the fields or ventures down to the river. In the interest of his wellbeing she continues to honor certain food taboos and refrains from sexual relations. The last restriction drastically curtails her male social contacts as she is no longer of sexual interest to her husbands or her lovers.

When the child is about a year and a half old, one of his grandfathers give him a haircut and a new name. Following this ritual the child may be seen publicly, and the restrictions on his mother's activities are lifted. The next period of seclusion for male children comes after their ears are ceremonially pieced, at about nine or ten years of age. After the ritual the boys are secluded behind palm wood partitions where some of them—especially those of chiefly descent—will spend the next two years. At the end of this time they leave for six months to a year and then return again for a second period of one additional year.

The restrictions observed in these types of seclusion are similar. The boys are expected to stay within their houses, behind palm wood barriers. Their mothers bring enough extra water from the river so that they can bathe three or four times a day by spilling the water over their heads. Urinating is managed through a short length of wood tubing that is forced through the thatch wall of the house. Defecating is ideally postponed until after sundown, when it is permissible to leave the house cautiously. Ideally, the boy's entire social life is curtailed, and he may only speak in a whisper with his parents and true siblings. He is expected to refrain from boisterous play, displays of anger, sexual activity, or any other expression of emotional intensity. In addition, he must honor numerous food taboos and take a variety of noxious root medicines, some of which are said to be very dangerous and even deadly. Although it is an unusual boy who wholly submits to these privations, they are thought to be necessary if he is to grow up into a strong man and become a good wrestler, a clever hunter, and a successful fisherman. For this reason many fathers supervise their sons' seclusion carefully and try to make sure that they honor all the rules.

Until he enters seclusion the young boy's life has been largely free of restrictions and responsibilities. Nevertheless, after an initial period of petulance and boredom he adjusts himself to a low-keyed restricted life behind the seclusion barrier. He may spend many hours each day doing little but stare out of a small opening that he makes in the thatch wall of the house. Ideally he is supposed to be concentrating his thoughts on wrestling and growing strong. From time to time, his father teaches him the skills and handicrafts he will have to know as a man, such as making arrows, baskets, canoe paddles, and feather headdresses.

A young Mehinaku leaves seclusion when he is physically mature and he has begun to break too many of the restrictions. When he regularly slips out at night to have sexual relations and carelessly allows himself to be seen on the central plaza, his parents may conclude that it is high time for him to leave isolation. Usually this termination of seclusion takes place without fanfare. The boy's father simply tears down the partition and evicts him. The young man is then ready to have affairs as an adult, go fishing and hunting with his companions, and think of getting married.

A girl goes through a similar period of seclusion in early adolescence. After her first menstruation, her parents construct a seclusion barrier which she lives behind for about a year. She honors most of the restrictions young men follow in seclusion, and learns women's skills from her mother. The reason given for isolating a girl is, as in the case of a boy, to make her mature. In most respects, however, a girl's period of isolation is a less serious matter than a boy's. She spends less time in seclusion, she never takes dangerous root medicines, and she is subject to less rigid restrictions.

A final period of isolation that every Mehinaku is expected to honor follows the death of a spouse. When a wife dies, for example, her cross-cousin supervises the widower's period of seclusion and mourning, which may last as long as a year. The restrictions associated with this type of isolation are very rigid and the mourner must never be seen by anyone other than members of his own household. His obedience is ensured by his fear that he will be bewitched by someone in his deceased wife's family if he fails to honor all rules.

The types of seclusion described are part of the ordinary Mehinaku social career, forming transitions between the sequence of statuses that all the Mehinaku ideally follow. In addition, there are periods of seclusion that precede statuses that only a few Mehinaku acquire, including voluntary periods of isolation for apprentice shamans and for those who wish to learn how to smoke or magically to increase their strength and wrestling ability.

There are, therefore, numerous opportunities for the Mehinaku to live in isolation. In fact, an individual could spend up to eight years of his life behind seclusion barriers, depending on the course of his social career. Many societies use periods of isolation to mark transitions in status, but the Mehinaku seem to have developed the practice beyond the ordinary. We suggest that Mehinaku seclusion can be understood in terms of its function of providing a measure of relief from socially abrasive interaction and surveillance.

It is apparent that seclusion practices reduce exposure for the individual behind the barriers, as he is living in a small private world. The boundaries of his world are established by the seclusion partitions and rules against leaving the house during daylight hours or talking in a voice louder than a whisper. In addition, he is also protected from exposure by symbolic barriers. Socially he becomes a "nonperson," physically present in a given situation, but often interactionally absent (Goffman, 1959). Thus a Mehinaku in seclusion who nevertheless appears in public will show by his demeanor and lack of ornamentation that he is unavailable for social engagement. He will be ignored and given no opportunity to participate in the polite encounters we have described or in any other public aspect of Mehinaku life.

Admittedly the psychological value of isolation for the individual is diminished by the fact that most periods of seclusion are not voluntarily chosen, but appear at predetermined points in the social career of the individual. Further, the duration of seclusion often goes beyond what we might expect if the custom were interpreted solely in terms of the isolated individual's psychology. A few days or weeks of isolation may provide relief from exposure, but a year begins to seem like too much of a good thing. The value of isolation as an exposure-reducing device becomes much clearer, however, when we examine not only the relief afforded the individual in isolation, but also the reduction in surveillance and exposure that his seclusion provides for the rest of the tribe. These are floor plans of Mehinaku houses showing several kinds of commonly used seclusion partitions. In general the type of partition used depends on the wishes of the person in isolation or on the wishes of his parents. A man in seclusion may seal himself off alone or he may include his wife and children, or even all his relatives on his side of the house. Each of these partitions greatly increases the privacy of everyone in the house, not merely of those who live behind them. This is true because there are, so to speak, two sides to every wall. If the Mehinaku who live on the far side cannot see the man on the inside, the insider's vision out is also obstructed. The partition, then, blocks communication in two directions.

I became dramatically aware of this effect when barriers were constructed blocking off one half of the house in which I was staying when I lived in the Mehinaku village. Everything became not only darker and less visible, but also quieter. Even the children seemed to cry less. There was almost no interaction between the residents on either side of the house except when they met in doorways and passed around food. It was as if they were living in separate residences. The lower rate of interaction and freedom from surveillance extended to persons in other houses, for they too were freed from the possibility of being observed and socially engaged by the Mehinaku in seclusion.

We can easily underestimate the significance of the total reduction in exposure unless we take into account the small size of the community and the events that precipitate seclusion. There are only 77 Mehinaku in the village. Since their social careers vary, and they occasionally fail to remain in isolation as long as they ideally should, it is difficult to say how many of them will be secluded at any one time. During my stay in the village the number of persons in seclusion varied from one to eight. On the basis of this information and Mehinaku life histories, I conservatively estimate that at any given time an average of four persons is likely to be in seclusion. The total reduction in exposure for any of the other members of the community is, therefore, nearly six per cent. Within the household of the secluded individual this reduction is even greater owing to the effectiveness of the seclusion barrier in limiting surveillance and interaction among the members of the residence. Consequently, the slackening of exposure for an average member of the community is likely to be even higher than six per cent.

Significantly, the Mehinaku are likely to enter seclusion in the largest numbers when community tensions are at their highest. Death, for example, invariably generates serious antagonisms because village witches are said to be responsible for almost every fatality. At such times, however, isolation taboos are rigidly enforced, and the seclusion partitions that limit potentially abrasive exposure are the most substantial the Mehinaku construct. After an epidemic or a series of witch killings, seclusion barriers are built in each household where a death has occurred, providing the Mehinaku with a refuge from unwanted exposure and limiting an important source of tension within the community. Seclusion practices thereby not only substantially slacken surveillance and involvement, but they also provide such relief when it is most needed.

EXPOSURE AND SECLUSION

The Mehinaku pattern of seclusion can be interpreted in terms of reduction of exposure. Isolation practices serve as a functional device to restrict the flow of information and limit socially abrasive involvement. This interpretation, however, raises a number of questions. For example, surely the Mehinaku could achieve a substantial reduction in exposure simply by building separate residences or permanently partitioning their houses. What need is there for them to have evolved such elaborate patterns of seclusion? Part of the answer to this question is to be found in the fragility of the Mehinaku community. Social cohesion is jeopardized by widespread fear of witchcraft, and by somewhat amorphous boundaries delimiting the tribe as a definite social unit. These amorphous boundaries permit the Mehinaku to go on extended visits to other tribes, and to retreat to gardens and houses several miles from the community. Their ties to their community are presently unsupported by warfare, intense out-group hostility, or definite rules of community exogamy that would structure in-group solidarity. Nevertheless, the Mehinaku's persistence as a tribal and village entity is important to their ultimate survival. In the long run, they depend on one another for cooperative labor and food. This dependency may only be significant during crop blights and sickness, but then it is vital.

Despite this ultimate need for cooperation village cohesion is tenuous, and hostility and fear threaten its fabric. Although I have pointed out in some detail how this hostility may be augmented by excessive exposure, it should now be noted that the opposite is also true: too little exposure may also build antagonism.[6] Were the Mehinaku permanently divided into separate neolocal households their mutual suspicions and fears would increase, perhaps past the point of village stability. This effect can be seen on a small scale within the present community. Villagers who live in the same residence have more certain knowledge about each other's whereabouts and social activities than they do of their fellow tribesmen in other households. Such knowledge tends to lessen mutual suspicion, so that residence mates are less likely to accuse each other of witchcraft than Mehinaku who live in separate houses. It is significant that in all of the witch killings I have documented, the victim invariably lived in a different resident from the killers.

Although too much knowledge of others may be an embarrassment, too little can also be disruptive. The Mehinaku can afford neither, for they are a society that is only tenuously held together. The advantages and need for community cohesion may be real, but they are not conspicuously apparent. In this setting there is a narrow, functionally optimal range between what constitutes too much exposure and what constitutes too little communication and social engagement. The practice of seclusion is well suited to helping the Mehinaku maintain this range. Thus seclusion practices not only provide refuge from exposure but neutralize the concern that the person in isolation would take advantage of his low observability to cast spells over his fellows. He excites neither curiosity nor suspicion.

Finally, seclusion is not permanent. The Mehinaku enter isolation for definite reasons at definite times and leave when their term is over. The custom does not become a precedent for a more enduring residential pattern. On the one occasion that this seems to have happened, a deviant individual entered isolation without justifying it in terms of the status passages that usually accompany seclusion. He honored none of the taboos associated with isolation and occasionally participated in the public aspects of village life. He was said to be a sullen unpleas-

---

[6]When devices that restrict information are more plentiful than is the case among the Mehinaku, special techniques may be developed that open lines of communication. See especially the study by Hotchkiss (1967) of the use of children as "spies" in the relatively low exposed setting of a Ladino community, and the analysis by Gluckman (1962) of gossip.

ant person, and he was greatly feared as a dangerous witch. His subsequent violent death at the hands of the kinsmen of one of his alleged victims was unregretted by the community. The periodicity of seclusion, then, prevents barriers to communication and interaction from becoming permanent and perhaps disruptive arrangements.

EXPOSURE AND THE STUDY OF SMALL SOCIETIES

I have interpreted Mehinaku seclusion as an adaptive device that maintains the flow of information and the rate of social engagement within tolerable extremes. The Mehinaku, however, are not unique among primitive peoples in being highly exposed to one another. Devices that separate role partners and limit their knowledge of one another are not readily available in small societies. In such settings, diffusely defined and relatively undifferentiated roles leave actors unusually accessible to social engagement. The face-to-face nature of communication greatly facilitates the flow of information that they would prefer to conceal. For these reasons exposure is likely to be a significant stress to which members of small societies must adapt.

The analysis of this stress and the devices used for managing it constitutes a useful and interesting way of examining social relationships in a small society. This approach regards such relationships as necessarily bimodal in nature. That is, from one point of view role networks may be examined in terms of how they engage actors in social relationships and incorporate them in well-defined groups. Similarly, communication with a society can be analyzed in terms of how people transmit information along well-defined channels, such as chains of command and gossip networks. These approaches are important, but they are only half the picture. Thus acting roles implies disengagement from roles, for to begin one encounter an actor must withdraw from another (Schwartz, 1968). Rules of incorporation for social groups must coexist with complementary rules of exclusion, for otherwise the boundaries of the group would be all-inclusive. Well-defined channels of communication between actors require that alternate routes be sealed off and that the informational content of messages be restricted to material that will not jeopardize the relationships upon which the system depends.

Since disengagement, social exclusion, and restrictions on

information are necessary aspects of involvement, inclusion, and communication, it is possible to analyze social events from either perspective. They are complementary and alike as are the negative and print of a photograph. Within the setting of the highly exposed primitive society, however, it is frequently the negative view that is most interesting. When devices that separate role partners and limit what they know about each other emerge even under the stress of intense social exposure, then these devices are likely to have special social importance. This is as likely to apply when these devices are informally maintained patterns of social evasion and concealment rather than highly institutionalized and somewhat bizarre practices such as Mehinaku seclusion.[7] A study of a small society, then, should require not only a full statement of how actors engage one another, form social groups, and communicate but a detailed analysis of how they evade interaction, exclude nonmembers from social groups and fail to communicate. Thus the ethnographer should be sensitive not only to determining kinship structures but to such subtleties as social avoidance, norms of privacy, and techniques of manipulating information. He or she may find that these are among the more important devices that make social relationships viable.

---

[7]In addition to their structural significance, devices that separate role partners and limit what they know about each other are of more than routine ethnographic interest. Since they do not spring easily from the process of social life in the setting of the small society, they often have a contrived and even bizarre appearance. See, for example, the description of the use of the veil among the Tuareg to establish social distance (Murphy, 1964).

References

Galvão, E. Cultura e sistema de parentesco das tribos do alto Xingu. *Boletim do Museu Nacional,* 1953, *N.S. 10,* 1–56.

Gluckman, M. Les rites de passage. *Essays on the Ritual of Social Relations,* M. Gluckman, editor. Manchester, Eng.: Manchester University Press, 1962, pp. 1–52.

Goffman, E. *The presentation of self in everyday life.* Garden City, N.Y.: Doubleday Anchor, 1959.

Gregor, T. *Social relationships in a small society: A study of the Mehinaku Indians of Central Brazil.* Ph.D. dissertation, Columbia University, 1969.

Hotchkiss, J. C. Children and Conduct in a Ladino Community of Chiapas, Mexico. *American Anthropologist,* 1967, *69,* 711–718.

Levi-Strauss, C. Tribes of the Upper Xingu River. *Handbook of South American Indians: The Tropical Forest Tribes* (Vol. III), J. H. Steward, editor, Washington, D.C., 1948, pp. 321–348.

Murphy, R. F. Social Distance and the Veil. *American Anthropologist,* 1964, *66,* 1257–1274.

Schwartz, B. The Social Psychology of Privacy. *The American Journal of Sociology,* 1968, *73,* 741–752.

Simmel, G. *The Sociology of Georg Simmel* (K. H. Wolff, tr.), Glencoe, Ill.: Free Press, 1950.

4

Privacy, Intimacy and Shame in a French Community[1]

Jeffrey S. Victor, Ph.D.
Jamestown Community College

PRIVACY AND INTIMACY: REVIEW OF RESEARCH AND THEORY

Behavioral scientists who have investigated privacy, have focused primarily upon its role in the political systems of societies (Westin, 1967). Such concern has dealt mainly with social and legal dilemmas involving rights of privacy and demands for public disclosure. Relatively few behavioral scientists have investigated the role of privacy in relation to intimate self-disclosure (Bates, 1964). Yet, there also exists a paradoxical duality of contradiction and complementarity between privacy and disclosure in interpersonal relations between acquaintances, friends and lovers.

Self-disclosure may be defined as the communication of personal information to others. In recent years, this process has become an important topic of social psychological research (Cozby, 1973; Derlega & Chaikin, 1975). Initial investigators were particularly concerned about understanding the relationship between psychotherapists and their clients, but attention has increasingly shifted to the study of intimate relations (Jourard, 1971). Privacy, on the other hand, may be defined as the ability to exclude others from information about oneself. The dilemmas of self-disclosure and privacy have long been recog-

[1] Paper presented to the Conference on: "The Impact of the Fifth Republic on France" State University of New York College at Brockport June 9–11, 1978

nized to be at the very heart of intimate relations (Simmel, 1906; Simmel, 1950).

It is unfortunate that most of the research into the interpersonal dynamics of self-disclosure has neglected consideration of privacy, as its complementary aspect. Yet, the substance of intimate self-disclosure cannot be identified without reference to privacy. A person who discloses all to everyone has nothing intimate to disclose to anyone.

Intimate personal information is essentially that which a person regards as being private (Bates, 1964). Therefore, most people are excluded from its knowledge. The more exclusive is the personal information, and the more discretion a person must take in offering the information about himself or herself, the "deeper" its level of intimacy. Intimate information is, then, a kind of secret shared between people that bonds them in trust to each other (Simmel, 1906). An intimate relationship is ultimately a relationship between confidants (Davis, 1973). Intimacy involves an exclusive relationship in which personal information is protected and limited from people outside that relationship.

The particular contents of self-information that is expected to be shrouded in privacy and guarded by confidentiality differs in different societies. A person's intimate information need not be dramatic or incriminating. It may even seem trivial to other people. The distinctive quality of intimate information is that a person regards it as a source of vulnerability and defines it as being private (Davis, 1973). In Western societies, sexual information about oneself is usually regarded as being private (Victor, 1980). However, there is a wide range of other kinds of intimate information. A person may regard his or her body as a source of vulnerability, due to real or imagined bodily peculiarities. A person's self-perceived shortcomings may also be guarded by privacy, as well as certain opinions and emotional responses. It is also common for people to want to conceal their financial affairs, at least from acquaintances. In many circumstances, people may want to conceal information about their social identities, such as their ethnic group origins or religious affiliation. Certainly, also, people usually wish to conceal information about behavior that other people consider immoral.

In everyday life, acquaintances must maintain a certain discretion (or personal reserve) about their self-disclosures (Simmel, 1906). When interpersonal relations are not bonded by confidentiality and trust, the communication of intimate information is always potentially threatening. The reasons for discretion in self-disclosure are numerous. A person's self-disclosure may result in ridicule, hostility, gossip, envy, and conformity pressures to change. This is particularly so in a society, where interpersonal relations are characterized by competition, rivalries, and conflicts of opinion. Therefore, people employ a variety of social distance mechanisms, in order to preserve their privacy.

Common social distance mechanisms include the suppression of spontaneous emotional expression, the ritualistic communication of superficial pleasantries, the avoidance of controversial matters in conversation, and formalistic good manners. In American culture, these social distance mechanisms take the form of maintaining a disposition of agreeable "friendliness," without presuming the trust and confidentiality of actual friendship (Kurth, 1970). This "friendliness" cannot be mistaken as an invitation for deeper involvement. Instead, it functions as a barrier to genuine intimacy, because it embodies an implicit expectation that serious self-disclosure should not take place.

The satisfactions of privacy and self-disclosure are often mutually exclusive, and pull people in opposite directions (Simmel, 1906). Privacy protects an individual from ridicule, vicious gossip, conformity pressures and conflict with others (Westin, 1967). Privacy may also play an important role in maintaining a person's sense of individuality (Schwartz, 1968). Yet, self-disclosure offers alternative satisfactions, especially within the confines of an intimate relationship. It enables people to obtain useful feedback information about themselves from other people, which may enhance their self-knowledge (Derlega & Chaikin, 1975). In self-disclosure, we learn more about ourselves, often by "thinking out loud" with an intimate. In addition, self-disclosure to an intimate may relieve the stresses of constantly maintaining a superficial public mask, in contradiction to one's own self-concept (Davis, 1973). We can confess our self-perceived vulnerabilities to our intimates and release the tensions generated by unexpressed self-doubt, guilt, and fear. Finally, in self-disclosure to an intimate, we build a bridge of trust to another person. In a relationship bonded by trust, lovers can find security from the uncertainties caused by being excluded from the intimate circles of others. A circle of intimacy excludes some people "out," just as it includes some people "in" (Weitman, 1970). The normal paranoia of everyday life generates suspicions about what is being said about them behind closed doors (Lemert, 1962).

The paradoxical duality of privacy and self-disclosure becomes clear, once it is realized that privacy is also necessary to protect self-disclosure (Westin, 1967). When intimates engage in the communication of intimate information, that communication must be protected by a circle of privacy. The bonds of trust are shattered once people communicate the "secrets" of their intimates to others outside their confidential relationship. There is nothing more disruptive to a friendship or love relationship than when one of the participants learns second-hand that their "secrets" have been shared with strangers. There is nothing more distressful in love, than the suspicion that one's lover has been "unfaithful."

THE RESEARCH PROBLEM

This paper has drawn from research data collected in a field study of individualist attitudes in a French village (Victor, 1974). The goal of the research project was twofold: 1) to determine the specific attitudinal components of French individualism; and 2) to determine the interpersonal conditions that psychologically reinforce French individualist attitudes.

The research question was provoked by an experimental laboratory study by Milgram (1961), in which he found evidence of significant differences between French and Norwegian college students in their abilities to resist conformity pressures. The French subjects exposed to conformity pressures exhibited a much higher independence of judgment. However, Milgram could offer no adequate explanation of this cross-national difference, in terms of variable cultural influences upon personality. The cultural pattern of this particular kind of individualism in France has been observed over a century ago by De Tocqueville (1955), and more recently by Wylie (1974).

Hypothesis—A key explanation for the persistence of individualist attitudes is found in the hypothesis that privacy in interpersonal relations functions to maintain individualist attitudes. This hypothesis was derived from theoretical explorations of the nature of privacy in relation to personal autonomy, in the works of Simmel (1950), Westin (1967), and Schwartz (1968). It was used to gather qualitative data in focused interviews and in participant observation.

RESEARCH METHODOLOGY

The research methodology employed three different techniques to gather data, in an attempt to answer the research problem.

1) A questionnaire was constructed, using items from previously published conformity attitude questionnaires (Barron, 1953; Crutchfield, 1955; Peterson, 1964; Pettigrew, 1958). The items were adapted to the cultural content of French society. The questionnaire was used in interviews, in order to gather quantitative attitude data for statistical analysis. In this way, a factor analysis could be carried out to identify the components of French individualist attitudes. In addition, sample subdivisions could be checked for statistically significant differences in response. The quantitative data also served as a check against the qualitative data.

2) Focused interviews in conversational format were used with the same subjects who filled out the questionnaire, in order to elicit detailed reactions to the topics of the questionnaire items. This technique provided valuable and unanticipated qualitative data about French interpersonal behavior, as contrasted with personal attitudes.

3) Participant observation of daily life was carried out in the village where the interviews were conducted. This technique enabled the collection of qualitative data about French interpersonal behavior. It was particularly useful in providing insight into the social context of privacy between acquaintances, as well as interpersonal relations between intimates. I was able to have access to intimate relations because the village is the hometown of my wife. Therefore, I was able to associate with friends and relatives, who are resident in the area. As a participant observer, I was simultaneously both a "stranger," and an integrated member of the community. (See Simmel, 1950(b), for a discussion of the social role of "stranger" and its usefulness in objective observation, due to the receipt of confidences.)

The Sample. Interviews were conducted with a sample of 120 people representative of the population in a French village, in terms of sex, social class, and age level over that of 25. Almost one-third of the households in the village were visited, choosing only one member of a household via a randomized selection process. The total population of the village, according to the most recent census figures available from 1968, was 1,164 people. The research was conducted during 1972.

The Villlage. The village chosen for the study, Orival, is located in the old province of Normandy. It is actually a bedroom suburb of the factory town of Elbeuf (pop. 19,401). The village, therefore, is not an isolated rural settlement but part of the industrial Seine River valley. In addition, it is located only ten miles from the large city of Rouen and its metropolitan area. The population of the village, and the region around it, is disproportionately (70 per cent) employed in working class occupations in local factories. Only about 25 per cent of the village is employed in lower-middle class occupations and less than 5 per cent in professional and executive positions. (The statistical analysis of the questionnaire data, however, was able to control for social class differences.)

While the village is representative of urban, industrial France, it does not reflect any particular ethnic minority region (such as does Brittany or the Basque area). Politically, the village and region tends to vote to the left. (See Victor, 1974 for specific data.) There is little party loyalty, except among Communists, but the modal political predisposition is probably vaguely Socialist (with a great attachment to the notion of private property). Religious participation is almost entirely absent in Orival, except during weddings and funerals. This pattern of religious indifference is typical of a majority of the French population (Coutrot & Dreyfus, 1965).

In essence, then, the village of Orival is reasonably representative of the mainstream of the French population, outside Paris.

RESEARCH FINDINGS: QUANTITATIVE DATA

Unfortunately, there is not sufficient space in this paper to present in deatil the results of the statistical analysis of the data. That information is available elsewhere (Victor, 1974). The most relevant findings are presented below.

A factor analysis of the attitude responses identified three distinct components, using the principal-axis technique of factor extraction (Mulaik, 1972). Factor I was identified as the attitude pattern called *méfiance* in French. *Méfiance* may be defined in English as a disposition of wary suspiciousness toward acquaintances. This pattern of wary suspiciousness has been described in detail by Wylie (1974), in his study of a French village. Factor II was identified as "stubbornness." Stubbornness may be defined as a disposition to resist attempts at persuasion and conformity pressure. It is consistent with the

French independence of judgment found in the experimental research by Milgram (1961). Finally, Factor III was identified as the attitude of "independence." This attitude component may be defined as a desire to avoid reciprocal obligations in relations with non-intimates.

The first research problem was to identify the attitudinal components of French individualism. A statistical analysis of the questionnaire data revealed these components to be: 1) a wary suspiciousness, 2) stubbornness, and 3) a desire for independence.

Internal variations between sample subgroups were also submitted to statistical analysis. A chi square check on the questionnaire data found little variation between social class levels, age levels, or the two sexes. Statistically significant differences in response to several of the questionnaire items were found only among middle-class men, and young people (ages 25–39). Examination of the relevant questionnaire items suggests that middle-class men may be more predisposed toward cooperation, than the other sample subgroups. It also appears that younger people in the sample are less likely to be suspicious of acquaintances (*méfiance*).

RESEARCH FINDINGS: QUALITATIVE DATA

Privacy. The focused interviews and participant observations enabled me to collect a considerable amount of data about the role of privacy in French interpersonal behavior. These data were crucial in providing answers to the second half of the research problem; that of determining the interpersonal conditions that psychologically reinforce French individualist attitudes. Without the qualitative data, the research findings from the attitude questionnaire would have been artificially abstracted from the particular social context of French individualism.

The qualitative data provide evidence for the hypothesis that privacy functions to maintain individuality. The social barriers constructed by privacy reinforce French individualist attitudes by enabling the French to be independent from acquaintances and stubbornly resist conformity pressures from others, outside their small circle of intimates. (They are able to avoid reciprocal obligations and attempts at persuasion.) In addition, the widespread use of social distance mechanisms to create the conditions of privacy generates a climate of wary suspiciousness of acquaintances—or what may be termed the paranoia of everyday life.

There are a great variety of social distance mechanisms used by Frenchmen to maintain their privacy by evading intrusions into their personal life. The barriers that appear most obvious to the eyes of an observer are the physical ones. Almost all the homes in Orival are surrounded by walls or fences, rather than the open lawns common to American small towns. Much like the hedgerows in the nearby bocage farmland, they are barriers to intruding eyes. Many of the gates are locked and can only be opened by the residents. Frequently, these gates support signs notifying the intruder of a *chien méchant* (dangerous dog) on the premises, should one decide to enter without invitation. A surprising number of homes actually sport menacing German Shepherds or Doberman pinschers prowling the yard, attached to long chains.

Most residents can refuse entry into their homes without any social contact at all. The standard procedure is to peek out a window when visitors acknowledge their presence by sounding the gate knocker or bell. Should the resident decide to deny entry to the intruder, he or she simply does not open the gate, leaving the impression that no one is home.

There are additional tactics of evasion designed to repel intruders, including misinformation and unfriendliness. On several occasions, I was told by a respondent's spouse that they were not at home, when this was untrue. I was also given appointments to return at times when the respondent would not be at home. Initial expressions of hostility also serve to ward off intruders. I was frequently greeted by people whose faces expressed distinct annoyance. A common verbal greeting was the curt reception: *"C'est à quel sujet?"* (loosely translated, as "What do you want?"). I was often told by the respondents that they were busy, before I could fully identify myself and explain my intentions. On several occasions, when a wife had given me entry, the husband rather bruskly expelled me from the house.

A total of 21 people refused to be interviewed. This amounts to 14 per cent of a total of 153 people contacted for interviews during the pretrial and actual research, which is a rather high refusal rate.

It should be noted that many respondents did greet me with an initial amiability. However, the weight of reactions tended more toward initial antagonism. I learned to expect resistance until I could fully identify myself and explain my purpose.

Then, this resistance shifted gradually toward curiosity and hospitality. Especially after I was offered and had accepted an aperitif, conversation became quite amiable. Most respondents asked me questions about life in the United States, and evidenced an enjoyment of dialogue. All gave me their full attention and interrupted any other household preoccupation. Several invited me to return for another chat.

The French concern for privacy is evidenced by the social distance maintained between co-workers and between neighbors. I asked whether women visited with neighbors and whether men socialized with co-workers after work hours. The overwhelming majority (81 per cent) of men maintain no, or negligible, social contact with their co-workers after work hours. The percentage of visitations between women neighbors is greater. Visitations are most common between elderly women. However, more than half (54 per cent) of the women have little contact with neighbors.

The comments of male respondents reveal why and how they maintain social distance from co-workers. Many men mentioned that they preferred not to choose their friends from among work associates. One respondent, a young technician, went right to the heart of the matter when he told me that he would not invite work associates to his home, because it would aggravate office politics. The lack of friendships between co-workers is consistent with similar findings by Crozier (1964) about French clerical workers.

An industrial psychologist at a large chemical factory with whom I discussed this matter articulated his considerations in great detail. He chose to live in Rouen and commute daily to the Elbeuf area, in order to avoid social contact with his co-workers. He said that such relationships constrain one's ability freely to choose one's friends. Social relations with co-workers lead to mutual obligations, formalities, and inhibitions. (These "constraints" involve obligations to reciprocate invitations, formal hospitality for guests as required by French custom, and inhibitions expressing opinions.) He told me that he had the experience of working in a Rhone Poulenc factory in Southern France, which was in an isolated location so that employees were forced to choose their friends from among co-workers. Consequently, "the atmosphere was very heavy and people felt constrained and unhappy."

In relations between co-workers, most Frenchmen prefer to compartmentalize their social life, by segregating their work associates from their family and close friends. This is a social distance mechanism, because work associates are excluded from information about a person's family life, friendship activities and perhaps personal opinions, wealth, and misfortunes as well.

On rare occasions when acquaintances are invited to a home, social distance is maintained by means of elaborate formality and ritualism. The food and wine must be truly memorable. Attire is expected to be formal, with men in suit jackets and ties throughout the visit. Conversation must avoid many points of possible disagreement, studiously detouring around religious, and even artistic opinions. Traditionally recognized good manners and good taste must be at their maximum exposure.

A relationship with an acquaintance is not presumed, even temporarily, to have bonds of trust. The constraints involved in the process of transforming an acquaintance relationship into an intimate relationship limit the possibilities of developing friends, as much as any lack of opportunities for meeting people. Consequently, the need for intimacy is intensified.

Intimacy. Intimate relations between French individuals enable them to find emotional relief from the social isolation created by the conditions of privacy.

An intimate friend in France is someone with whom one can relax the social distance barriers of formality and ritualism. A friend must, therefore, be a social equal and have equivalent wealth and prestige ranking. Invidious factors must be concealed, distant, or irrelevant in the relationship. A friend was described by my respondents as being someone who may enter one's home, not spy with envy one's material possessions, and not leave with the intention of back-biting gossip.

When I made inquiries about sources of friends, several people said that they developed friendships from encounters during leisure time activities, especially during vacation travel in places where informality prevails. This, of course, usually meant that friends lived in distant places, and consequently visits were infrequent. Other people reported that they retained their friends from youth. They were able to continue with them, the informality and egalitarian spirit of the youth *bande*. Many people told me that when they have informal visits, they usually choose family members. My observations suggest that visitations between kin (nuclear and extended) are normally frequent. They may function as a partial alternative to friendship relations; just as in American society, friends function as alternatives to kinship relations. I asked a class of French high school students, if they would prefer to stay with their friends during summer vacations or go somewhere with their parents. All of them responded that they prefer to be with their families during vacations, as if the question was a bit absurd. I doubt that a corresponding group of American adolescents would respond similarly to the choice.

Even when friends and family visit each other, the informality that prevails includes a certain polite hospitality. Some ritualism is enjoyed for its own sake. French informality, even among working class families, exhibits a studied style known as traditional good taste. To entertain without good taste is an insult, even to friend or relative. The rules are not rigid, but there are distinct limitations on behavior. It is simply good taste for the host to offer guests their full attention and avoid distractions like watching television. Hosts are expected to provide entertaining conversation, stories, gossip, and jokes. It is polite to offer an aperitif in the afternoon or evening. Find food and interesting conversation provide the source of fond memories during later times.

Intimacy involves an exclusive relationship, in which personal information is protected and limited from people outside the relationship. Intimate interaction is personal and unguarded, involving self-revelation and mutual psychological exploration. Opinion and personal idiosyncracies are unconstrained. Frenchmen savor the *ambiance* of intimacy as a fundamental joy of life. Indeed, it may be the essential element in what the French call *joie de vivre*. In intimate relations, the French learn a deep emotional dependence upon a small circle of family and close friends. At the same time, the psychological gratifications of intimacy enable them to be emotionally independent from their many acquaintances, such as peer group associates, co-workers, and neighbors.

Conversation is the medium in which intimacy exists, and the content of intimate conversation in France is distinctly expressive. It is expressive in the sense that it focuses on the pleasure-pain dimension of experience: feelings, evaluations, emotional responses. For example, one particularly recurrent topic of conversation is food. Past meals at weddings or restaurants are recalled in all their savory detail. The emphasis is never upon the quantity, but the quality and variety of tastes. Another even more common topic of conversation is people. Gossip and life histories are exchanged. More important is evaluative commentary on people's pleasing or disagreeable personality traits. Less common is concern about a person's psychological motives.

The expressive orientation of intimate communication may account, in part, for the great deal of personal criticism of others that I heard. Intimates exchange their reactions to, and evaluations of movies, vacations spots, clothing, and furniture. Special enthusiasms and joys are shared, such as mushroom hunting, antique collecting, or jazz music. Most important, intimates exchange in colorful detail descriptions of their separate experiences, so that the emotional life of one becomes through empathy, part of the life of another. The emotional intensity of intimacy exists among the French, not only because of the difficulties in getting to know others, but also because of the expressive nature of intimate interaction.

The psychological closeness of intimacy is symbolized in the extent of physical contact that is customary. Girlfriends, young and old, are frequently seen walking arm-in-arm, hand-in-hand. Women friends often kiss on greeting each other. Displays of affection between lovers in public are commonly seen. Family members, including fathers and their sons, usually embrace and kiss on greeting each other, in a symbolic expression of affection.

Shame. The "others," those outside of one's private circle of intimates, are not seen as a potential source of psychological satisfaction. Instead, they are seen as a source of threat to one's well-being. The threat is seen to derive from the inevitability of envy, jealously, gossip, and disputes. A common predisposition toward other people was the "other people cannot be trusted." (This is the attitude component of *méfiance* in French individualism.)

There is considerable fear of ridicule. Many respondents reported to me that the French are very critical of each other. In fact, I did observe that they are quite critical of each other. They seemed to be much more critical of each other (and of their social institutions), than are Americans. It is not unusual to hear a blanket condemnation of all other fellow French. "Other people" were accused of all sorts of maliciousness and injustices. The potential for interpersonal disagreement is aggravated by widespread ideological and social class conflict in French society (Victor, 1975). As one respondent put it, "the ideal of *fraternité* is not really taken seriously in France."

The attack on anonymous others seems to take the logic that a good defense is a good offense. Much of the criticism is expressed in anticipation of being similarly criticized. That anticipation is consistantly fulfilled. The result is a vicious cycle of distrust and fear of being shamed. These observations are consistent with similar ones made by Wylie (1974) about the effects of shame in French society.

The pervasive fear of criticism from anonymous others indicates the nature of informal social control in French society. It is shame more than guilt that controls possible deviation from cultural norms. French culture is a shame culture, as contrasted with a guilt culture. A shame culture facilitates the articulation of the distinctiveness of personal identity, by heightening the tension between self and others. (Gouldner, 1965).

In guilt cultures, group norms are strongly internalized and regarded as having intrinsic value of their own. Even the thought of deviating from group norms evokes self-criticism. The individual conforms inwardly, due to self-censorship and the need for self-esteem. In such cultures, the group and the self are closely bonded together, psychologically. Guilt is felt as a response to something seen as part of the self; a reprehensible thought or action. Consequently, the individual's self-esteem is constantly in need of support, gained through seeking approval from others. I believe that the social context of a guilt society is much more characteristic of American society, than of French society.

In contrast, in a shame culture the locus of social control is censure from others, rather than direct self-censure. This creates an antagonism between the self and anonymous others. It is the contemptible others, who are the source of condemnation. In a shame culture, the individual's private thought and motives are less relevant to such condemnation, than are visible actions. Therefore, the individual conforms outwardly due to fear of punishment. Group norms are less apt to be perceived as being intrinsically moral. They are experienced as part of the environment with which the individual must deal; as conveniences perhaps, but not necessarily worthy of great sentimental attachment. Social control through shame results in a polarization between self and society.

CONCLUSIONS

Social control through shame in France intensifies the individual's sensitivity to the scrutiny of others. It creates a climate of fear of criticism and ridicule. Such a social context of personality generates a pervasive concern for privacy. Privacy functions to protect individuals and their intimate circles from possibilities of envy, disputes, and malicious gossip. A great variety of social distance mechanisms are used to create the conditions of privacy by excluding others from personal and family information. In this sense, then, privacy can serve a boundary maintenance function in interpersonal relations. However, privacy also isolates acquaintances from each other. It inhibits feelings of mutual trust and provokes interpersonal suspicion.

The social isolation of French people could result in emotional deprivation if it were not for the emotional rewards found in relations between intimates; family, friends, and lovers. The intense intimacy both complements and contradicts the strong social demand for privacy in the form of personal reserve and discretion. Intimacy involves extensive self-disclosure in a relationship, in which intimate information is protected and excluded from others. Intimacy psychologically reinforces an emotional dependence on the family and a few friends. In addition, it simultaniously enables emotional independence from acquaintances.

The social psychological roots of French individualist attitudes can be found in the emotional independence of French people from the conformity pressures of acquaintances. The attitudinal components of French individualism include a wary suspiciousness, stubbornness, and a desire for independence from non-intimates. It does not include any rejection of emotional dependence on intimates, as American individualism has been described to include (Slater, 1970). Indeed, the research suggests that independence of judgment is facilitated by emotional dependence on a small circle of intimates, rather than by openness to the influences of acquaintances. French individualist attitudes are psychologically reinforced by: 1) informal social control based upon fear of shame, 2) privacy in relations with acquaintances, and 3) the psychological rewards found in intimate relations.

In summary, the French do not learn to regard peer group associates, co-workers, and neighbors as sources of psychological gratification. This social context of interpersonal relations, when compensated by emotional gratifications found in intimate relations, enables considerable psychological automony and independence of judgment. The data provide support for the hypothesis that privacy in interpersonal relations functions to maintain individuality in personality.

References

Barron, F. Some personality correlates of independence of judgment. *Journal of Personality,* 1953, 21, 287–297.

Bates, A. P. Privacy—A useful concept? *Social Forces,* 1964, 42, 429–434.

Coutrot, A. & Dreyfus, F. G. *Les forces religieuses dans la société française.* Paris: Librairie Armand Colin, 1965.

Cozby, P. C. "Self-disclosure: A literature review." *Psychological Bulletin,* 1973, 79, 2, 73–91.

Crozier, M. *The bureaucratic phenomenon.* Chicago: University of Chicago Press, 1964.

Crutchfield, R. S. Conformity and character. *American Psychologist,* 1955, 10, 191–198.

Davis, M. S. *Intimate relations.* New York: Free Press, 1973.

Derlega, V. J., & Chaikin, A. L. *Sharing intimacy: What we reveal to others and why.* Englewood Cliffs, N.J.: Prentice-Hall, 1975.

De Tocqueville, A. *The old regime and the french revolution.* (Translated by S. Gilbert). Garden City, N.Y.: Doubleday, 1955.

Gouldner, A. W. *Enter Plato.* New York: Basic Books, 1965.

Jourard, S. M. *The Transparent Self.* New York: Van Nostrand, 1971.

Kurth, S. B. Friendships and friendly relations. In McCall et al. (Eds.). *Social relationships.* Chicago: Aldine, 1970.

Lemert, E. M. Paranoia and the dynamics of exclusion. *Sociometry,* 1962, 25, 2–20.

Milgram, S. Nationality and conformity. *Scientific American.* 1961, 205, 45–51.

Mulaik, S. A. *The foundations of factor analysis.* New York: McGraw-Hill, 1972.

Peterson, R. A. Dimensions of social character: An empirical exploration of the Riesman typology. *Sociometry,* 1964, 194–207.

Pettigrew, T. F. Personality and sociocultural factors in intergroup attitudes. *Journal of Conflict Resolution,* 1958, 2, 29–42.

Schwartz, B. The social psychology of privacy. *American Journal of Sociology,* 1968, 73, 741–752.

Simmel, G. Friendship, love and secrecy. (Translated by A. Small). *American Journal of Sociology,* 1906, 11, 457–464.

Simmel, G. The secret and the secret society. (Translated and edited by K. Wolff). In *The sociology of Georg Simmel.* New York: Free Press, 1950.(a).

Simmel, G. The stranger. (Translated and edited by K. Wolff). In *The sociology of Georg Simmel*. New York: Free Press, 1950(a).

Slater, P. E. *The pursuit of loneliness*. Boston: Beacon Press, 1970.

Victor, J. S. Individualism in France: An empirical study of a national characteristic. Unpublished doctoral dissertation. Buffalo: State University of New York at Buffalo, 1974.

Victor, J. S. Social conflict and individualism in France. Paper presented to the Eastern Sociological Society. April 1975.

Victor, J. S. *Human sexuality: A social psychological approach*. Englewood Cliffs, N.J.: Prentice-Hall, 1980.

Weitman, S. R. Intimacies: Notes towards a theory of social inclusion and exclusion. *Archives Européennes de Sociologie*, 1970, 11, 348–367.

Westin, A. F. *Privacy and freedom*. New York: Atheneum, 1967.

Wylie, L. *Village in the Vaucluse*. New York: Harper & Row, 1974.

Unit 3

The Politics of Secrecy

Introduction

Politics encompasses all those social strategies employed by political leaders for acquiring political power, attaining political office, and establishing and maintaining the legitimacy of their political rule. Politics also involves organized efforts by dissident or opposition groups or factions either to replace existing governing authorities or to subvert or change the existing political institutions. Secrecy is an inherent part of this political process. Secrecy either enables political leaders to carry out their administrative duties in ways not sanctioned by law or custom while maintaining their legitimacy; or it enables political dissidents to organize opposition to the government while avoiding political persecution or coercion.

Often secret associations or cults play a significant role in community politics. Some secret organizations, the conformative types, may actually support the existing social and political order and the values on which this order is based. However, many secret societies oppose the political status quo and challenge the value structure on which the political system is based. These latter secret associations, the alienative ones, differ from conspiratorial groups in that the conspirators constitute a short-lived secret grouping while the secret societies are more enduring. Moreover, conspiratorial groups usually make little use of secret rituals as a unifying device.

The selections in this unit discuss the role of secret organizations in the politics of several different types of political systems. Elizabeth Brandt discusses the role that Taos pueblo religio-political leaders play controlling information flow within and outside the Indian pueblo. The leadership of moiety, clan, and secret kiva groups enables traditional Taos leaders (the "Old People") to maintain their political power by control of religious knowledge. Such positions enable the Old People to restrict the spread of certain mystical, theological, and liturgical knowledge necessary for the attainment of influential religious as well as political leadership. Taos leaders must control, as well, the dissemination of such religious and ritual information outside the pueblo; for outsiders might, for various reasons, transmit this information back to pueblo factions hostile to the traditional leadership, thereby enabling such political opponents to claim rights to secular power and to challenge the rule of the Old People. Thus, the traditional leaders, by limiting access to the religious system, limit access to the political system.

While political leaders can maintain their authority through control of secret cults, as in the Taos case, dissidents can employ secret associations to challenge or subvert prevailing governmental power. Michel Laguerre reports on the Bizango, a secret society in French-colonial Haiti, which helped organize and protect rebel Haitian communities as well as made guerrilla raids on French plantations. Later the Bizango supported revolts against the U.S. occupation of Haiti (1915–1934). In postindependence Haiti such maroon secret orders have enabled the peasants to protect peasant land from the black and mulatto elite, who have tried to appropriate peasant estates for their own use. The Voodoo religion has given cohesion to secret society activities as well as an ideological rationale for their rituals.

Like the Bizango, the Ku Klux Klan has, at one time or another throughout its history, come into conflict with the prevailing political authority, at least at the national level. Even so, as Richard Schaefer suggests in his paper, the Klan has often supported values that are shared by "significant segment of the population." While essentially a conformist secret order resisting change in racial relationships within local communities, at times it has also promoted political change in order to achieve its racist goals.

Like many secret societies the Klan has stressed the importance of reciprocal confidence among its members, demanded total loyalty, used binding oaths to assure such loyalty, established strict codes governing written and verbal communications, and conducted secret rituals that have provided both intrinsic satisfaction as well as have served as an instrument by which the ideology has been made known to the membership. The Klan has a hierarchy of officers with an inner governing body or core leadership privy to the most carefully guarded secrets. The status hierarchy as well as the impressive rituals enable the Klan members to set themselves apart from outsiders, thus making them feel exalted and superior to nonmembers.

In recent years there have been many published accounts of military conspiracies. None of these studies have given us such an in-depth description of the secret politics of such military coups as does the case study of the 1960 Turkish military coup presented in the selection by Kenneth Fidel. Fidel's study can help us better understand the secrecy process within more recent military conspiracies, for the problems faced by the Turkish military plotters are common to most coup organizers.

Of course many of the security problems faced by the Turkish military conspirators are also common to alienative secret societies, those pursuing goals that subvert established authority. Since the conspirators' activities and plans had to remain secret for fear of political reprisal, they conducted their secret meetings in secluded settings. Strict canons of silence about the conspiracy were placed on members in their communications with those fellow military officers who might possibly side with their enemies. The conspirators also faced the same internal security problems (e.g., membership loyalty and protection from their enemies' espionage). Coded messages were necessary when public means of communication were used (e.g., telephone communications).

On the other hand, unlike the members of secret associations, the Turkish conspirators belonged to a single occupation. Members of the conspiratorial organization were in little agreement over goals, strategies, and tactics. Officers who joined the conspiracy did not go through a long period of testing and indoctrination to establish their loyalty; nor did the conspirators develop rituals or ceremonies to dramatize their ideology or promote solidarity.

What solidarity the conspiratorial organization achieved was based on fear of government punishment. Once in power the conspirators fell into conflict with one another. The earlier unity was destroyed.

The Turkish conspiratorial organization was, of course, characterized by a status hierarchy. But unlike the hierarchies of secret societies, which contribute to group cohesion, the hierarchy of the Turkish organization created tensions between members. Those leaders who claimed authority by nature of their conspiratorial role resented other members exerting leadership by nature of their military rank outside the organization itself.

Irrespective of the differences between these secret organizations the secrecy process is similar among all of them. Security is a common concern. Similar procedures are developed to screen initiates, indoctrinate them, maintain their loyalty when they become members and to guard against either accidental discoveries by outsiders or actual espionage.

5

On Secrecy and the Control of Knowledge: Taos Pueblo[1]

Elizabeth A. Brandt
Arizona State University

The central problem confronting any Pueblo scholar is secrecy. Pueblo society presents two fronts, a complex secular organization and a religious grounding of like complexity. The first aspect can be understood, but the second is always shrouded by secrecy; yet both are essential to a complete understanding of Pueblo society. Anthropologists such as Bloom, Parsons, Scholes, Dozier, and Spicer have attributed secrecy to the pressures of external contact, but I believe that this emphasis is mistaken and has obscured the real issue, which is internal secrecy. External secrecy directed toward outsiders is merely a special case of a much larger process. The genesis of secrecy lies in the nature of religious societies, their ritual and political functions, and the fact that all esoteric and much secular

[1] The initial idea that stimulated this paper was a remark by my colleague, Donald Bahr, on the nature of oral cultures. I am grateful to George L. Trager, M. E. Smith, William Leap, Jay Miller, Amy Zaharlick, and James Bodine without whose willingness to share data and ideas this paper would not have been possible. I would also like to thank those who read earlier drafts of this paper and by whose criticism I have benefited: M. E. Smith, Alfonso Ortiz, Donald Bahr, Melvin Firestone, and Joseph Gross. I am solely responsible for any misinterpretations in the data and the opinions expressed do not necessarily represent the views of these individuals. I also wish to thank individuals at Taos who were willing to explore the whys rather than the whats of secrecy. Data were collected in 1967 while at Ft. Burgwin Research Center and during summer 1975 and 1976. This research was funded in part by a grant from the Research Board of Arizona State University and the American Philosophical Society. An earlier version of this paper was published as "The Role of Secrecy in a Pueblo Society" in *Flowers of the Wind,* edited by T. C. Blackburn (Socorro, N.M.: Ballena Press, 1977).

knowledge is communicated through speech in the Pueblos.

This paper explores the sociology of knowledge of the Pueblos in a preliminary way, and the structure and function of the societies insofar as it is known, using Taos Pueblo as a case study in secrecy. The details of organization will differ from village to village, but I am confident that the general model presented here is applicable to all the Pueblos.[2]

The classical view of Pueblo secrecy began early and has been commented on by many authors (Bloom, 1931; Scholes, 1942; Parsons, 1939; Spicer, 1962; Dozier, 1961). Dozier is the most articulate statement of this historical theory. Secrecy is attributed to the program of forced culture change in political structure and religious belief and practices imposed by the Spanish conquest. The forced Christianization of the Pueblos and incidents of kiva destruction and mask burning, the whipping and imprisonment of religious leaders, and witchcraft trials for practice of native religion caused the Pueblos to adopt an attitude of outward compliance with Christian belief while religious ceremonies went underground and secrecy became important (Spicer, 1962). Both Dozier and Spicer attribute the continued maintenance of religious secrecy to unfavorable publicity about Pueblo beliefs and acts by the church and the Indian Service under the Religious Crimes Code in the 1920s. Taos Pueblo was investigated at this time for breach of the code and was able to argue successfully for First Amendment rights in the courts. This interpretation has protected the politico-religious nature of tribal government ever since. Dozier (1961) states:

> The unsuccessful attempts of recent ethnologists to break the Pueblo iron curtain appear to demonstrate that these Indians still believe that the release of ceremonial knowledge will be used against them. They, therefore, guard tenaciously their native ceremonial system from all outsiders, offering only the Spanish-Catholic and some less sacred aspects of the native system to public scrutiny (p. 97).

While the historical explanation is logical and certainly useful in explaining slight shifts in the degree of openness of the Pueblos to outsiders, it diverts us from more general questions about the sociology of knowledge in the Pueblos. It is a case of

[2]This paper is a preliminary exploration of the nature of information transmission and nontransmission in Pueblo societies. It ties into the literature on secret societies and has a number of aspects that will be elaborated in later papers.

misplaced emphasis that obscures the real issue of how knowledge is used and transmitted in Pueblo society.

For secrecy, selective transmission of information is the key point—what you tell and to whom you tell it. Access to knowledge and proper use of knowledge are primary concerns of Pueblo people. Rather than seeing secrecy as a bar to understanding Pueblo societies, we should see it as a striking phenomenon, one deserving of investigation in its own right. The classical explanation ascribes only one function to secrecy, the maintenance of traditional religion in a hostile context. It also implies that secrecy is a phenomenon practiced only against outsiders, which is definitely not the case. This paper will show that secrecy is a dynamic rather than a static phenomenon, a tactic that serves a variety of functions.

SECRECY

Pueblo people make a conceptual distinction between insiders and outsiders. In its broadest sense, the term "outsiders" refers to Anglos, Spanish-Americans, and Indians of other tribes who exist outside of the symbolic and spatial limits of a Pueblo village. It distinguishes those who are not integrated into the social networks within a village. The term may also be used in a narrower sense to distinguish the social roles and statuses of individuals based on their participation in village information networks. Thus, an individual may be an insider with respect to one's own kiva group, but an outsider to others. An individual married into the community may be an insider in all respects except religious participation. The distinction is thus a flexible one that can be used to include or exclude any individual from social participation in any activity or context. This conceptual distinction creates a web of social boundaries that cross-cut a village and extend outside it.

Inhibition of information flow across any of these boundaries is secrecy. Anthropologists, including Dozier, have misinterpreted the process of information flow. They have tended to use the imagery of a wall, an "iron curtain," or a similar physical or spatial boundary that demarcates the limits of information flow from within a Pueblo community to the outside. The outsider also accepts this distinction and focuses on the external boundary, rather than seeing that this boundary is not the only one, but merely one of many. If a spatial analogy is needed at all, a more appropriate one would be the multilevel architectural massing of individual living units at a pueblo such as Taos. The boundaries are not rigid, though they may be relatively permanent for any one individual given his or her status or social role. The outsider's view of self as locked out of information channels by a wall of secrecy can be called external secrecy. As I have discussed briefly here and continue to elaborate in this paper, this view is incorrect. There is also a sense in which this view implies a homogeneity of knowledge within a community, a serious error.

I have used the term "internal secrecy" to contrast with the term "external secrecy." Free access to all information does not occur within a community. There are outsiders within the village for certain kinds of information. Though I will continue to use the two terms, they must be understood as two superficial aspects of a single process, inhibition of information flow across any boundary. The relationships between internal and external secrecy may be unclear at this point, but will be explained much more fully later in the paper. Briefly though, internal secrecy is primary; external secrecy is maintained to prevent information from going back into pueblo communities from the outside where it might have disruptive effects if the wrong individuals possessed it. There can be little control over insiders and information can be channeled and controlled in a very precise way.[3] It is also true, though, that external secrecy is a powerful boundary-maintenance mechanism.

Knowledge or information is power in both a spiritual and a secular sense and the use of power must be controlled. Power is here defined as the ability to influence the behavior of others. The asserted belief in supernatural power and supernatural sanctions is a powerful determinant of behavior for some individuals. Information as power is also discussed more fully in a later section.

The social boundaries are permeable to some kinds of information flow but not to others. Certain kinds of information are declared secret, particularly information concerning religious matters, and there is a high degree of concern over the "secrets." The content of a secret is variable to some extent and what is secret is defined by religious leaders not left up to indi-

[3] I believe internal secrecy is a prime factor in Pueblo factionalism, though, of course, it also owes much to the changing demography of the Pueblos, increased education, and outside employment. At Taos, the leaders have reacted to the threat of the outside world by increasing internal secrecy and this has created a bitter factional dispute of a decade's duration, which erupted in 1976. The role of secrecy in factionalism is explored in a forthcoming paper (Brandt, 1978; Smith, 1969, 1974).

vidual choice of community members. For the most part, the secrets consist of esoteric information underlying the meaning and symbolism of a ritual or part of a ritual, the ritual paraphenalia used, the sequencing and timing of ritual, and the figures responsible for conduct of ceremonials and their activities.

There is a relationship between the kinds of knowledge and the ability to communicate it that is nonarbitrary. It may be profitable to explore different categories of religious knowledge and determine how they relate to secrecy. While the categories are Western, I believe they are adequate cross-culturally, although they are not exhaustive or comprehensive. The five categories are: (1) mystical; (2) theological; (3) liturgical; (4) dogma, or catechism;[4] and (5) participatory. Each kind of knowledge has some restriction on transmission and media of transmission by its very nature and thus is "secret" automatically. This is especially true of mystical knowledge, Category 1, which is private, ineffable, and nonverbal. To communicate this kind of knowledge is to destroy it. It is always secret.

Category 2, theological knowledge, is a kind of deep knowledge that penetrates below the surface Categories 3 through 5 and may result in new information, interpretations, or innovations. It is the source of new information in a relatively closed system. Prophets would draw on this kind of knowledge. It is frequently the result of a long process of familiarity, experience, and meditation on the part of the knower. It may be communicated in narrative form, chant, or in visual or gestural symbols; but it is difficult to communicate without a long period of training on the part of the information recipients. It may be either public or private and may not be communicated at all. In some senses it is also secret by nature, except to those who are willing to expend the time and effort it takes to acquire this knowledge. It may be acquired individually or by a formal learning process.

Category 3, the liturgical level, deals with knowledge about behavior—in a sense, knowledge of the participatory technology of a ritual. This kind of knowledge is unlikely to be transmitted verbally, but some information must be acquired by viewing and participating in ritual and ritual preparation. Because of this, it is possible for an outsider to gain some liturgical knowledge by witnessing ceremonies, although knowledge

[4]I have used the nominal form of dogma to avoid the unpleasant associations of the adjectival form.

thus gained may be fragmentary or trivial.[5] When communicated formally it involves memorization of a large corpus of material and frequently involves gestures as well. It deals with the how, when, and why rituals are performed and may also deal with the overt symbolism present in performances.

Knowledge of the dogma or the catechism, Category 4, is essentially a superficial form of knowledge in contrast to the preceding levels. It typically involves a rote form of learning and represents the officially "received" view on religion, both asserted beliefs and practices. It is always public; not private knowledge. It may be communicated in highly structured verbal and narrative forms, such as myths or prayers, to initiates. It is always explanatory material about behavior and belief. It is typically taught to initiates as the first stage of their religious education. It is restricted to initiates and is not generally public knowledge, although it is much less secret than the preceding levels. Some outsiders may be in possession of some catechismic knowledge without being considered to have violated secrecy.

Category 5, or participatory knowledge, is essentially a miscellaneous ad hoc category. Participants in ritual may be a very diverse group in terms of the knowledge they control. They may receive explicit instructions on their roles and perform them but never go beyond this level to understand any others. In many cases they are prohibited from asking any questions that do not pertain to their roles. In this category I am also including spectators to public ceremonies, many of whom will be total outsiders. They possess little or no knowledge about what they witness, but they are under some restrictions if they attempt to find out more about what they witness. By analogy, we might think of an individual attending a mass in Latin, knowing no Latin, who participates by watching what others do, but has no deeper understanding of what it all might mean.

All these categories are present in Pueblo religion. There may be other categories and some of them may overlap as they are not intended to be mutually exclusive. But it is important to consider them as a background for understanding secrecy. We must realize something of the nature of knowledge in general and realize the diversity of knowledge among individuals.

[5]This explains some of the opposition to data gathering devices that provide more complete retrieval of information. Taos Pueblo attempted to suppress Parsons's *Taos Pueblo* (1936) when it first appeared as it "gave away the secrets." Parsons's *Isleta Paintings* (1962), much of Leslie White's work, and Ortiz's (1969) are also considered to contain secrets.

From this background, cultural mechanisms that disseminate and control knowledge can be understood.

STRATEGIES MAINTAINING SECRECY

There are a number of strategies for practicing secrecy. Outsiders are barred from the village for specific rituals, and the private performances of ceremonies in such ritual spaces as kivas, society houses, and shrines prevent outsiders from witnessing them. Other strategies are prohibition against photographs, drawings, and tape recordings at otherwise open ceremonies and villages. Another strategy is the well-known Pueblo propensity to construct false and misleading information for benefit of the curious. Another is polished evasion of questions. Trager and Leap (1968) found a pattern in speaking, which they called "the purist tendency." Loanwords from Spanish and English are purged in the presence of outsiders who might understand them. Elaborate circumlocutions are employed in the native language to convey information without using a term that might be understood. Some of these circumlocutions have become well-known idiomatic expressions in the native language. At the beginning of an encounter with native speakers of an Indian language, if there is an outsider present who understands some of it, the other parties will be warned to watch their speech.

The presence of ritual speech in religious contexts, which contains archaic words, borrowings from other languages, and a different semantic system with nonordinary referents, also preserves secrecy. There are also special styles of speaking, such as the speech of the Black Eyes, the Chiffoneti clown group at Taos, and "talking backwards," which serves to exclude the curious. Simple use of the native language in religious and political contexts serves effectively to exclude outsiders. It is quite frequent for leaders to use the native language with an interpreter when engaged in political meetings with Anglos and Hispanos even when the leader speaks English or Spanish. This is an important dramatic speech act and serves to distance the hearers and enhance the status of the Indian leader. In many communities, though not at Taos, use of the native language in religion and politics serves to exclude the younger members of the community, who do not speak the language.

CONSEQUENCES OF SECRECY

It has been demonstrated earlier that there are certain forms of knowledge that are secret due to inherent restrictions on the type of knowledge and that there is diversity among individuals in the kinds of knowlege they possess. This creates some internal secrecy and also has consequences for external secrecy. Individuals cannot transmit information that they do not possess, either within the community or outside it. Internal secrecy in the sense of deliberate exclusion of individuals from witnessing ceremonies, asking about them, or participating ensures that relatively few individuals in a community will actually be in possession of secret information. The majority of the community simply does not know secret information; or if they do know any they may be in possession of a very small amount.

A major consequence of internal secrecy is the establishment of status hierarchies based on access to knowledge communicated only in oral form. Pueblo communities contain a number of small-group cultures that store, retrieve, and transmit different kinds of information (McFeat, 1974). For the Pueblos as a whole, the important small-group cultures we are concerned with in this paper are dual organizations, clans, societies, and kiva groups. There is relatively little overlap or information leakage between the groups. Since Pueblo governing systems are linked in important ways with these small-group cultures, the establishment of status hierarchies based on secret information in the possession of one group rather than another can have important political consequences.

Possession of religious knowledge and participation in religious works are prerequisites to full participation in the political system. While most individuals know the theory of their governing system and can observe its overt acts, many are excluded from significant roles and have little real conception of what actually occurs. The inability of individuals to obtain certain kinds of information makes any challenge to internal governing risky and generally doomed to failure. Internal secrecy thus slows innovation in Pueblo communities and provides a stabilizing influence, though at times this is seen as oppressive and unresponsive by those without full participation.

The focus for secrecy is internal, not external. The society can bring a full range of sanctions into play against a community member, but can do little against a nonresident. Thus, if you can control the information sources within a community, you can also control information transmitted to the outside. Religious knowledge is necessary for political power within the community. If this knowledge can be restricted to a very small group, that group can control the community. External secrecy primarily prevents back contamination, or information that could threaten the established leadership hierarchies from coming back into the community. Secrecy is also maintained within the community on a great many political matters.

This last point requires some amplification. I do not mean to imply that secrecy is a relatively new phenomenon or that there are not legitimate secrets and nonpolitical reasons for keeping them. One reason often adduced for secrecy by Pueblo leaders is that religious ceremonies lose their power if they are known by the wrong people. This is certainly an attitude commonly encountered in many parts of the world.

Nonreligious secrecy has received little attention from anthropologists because of the tremendous interest in Pueblo religion and the texture and complexity of Pueblo ceremonialism. While some secrecy surely existed in the past as a way of integrating culturally diverse groups, within the historic period it has expanded from its original contexts.

Archaeological evidence, historic documents, and Pueblo tradition all confirm that Pueblo villages were internally diverse communities that periodically received groups of immigrants from other areas. These migrating groups must have brought their own traditions and religious beliefs with them. Secrecy about religion would enable the community to achieve a measure of religious freedom for its members and minimize conflict over ceremonial practices. Differing groups could be accommodated and the Pueblo might gain ceremonial specialists it did not originally possess. With the advent of Spanish colonization, secrecy took on new dimensions as Dozier theorized and the Pueblos added yet another religion. In the twentieth century yet another vector of secrecy came into play.

Secrecy becomes a conscious political strategy adopted to maintain political autonomy and freedom in a hostile world, but in a different sense than envisioned by Dozier. Beginning in the 1920s and 1930s, a cloak of secrecy has been thrown over a great many things that were formerly open. This new use of secrecy is especially pronounced at Taos. I believe that it correlates with three events: (1) increased population surrounding the Pueblo communities; (2) the advent of extensive tourism in the Pueblos; and (3) the discovery by Pueblo leaders that the U.S. Constitution protects freedom of religion. Events 1 and 2 made it difficult to control information due to the sheer numbers of nosy individuals poking around and asking questions. Event 3 enabled Pueblo leaders to throw a cloak of obscurity over any internal matter and to gain a greater degree of internal control and freedom by claiming outside interference in traditional religion at Taos, the refrain for any denial of information on anything is that it is part of the religion. A political proposal may be justified or denied by an appeal to religion. If pressed for a reason, tribal leadership may assert that the reason is part of the religion and therefore secret.

The foregoing discussion does not mean to suggest that there are not legitimate reasons for secrecy and legitimate secrets, only that leadership has learned to use secrecy in a new manner for explicitly political purposes. It also does not imply that secrecy is not broken upon some occasions. In some cases violations are inadvertent or the result of sophisticated digging by outsiders. In a majority of cases when secrecy is broken, however, it is done for a specific political purpose by those in possession of the secrets and is a deliberate strategy, e.g., in the Taos case for the necessity of winning outside support and understanding in their attempts to win back the Blue Lake area.[6] Secrecy is a dynamic complex of behaviors that serves a variety of functions and whose function has changed through time.

In the next section of the paper, I will examine the ceremonial and political organization of Taos in some detail to show how information is controlled and political power is allocated within the community. The following points provide the structural sociocultural groundwork for the secrecy dynamic.

(1) The existence of cross-cutting religious societies or groups that have secular political functions as well is the most important factor in Taos social organization and possibly in other villages as well. While dual organization is also an important organizational principle in some villages, especially the Tewa (Ortiz, 1969), there is no evidence for its importance at Taos.

(2) As a consequence of these societies, the specialization of their functions, and the differential training involved, no one individual in any village serves as a repository for *all* cere-

---

[6]It is also possible for other individuals to break secrecy if they have strong kin and/or political support.

monial and religious knowledge (this would be true in dual organization as well). This is a controversial assumption as some Pueblo scholars have placed the cacique in this position, but a careful review of the evidence, both ethnographic and linguistic, shows little support for this view.[7] The cacique may coordinate activities and perform an integrative role, but I do not believe he possesses all the knowledge relevant to each group. My own fieldwork at Taos and Sandia also supports this view.

(3) Categories and levels of being such as those described by Ortiz (1969) are a universal in Pueblo society. Ranked status categories are based on access to ritual knowledge and exist in every village.[8] These categories also serve to define the extent of political participation in many Pueblo communities, especially Taos. There is some evidence at Taos that they may represent incipient social classes and research is continuing on this topic (Brandt, 1975). Interestingly, Parsons (1939) states:

> In Zuni definition, poor people are people without ceremonial property or connection, belonging in no rain or curing society—people who are not valuable. In this sense the poor of Zuni are about half the population. The proportion of poor would be very

---

[7]The last cacique at Taos was not considered the legitimate heir for the position by many. In addition, he was incapacitated by age and blindness. In testimony in U.S. District Court in 1975 he was criticized by some community members for misrepresentation of his position and power. After a severe factional dispute culminating in 1976, he left his position. He died in 1978.

[8]I have quoted Parsons's (1939, p. 112) footnotes in their entirety for their clarity. She gives important terms for these categories.

> Keres *sishti,* which denotes any person not actually engaged in ceremonial work or any common person without ceremonial or governmental affiliation. Santo Domingo (Acoma, White, Chap. 4, p. 167, Chap. 7), or anyone who knows all about the kachina (San Felipe, White, Chap. 3, p. 27). Compare Laguna and Cochiti, *shuts, shurdze* (Dumarest, 198). The kachina dance cult is everywhere that of the "poor man", or commoner. Distinctive terms or references are applied or made by Hopi of Second Mesa to chiefs, neophytes, or members merely, *pavunshinum,* small mound caused by corn just starting to come up out of the ground (Nequatewa, p. 103; Stephen, 4, glossary) and to non-members or commoners.

> In the quote given above, I am following the Hopi distinction between belonging to a ceremony (or society with ceremony) and belonging to a dance group (or society without ceremony). Dance groups or societies are large in all the towns, since they are generally inclusive of all the males. Kiva memberships are similarly inclusive, and of course, moiety membership. The memberships of the clown societies at Cochiti and Jemez are strikingly large, showing moiety influence.

> See also the term used by Tewa in Ortiz (1969, p. 17), "Dry Food People" *whe towa* and *nayi wha towa,* "Dust Dragging People."

much larger in the East, but I doubt if the distinction would be made at all there; the society membership lists are too small (p. 112).[9]

(4) Religious societies and their leaders are socially ranked with respect to each other. There is differential access to knowledge within and between the societies. Rewards for participation in the secular sense are primarily political and, in the last decade or two, economic.

(5) Processes of society recruitment and training within a society lead to extreme variations in the nature and amount of knowledge that individuals possess. This makes it possible to control information in very explicit ways and to ensure a high degree of conformity.

(6) Oral transmission of religious information provides a high degree of control over information impossible with any other system of data storage and retrieval. This is a crucial factor in the maintenance of the religious and political systems of Pueblo communities. As such it explains much of the opposition of Pueblo communities to any relatively permanent forms of data storage such as writing, recordings, and photographs.

Systems without the rapid fading characteristic would allow unqualified and potentially unsocialized individuals access to the deepest and most central concepts of Pueblo life without the cautionary experiences and explanations of those more knowledgeable. This would be true whether they were insiders or outsiders. We might liken this to the control Anglo society attempts to exercise over classified material.

(7) Since the society leadership is, in effect, coterminous with the technical secular political organization, it is able to exercise a variety of both religious and secular sanctions against potential or actual violators of secrecy. At the same time such leaders are also able to violate secrecy if political consider-

---

[9]The distinction *is* made between categories of people even in the eastern Pueblos. Normally this is translated in English, the Made People or Cooked People opposed to everyone else. At Taos it is the *lulina* ("Old People") as opposed to *'it' oysemayana*, ("New People"). Among the Keresans we find the terms *shurdze* or *sishti* applied to individuals without ceremonial affiliation (Parsons, 1939). Ortiz (1969) gives *patowa* as the term for Made People. Another suggestive term for the Cooked People is *nalent'óynema* as recorded by Trager in Parsons (1940). *Nalen* was not translated, but *t'óynema* is "people." The number of people in the Made category at Taos is approximately 50. This agrees with Ortiz's (1969) figure for the Tewa of 52, though of this maximum number not all participate. At Taos only 36 individuals are active society leaders and council members (Brandt, 1976).

ations warrant it without fear of reprisal other than gossip and factionalism.

Supporting data for the points mentioned above is discussed in the following section.

TAOS CEREMONIAL ORGANIZATION

Dual Organization

Taos possesses a dual organization with membership inclusive for all individuals in the named segments—north side, south side. Membership in these groups is the basic common denominator for the community, but the two groups seem to have little structural importance at the explicit level. Ortiz's (1965) useful distinction between moieties and dual organizations can be applied to Taos. The groups are not exogamous and have no connections with residence or political organization. Although Taos has six functioning kivas, three on each side of the village, their location does not seem to reflect dual organization. It is possible that the details of dual organization at Taos are secret.

Cross-cutting Societies

Within each kiva are two societies, each with its own leadership.[10] The true nature of the kiva societies is still somewhat unclear. Some societies have overlapping membership in two kivas, such as the Big Hail people, who are found in both Big-Earring Kiva and in Water Kiva (Parsons, 1936). Other societies are restricted to one kiva. Some of these societies do not formally initiate members. A category of membership is reserved for those who sing but do not dance. The uninitiated membership is larger than the initiated membership. Each society gains members by dedication, trespass, and trapping. The most common way is by dedication, either by a personal vow or being promised by one's parents. Dedication may occur shortly after birth, but formal society initiation will take place later when the child is between 10 and 12 years of age. Trespass occurs, usually, when a male individual is in a position to witness some secret ritual, touches a taboo society member or ritual object,

---

[10]At Taos, a kiva is a semisubterranean chamber used as a meeting place for some societies. Additional societies exist, some using kivas, others society houses.

or encounters an individual on ritual business (Parsons, 1939). Trapping is rare and occurs only when a society is in need of a replacement and an individual must be coerced. In trespass, an individual becomes contaminated by power and must join the society to deal with the burden. It also serves to prevent an individual from divulging privileged information.

Each society is responsible for certain ritual activities and must inform the next group of its part if it is a cyclic or joint ritual. Authority over a ceremony and its participants is limited to the society directly concerned. An individual may not interfere with another society's rites.

While most individuals know the kiva and kiva society affiliation of most adult males, they do not have access to or knowledge of the specific details of internal group organization, nor knowledge of ceremonies held within other kivas. A rigid etiquette governs a man's participation in his kiva work. A Taos consultant stated:

> I've talked to a lot of people up at Taos, and got a lot of friends and that kind, but we *never* do talk about that kind of thing, about what clan or society they belong to. They don't talk about themselves either. And I guess, that's where the questions comes in, as secrecy things.[11]
>
> Well, naturally, they don't want you to know what society they belong to. Naturally, you don't ask either. If you did, well, what is it to you? Just the way the answer comes out, you know. So I'm always afraid to ask, unless they come up and tell me. Unless you watch 'em and see where they go, like you watch an individual, like your close friend, and still you don't know which group he belong to, and he might tell you, 'All right, I got to go tend to my society.' When he tell you that, well you might follow him, watch him, see which kiva he goes into. That's one way of finding out. (Brandt, 1975).

If an individual wishes to know about a particular society, he must join to find out. An individual does not ask questions. If he does, he will be firmly put off or asked to join. If he persists, he may lose face or risk expulsion from the community. Once in a society an individual may not divulge his information to outsiders without fear of sanctions. Noninitiated or short-term initiates are also put off. As one short-term member stated:

---

[11]The Taos use the term *clan* to refer to societies and kiva groups. There is no notion of unilineal descent at Taos.

Well, all you do is just cooperate. Just follow the leader and forget the rest. That's the way it works, I mean the secrets that they keep. I mean I'll never go any farther than, 'You do what I say and then forget it.' Then you respect them, so you have to forget it. Do just what they ask you to do, that's all (Brandt, 1975).

INITIATION

In addition to inclusive dual organization membership and general kiva membership, males may also belong to one or more societies in the kivas. There are two categories of membership, long-term and short-term, or easy-term, reflecting the differing degrees of training and knowledge that individuals receive. Initiation is a two-stage process beginning with registration or dedication at age 6 or earlier and formal incorporation between the ages of 8 and 12.

Fully trained or long-term initiates undergo an 18-month initiation period, beginning in February and coming out at the time of the annual Blue Lake pilgrimage the following August (Parsons, 1936; Bodine, n.d.). Short-term initiates receive only a 6-month training period beginning in February or March, and coming out in August. The kiva societies rotate initiation over a long period. Kiva leaders are drawn from the long-term group.

Short-term members are not fully trained and have little access to secret knowledge. Their training and the ritual prohibitions on their private lives are less strenuous. Their access to knowledge is on a "need-to-know" basis necessary for the performance of their duties, which consist of running errands, procuring supplies, and singing. Membership consists of individuals who have earned rights in the community by performance of community duties, but who have refused full initiation, were away when it normally would have happened, or who have come from other villages, but have shown their willingness to participate and reside at Taos. They are called in English the "in-between" or "middle people" by the Taos; there is no term in Taos for this category. Adult individuals are sometimes recruited into this category to serve the community politically if they have special skills or information the community needs (Brandt, 1975). Essentially, short-term individuals are lay assistants (Parsons, 1939).

Women also belong to the dual divisions and have in addition to their own societies (which are very few in number) a type of auxiliary kiva affiliation normally derived from their father's membership and changing to their husband's kiva upon marriage. Women prepare food, grind corn, and repair and plaster kivas; but at least at the formal or technical level they do not have access to esoteric information except as it is relevant for their duties. Women do not actually hold kiva membership, though they do perform functions for the kiva societies.

There are three groups present in Taos society, each with differential access to esoteric knowledge. One group, *'it' oysemayana* ("The New People"), consists of women, uninitiated adult males who have moiety affiliation and may have general kiva membership. The second group, the Middle People, consists of short-term initiates who have somewhat greater access to knowledge than the first group. The third group are the *lulina* ("The Old People"), who are fully initiated and often kiva leaders or society leaders.

The New People are poor ceremonially and may be poor in other respects as well. They are disenfranchised and may lack kin support, which would enable them to obtain favorable grazing permits and access to land. They are unable to hold political office and rarely have friends in high places. The Middle People are in a somewhat better position, but may not hold major offices. They are also ceremonially poor. The *lulina* are leaders and produce leaders. They allocate land, water, and permits. Certain families tend to develop power bases in kiva societies and allocate resources to their kin.

KIVA LEADERSHIP

Each society has a leader and there is an assistant leader for each society.[12] Leadership is lifelong. Some special training is given to leaders, assistants, and potential leaders at the time of initiation and continues most of an individual's lifetime. This long period of training is necessary to commit to heart the details of the ceremonies and the language that accompanies them. As positions become vacant and an individual is judged competent, he may move into a position of leadership. There is apparently a line of succession for leaders and assistants and occasionally a young man is chosen in preference to an

---

[12]My earlier data and that of Smith (n.d.) indicate that Taos uses the general Tanoan body analogy for leadership (e.g., a head and a right-hand and left-hand assistant). Parsons did not find this and my data from 1976 contradict my earlier data. At the request of some Taos, this statement reflects the more recent position; but it is still controversial

older one in the line, but my data is very incomplete in this area.

Leaders, by virtue of their positions in the religious hierarchy, are also automatically members of the Pueblo Council and thus receive political training by kiva society participation It is also possible to become a council member by holding major office, such as governor or war captain. A survey of current council membership (Brandt, 1976) indicated, however, that the majority of members had attained major office after they became leaders or assistants. If we count kiva leaders and their assistants and society leaders and their assistants, we arrive at a figure of 36 individuals, which coincides exactly with the current active membership of the Pueblo Council, assuming a long-term and a short-term leader and their assistant for each society.[13] This may merely be a coincidence as there are other members eligible for the council who do not actively participate and it includes three individuals who are not leaders and assistants. In any case, it demonstrates the interlocking nature of the secular and the ceremonial systems. Since basic governing positions in the Pueblo are chosen from this group, it follows that the secular governing officials will also be religious leaders at some level. The positions in the political systems and the religious system thus have the same occupants.

The levels of leadership and the reservoir of trained people provide a continuity of religious knowledge, a necessity in a society relying on oral transmission. If only one or two individuals possessed the knowledge, it would be easy to lose precious cultural information at the death of a leader. In fact, this has happened in other villages and also at Taos. The longer period of apprenticeship serves not only for technical mastery of a leader's duties, but is a powerful force in molding proper attitudes and respect. It allows the existing leadership a high degree of control over attitudes and behavior of members and provides a political leadership that is firmly grounded in religious principles. It denies major political participation to those who do not have the proper religious training and bars them from access to religious knowledge. In other words, religious training is a prerequisite for secular office-holding at the senior level. Nontraditionalists cannot gain technical or formal power, and secrecy prevents them from learning the underpin-

---

[13]If the data for two assistants is used as in Footnote 12, the figure becomes 48 which correlates well with an approximate figure of 50 individuals in a village who are "Made" people. If the lower figure is used, we could include leaders of other societies not considered as kiva societies. The exact number of these groups is unknown (see also footnote 8).

nings of certain political acts because the rationale of such acts is frequently attributed to religious reasons.

POLITICAL ORGANIZATION AND PROCESS

While Taos accepted the provisions of the Indian Reorganization Act, it has never been fully implemented. For details of the governing system, see Smith (1969, 1970). Only fully initiated members can fill any of the major governmental roles, such as governor or war captain or their first lieutenants. Short-term initiates and even noninitiates can fill appointive positions in the secular government, such as secretary, interpreter, sheriff, or be on the staff of the governor but cannot hold any major office. Since only approximately 50 people are fully initiated, the pool of potential officials is very small when compared with the total resident population of more than 1,000 (Bodine, n.d.). This pool also remains relatively constant over time. With the exception of the appointive positions, government is a closed system with the *lulina* choosing one another for major positions again and again. The same individuals occupy positions of authority and power in both the religious system and the political system. They also use their esoteric knowledge to direct the course of the village. As one informant put it:

> What you call our self form of government, it's all based on a religious ground. So those that doesn't belong to the kiva religion or society, we have no right to hold office. We can be appointed to help the Old People in terms of interpreting what the non-Indians, you know, want to do... or we can be selected as one of the ten staff officers, but we—like myself, I can't be a Governor up there, cause I was never initiated into the clan. So that makes the Old People carry on all the government to themselves, and they can appoint whoever they want. And then in another way, they have more advantage, appointing themselves, even if they have to appoint their own nephews or brother and sister (Brandt, 1975).

The Old People also use their knowledge of the "secrets" to prohibit undesirable behavior. For years, certain Taos have asked that the village have electricity everywhere.[14] The Old

---

[14]Electricity has recently been allowed on the west, south, and a limited portion of the north side outside the walls of the village. Members of the People's Committee, an internal faction, recently lost a suit in U.S. District Court against the council to force electricity on the east side of the village. The council claimed that the east side was sacred ground and would be harmed by the introduction of electricity.

People prohibited electricity (inside the walls) in the village proper on religious grounds but would not explain to the rest of the population the details of the reason because it was secret. One Taos says:

> We have been restricted all along—like electricity. Nobody up to this time tell us as to why it was restricted or against the religion. Course, that's a most sacred thing and they won't tell us (Brandt, 1975).

Rights in the community are inherited bilaterally. For an individual to hold his rights in the community, he should participate in the kiva religion and should have undergone at least short-term initiation. A current factional dispute at Taos concerns the whole question of tribal enrollment and community rights and duties. Some of the New People, *'it' oysemayana* have formed a political group, the People's Committee, to fight for their rights in the federal courts and are suing the tribal government, the Old People, under the Civil Rights Act. They want an end to what they see as abuses in tribal government; they want certain rights for themselves and their children as tribal members—rights that they are denied access to; and they want a democratic form of government. They have approached the tribal government on many occasions with their grievances, but as much of this group consists of women who have married out or married in, males who have married in, and non-Taos men who are not initiated, the group has little hope of success. In 1975, one of their members who was initiated became governor and for the New People this was seen as a sign of success. However, he was quickly co-opted and lost or denied his affiliative ties with the *'it' oysemayana*:

> Well now, in term of talking about the Old People is not the age of a person at the pueblo. Alright, we have a young governor, now ... and he's been initiated into the clan. Alright, when that young man get into the, become one of the officers, he became one of the Old People. That's why I say the Old People, they are so influence. So automatically, within his knowledge in himself, he feel that civilization is alright, but the same time he have to deny the civilization to make the Old People happy or satisfied. So he got to do what the Old People according to the functions of their government. So the Old People, they don't talk about age. They talk about the things that function (Brandt, 1975).[15]

[15] This quotation is interesting since the individual referred to was 64 at the time. He was chronologically young for office-holding in this village. But at the same time it illustrates the central point of the quotation—that a "young" or "new" person is one who is not fully socialized, ritually, socially, or politically.

142 • THE POLITICS OF SECRECY

> You can't do as you please when you are initiated, cause you have to do just what your society tells you to do... I was told when we were fighting this paved road up to the Pueblo and the electricity and what have you, we bring in, try to bring in the modern type of things, better living conditions in their home and that's one of the things I was told, that the signs say well, that's not allow here. It's against the religion. And everything was against the religion (Brandt, 1975).

The Old People have a firm grip on the society through control of the secular political system, which their access to knowledge gives them. Through secrecy they can invoke dire but unnamed supernatural sanctions on the rest of the population. They can ban anything they wish without the necessity for explanation by invoking secrecy. The *lulina* are the judicial system within the village and the legitimate agents of social control with the power to fine, imprison, whip, or expel anyone who threatens their authority. The tribal government is also backed by the support of the federal government. The secrets can only be revealed if one of the *lulina* chooses to reveal them. Secrecy is thus an internal political tool of great utility.

SUMMARY

Secrecy is a complex of behaviors and a dynamic process, which has changed through time. Pueblo leaders control information by limiting access to information to small numbers of individuals who must be socialized into the proper uses of information through a lengthy and complex process of group recruitment and training. Since information is transmitted primarily by oral means, their degree of control is high. The opposition of Pueblo leaders to permanent sources of data storage such as writing, filming, or recordings becomes quite clear on two levels. The religious objections that this sacred information should not be known by those who are not properly socialized into its uses and who do not have proper respect for it is also true at the secular, political level. The religious knowledge possessed by the Old People is a source of natural power as Pueblo religion deals with the forces of the universe and nature generally; and as leaders they are required to fulfill their duties, responsibilities, and rights to the community to keep these forces in balance. Their authority (the technical rights of their status and role) proceeds from their sacred knowledge: their power (the informal extensions of their authority) from their coterminous positions in the political system and the religious system. By limiting access to the religious system, they limit access to the political system. Their power and authority are reinforced by the complexity of the political and religious systems. In both the religious sense and the political sense, the New People are too rash, to unbalanced, and too dependent on others to exercise power and authority. In the view of the Old People, they do not have the knowledge or the social maturity to weigh all the considerations before making decisions. A long period of training provides the seasoning necessary to make decisions that are in harmony with nature and the universe and a Pueblo's special relation to the forces there. On the political side, a young man must learn balance on the person-to-person level and respect his culture's ways.

Religious leaders are the only ones who possess the secrets; and in order to retain their internal control over the community, the secrets must not be exposed. External secrecy is an attempt to prevent the spread of information to the outside world; from the internal perspective, however, it functions more importantly to keep such information from coming back into the community and effecting a radical shift in the internal organization of the community. Outsiders who gain information cannot be controlled effectively and may spread information into the wrong hands. As such, I believe it has proved adaptive for the maintenance of a power elite.

Traditional leadership at Taos has been criticized extensively by the People's Committee. One of the first activities of this group was to have Parson's *Taos Pueblo* (1936) read to them and to request its reprinting so that every disenfranchised individual could own a copy. This gave members some understanding and access to the secrets so necessary for a secular political challenge to Pueblo leadership. In a very real sense, knowledge is power and Parsons spoke the truth when she said:

> Our ways would lose their power if they were known. People have learned about the ways of other pueblos and those pueblos have lost their ways (Parsons, 1939, p. 433).

I believe it could be demonstrated that secrets would not be given away unless the traditional religious organization had begun to disintegrate. After this process got underway, we would expect that the political system would show serious changes and realignments, and that a village would accept writing and other forms of data storage.

The secrets as the source of power and authority also explains a fact that surprises many investigators. When a factional split becomes so intense as to cause village fission, it is the conservatives who leave, taking their information with them.[16] They have the ability and the techniques to reconstitute a complete new village, but those who are left behind are in the same position as an American community might be if all the utilities were abandoned and the trained personnel were gone as well as all the religious and political leadership. The fear of this happening is sometimes enough to effect a reconciliation of sorts. Today, of course, it is difficult to found a new village, given the reservation system, but secular villages do exist and leaders do walk out abandoning their people until they find the right "path" again.

Secrecy is intimately tied up with political factionalism and the stresses and strains of continued existence in the modern world, but I believe I have demonstrated that the process is of a different nature than that envisioned by Dozier. While I have stated that I believe secrecy of the sort we currently see is a relatively recent phenomenon, I also believe that institutionalized secrecy was present even in precontact times and was necessary to preserve the coherent social organization that we know was present. It is debatable whether there was a need to maintain an external form of secrecy, but if my argument is correct, there *must* have been a necessity for internal secrecy. I hypothesize that in this same aboriginal period (from, say, at least Pueblo II on) the number of initiated members and societies was larger and/or that there was greater overall involvement in the political organization. Many of these themes must be explored in later papers. On the ground, socioceremonial and political organization differs from village to village, but I believe that an examination of the data would show a similar function for secrecy.

---

[16]M. E. Smith enlightened me on this point and is responsible for many suggestions that I have incorporated in this paper.

References

Bloom, L. B. A campaign against the Moqui Pueblos. *New Mexico Historical Review,* 1931, 10, pp. 242–248.
Bodine, J. Personal Communication, n.d.
Brandt, E. A. Transcripts of taped interview, Summer 1975.
Brandt, E. A. Transcripts of taped interview, Summer, 1976.
Brandt, E. A. Factionalism and Communication. Paper presented at the Conference on Pueblo Politics, Santa Cruz, California, 1978.
Dozier, E. P. Rio Grande Pueblos. In E. H. Spicer (Ed.), *Perspectives in American Indian Culture Change.* Chicago: University of Chicago Press, 1961.
Dumarest, N. Notes on Cochiti, New Mexico. *American Anthropological Association Memoirs,* 1919, 6(3), Lancaster, Penn.
McFeat, T. *Small-Group Cultures.* New York: Pergamon Press, 1974.
Nequatewa, E. Truth of a Hopi. In M. R. F. Colton (Ed.), *Museum of N. Arizona Bulletin,* 1936. 8.
Ortiz, A. Dual organization as an operational concept in the Pueblo. *Southwest Ethnology,* 1965, 4, 389–96.
Ortiz, A. *The Tewa world: Space, time, being and becoming in Pueblo society.* Chicago: University of Chicago Press, 1969.
Parsons, E. C. *Taos Pueblo* General Series in Anthropology, 1936, 2.
Parsons, E. C. *Pueblo Indian Religion,* Chicago: University of Chicago Press, 2 vol., 1939.
Parsons, E. C. *Taos tales.* New York: American Folklore Society, 1940.
Parsons, E. C. *Isleta paintings.* E. S. Goldfrank (Ed.) Washington: Bureau of American Ethnology Bulletin 181, 1962.
Scholes, F. V. Troublous times in New Mexico, 1659–1670. *Historical Society of New Mexico, Publications in History,* 1942, 2.
Smith, M. E. Personal communication, n.d.
Smith, M. E. Governing at Taos Pueblo. *Eastern New Mexico Contributions in Anthropology,* 1969, 2(1).
Smith, M. E. Notes on ethnolinguistic study of governing. In M. E. Smith (Ed.), *Studies in linguistics in honor of George L. Trager.* The Hague: Mouton, 1970.
Smith, M. E. Tourism as a force for tradition and change in an American Indian community. Paper presented at the XLI International Congress of Americanists, Mexico City, 1974.
Spicer, E. H. *Cycles of Conquest.* Tucson: University of Arizona Press, 1962.

Stephen, A. M. Hopi journal. *Columbia University Contributions to Anthropology,* 1936, 23.

Trager, F. H., & Leap, W. L. Vocabulary acculturation in two Rio Grande Pueblos. Paper presented at the AAAS Meetings, Dallas, Texas, 1968.

White, L. A. The Pueblo of San Felipe. *AAA Memiors,* 1932, 38, Lancaster, Penn.

White, L. A. The Pueblo of Santo Domingo, New Mexico. *AAA Memiors,* 1935, 43, p. 167, Lancaster, Penn.

White, L. A. Supplementary data on Acoma, New Mexico, n.d.

6

Bizango: A Voodoo Secret Society in Haiti

Michel S. Laguerre
University of California at Berkeley

INTRODUCTION

Bizango is the name of a secret society operating in the western and southern portions of the island of Haiti.[1] It is also the name of one of the African tribes from the Bissagos Islands, whose members were brought to colonial Haiti for plantation work (Moreau de Saint-Mery, 1958). The Bissagos, or Bijago's, Islands, an archipelago, are located off the Coast of Kakonda, between Sierra Leone and Cape Verde. Referring to slaves coming from the Bissagos Islands, Moreau de Saint-Mery (1958) writes, "these blacks are good hunters and sure guardians of living quarters in the plantations." The participation of Bissagos slaves in the formation of maroon communities has already been acknowledged (Debbash, 1961; Laguerre, 1973a; Débien, 1966). However, the reasons why a particular tribe has left its name to a secret society have not been explained yet.

The concentration of slaves of same ethnic origins in a same region or the leadership role played in a secret organization by a slave whose ethnic identity was known are the two main

---

[1]The data upon which this paper is based were collected while I was doing field work in Haiti during the summer of 1976. I wish to thank the Research Institute for the Study of Man, the University of Illinois Research Board and the InterAmerican Institute of Agricultural Sciences for their financial assistance. I am also grateful to Norman Whitten, Vera Rubin and Robert Bellah for their encouragement to write this paper. I am finally indebted to Dr. Stanton K. Tefft for his insightful comments on an early draft of this article.

reasons which might explain the identification of Haitian secret societies to the names of specific African tribes. It was a common custom in colonial Haiti for slave leaders to leave their names to organizations that they formed. There are a few examples of those cases throughout the history of the island. Don Pedro, a maroon, has left his name to the *Petro* cult group that he founded (Métraux, 1972). Makandal, a rebel who organized slave revolts in the northern plantations, has also left his name to the *Makandal* society, which is based in the North (Fouchard, 1962). The *Mandingue* secret society—*Mandingue* is the name of an African tribe—is still a strong association in the Valley of Artibonite (Peters, 1965). Other secret societies such as *Zobop, Vlinbinding,* and *San Poèl* which function in the West, carry rather names of creole origin (Courlander, 1960).

Maroons, or fugitive slave rebels, constituted during the French colonization of Haiti (1625–1791) a constant threat to the local French establishment (Price, 1973). They were revolutionary slaves who used a large range of strategies and tactics in their day-to-day resistance to slavery. In more specific terms, the maroon can be defined as

> the fugitive slave who has broken with the social order of the plantation to live, actually free, but as an outlaw, in areas (generally in the woods or in the mountains) where he could escape the control of the colonial power and the plantocratic establishment.
>
> The first element in this definition is the existence of a social organization (the plantation system) with a structure and laws, within which the *servile condition* is set down, and with which the maroon breaks by fleeing ...
>
> The second element is the possibility of taking refuge in a space not actually controlled by the ruling authorities and their repressive forces, so that he can escape from the hold of the center by putting himself on the periphery, in a marginal but independent situation ...
>
> The third element is the insecurity of his new life.... It is a material, psychological and political insecurity. To resist and survive means a psychology of risk-taking and a determination to brave adversity and face danger ...
>
> The fourth element comes from the necessity to survive by his own means. The three main problems of survival are food, shelter and defense ... (Manigat, 1977).

In colonial Haiti, there were three types of maroons: urban, rural, and nomadic (Laguerre, 1973(a)). Colonial maroons were all slaves who fled the plantations in search for freedom. Both rural and urban maroons established maroon communities with genuine political, economic, and religious systems of their own. Nomadic maroons wandered in streets and rural roads begging and stealing from plantations whatever they could find. Maroon villages, placed in mountainous areas of difficult access to colonists, served as training grounds for maroon guerilla warfare.

This paper argues that, after independence of Haiti in 1804, cells of maroon communities have continued to exist through the formation of secret societies. Secret societies are seen then as the channels that "maroons" of contemporary Haiti use to protect their personal interests and that of their own communities. The colonial maroons fought against the slave system and all of its evil forces; this was a racial war, a fight against French planters. In contemporary Haiti, maroons, which constitute the membership of secret societies, continue to fight not against white people, but still stand strong to keep safe the boundaries of power of their local communities and to keep other groups of people from being a threat to their communities.

Simmel (1950) distinguishes two types of secret society: on the one hand, the formation of the group is concealed; and on the other hand, "the formation of the group is completely known, while the membership, the purpose, or the specific rules of the association remain secret" (Simmel, 1950). The Bizango secret society belongs to the latter, for its existence is known not only to people who hold membership in that association, but also to outsiders. Since Bizango people walk in bands in the streets at night, one may be able to encounter a group in one's lifetime and find out who they are.

The information on the Bizango secret society was given to me by informants who were invited to join the association and who, later on, converted to Protestantism. These informants live in the Artibonite Valley and the Central Plateau of Haiti. They were willing to talk about the functioning of the association, but not to reveal secret languages, strict rules, and individual members' names. One informant has even allowed me to have a Xerox copy of a Bizango passport that he used to carry with him at night for protection from other competing secret societies.

THE FUNCTIONING OF A SECRET SOCIETY

The importance of secrecy in the formation and functioning of secret societies cannot be overestimated. For Simmel (1950), "the secret determines the reciprocal relations among those who share it in common." Secrecy is the principle at the base of the formation of such groups. However, secrecy cannot be maintained without proper initiation and training of neophytes. Initiation and training are specific moments when one learns about the rules of the game. An initial training is not enough for one to become a full member; cyclical rituals must be performed to strengthen linkages among members and obedience to the leaders and faithfulness to the purposes of the secret society.

Not everyone can become a member of the Bizango society. One must be invited by a member to do so. The acceptance of such an invitation does not make one eligible to be briefed at once about all the rules of the secret society. These rules are revealed step by step to the newcomer as the person is being tested on other grounds.

The recruitment process is done through a kind of selective and elective brotherhood. The initiation ritual—consisting of the recruitment process, the participation in formal rituals, and the teaching of rules of the society—is a way of integrating newcomers to the group. To maintain the unity of the society as one body, other rituals are also performed.

Mackenzie (1967) has mentioned the following variables as characteristics of secret society, "the initial ritual, the ordeal, the oath, the myth or legend that supports the secrecy and the segregation of men from women". The Bizango society will be described here in light of those characteristics.

The Bizango society has developed over time its own Voodoo tradition. During the colonial era, Bizango was the spirit protector of Bissagos slaves. He is still known in Voodoo mythology as a warrior and a violent spirit. The Bizango mythology is not well known in the Haitian literature because of the secrecy to which the members of the society are bound.

Members of the Bizango society, as well as other Voodooists, believe that the universe is governed by *weak* and *strong* spirits. Some of them are of African origins while others are Creoles, that is born in the New World. Bizango belongs to the family of strong spirits, born in immemorial times in Africa. His function in Voodoo mythology is to protect the interests of his followers. The main reason for his protection is to bring them back to Africa when they die so that they may live in the land where he holds a residence.

In the context of Haitian peasantry, the belief in Bizango means for the peasant assured protection against individuals who may try to rid them of their lands and a guarantee to return to live in Africa after death. These two elements serve as the practical and eschatological base from which they operate.

The first phase in the educational process by which one becomes a member of a secret society is the "initial ritual." During the initial ritual, or ritual of initiation, the individual learns about the peculiar belief system that serves as a philosophical basis to the existence of the group. As mentioned earlier, this philosophy, which presents Voodoo spirits as guardians of peasant lands, is a combination of peasant political thoughts and Voodoo beliefs. While going through the initiation phase, the individual also becomes aware of the identity of fellows who belong to the group, as well as of the group stratification, the function of each individual, and the existence of competing groups in the district or elsewhere on the island. The individual is also admonished about the importance of secrecy for the survival of the society, the role that he will play in the association, and the financial contribution (monthly fees) that he will be called upon to give. Moreover, the neophyte is invited to attend meetings for an entire year before he can be accepted as a full member. During this probation period, he is also called to perform what might be considered by Haitian standards "dirty tasks," for example, to clean someone's outhouse.

The novice must be tested on certain grounds before the elders can decide to accept his request to join the society. They must find out through various testings if the individual can keep the secret of the group. As it happens also in other secret societies, "the novice is treated as a stranger, a spy, an alien, or some other outsider, who must submit to various tests" (Mackenzie, 1967). To find out about a novice's ability to keep a secret, elders may send individuals who do not belong to the group to check on him and to see if he is going to reveal to others what might have been done and said in group meetings. He may even be tempted to do so for a woman's favor or for financial rewards.

When the elders accept to elect someone as a permanent member of the group, an ceremony, full of an atmosphere of magic, is organized. The role of such a ceremony which is not peculiar only to this voodoo secret society is "to impress the candidate with the seriousness of the step he is about to take" (Hobsbawn, 1959). During such a ceremony, the rules of the association are once clearly explained to the individual and names of the membership are fully revealed to him. At the same time, they make sure that he understands what might happen to him if he decides to leave the society or reveal its secret and names of individual members to outsiders.

The candidate must also make a speech explaining that he is definitely ready to join the association and that he agrees not to reveal to anyone the secret and names of individuals. To ratify his agreement, the candidate is invited to drink from a cup some pig blood that is presented to him. This is a kind of oath that binds the individual to the group.

Like other secret societies, the Bizango association holds periodic meetings "to reaffirm the unity of the members" (Hobsbawn, 1959). Once a month, they organize a nightly march or rally; and once a week, they meet for a couple of hours to worship together, during which time a member may be possessed by Bizango, the spirit-patron of the association.

The Bizango society has such "ritual furnishings" as banners, flags, passports, and uniforms. Banners and flags are of black and red. These are also the colors of the Haitian national flag, symbolizing the solidarity that must exist between blacks and mulattoes in the case of eventual threats by enemies of the nation. The members of the Bizango society wear black pants or skirts and red shirts or blouses with a black cross drawn on the back of the shirt or the blouse.

Every member of the Bizango society must carry with him at night a special passport for protection from members of the other competing secret societies. Secret societies compete against one another for power, and by becoming powerful, they may attract many followers to the Voodoo temple to which they belong. In so doing, they may exert control over an entire district.

The Bizango passport is a sheet of paper with a stamp on its upper left corner. Such a paper can be bought from the *Bureau des Contributions* (internal revenue service). On its borders, there are color lines, which are the same as the colors of the flag of the society. Under the stamp, there is a prayer, then the passwords, and there follow the names of villages and secret society leaders that have agreed to acknowledge such a passport. In the middle of the passport, stands a black and red cross.

Individuals who walk at night without a passport may be admonished by secret society members not to do so again. They may be invited to join the association if they must walk at night. A few cases were reported where individuals were beaten at night by their enemies who happened to be members of the Bizango society. However, the Bizango secret society can by no means be considered as a criminal association.

EVENING RALLIES

Evening rallies are rituals performed monthly by the society to strengthen the unity of the group. Drumming and the use of a conch *(lambi)* signal to the membership that the association is about to hold a meeting. Males and females take part in those rallies. The members gather in the Voodoo temple before they start the procession where they carry with them flags and banners.

Before leaving the temple to start the march, neighbors are admonished through songs not to talk about what they might have seen or heard. Voodoo temples are sometimes so close to surrounding houses that when they are having a meeting, neighbors can be aware of what's going on. If they are awake at night, they can hear songs sung by the society and recognize voices of some members. This following song invites neighbors not to reveal the identity of the society.

> La fanmi bizango io pinga diol nou
> La fanmi io pinga bouch nou
> Moin été ion band bizango asouè ia déio
> Nou lévé matin na pale ki jan mtap dansé
> Pinga diol nou.
>
>> Neighbors and friends of the Bizango society,
>> Be careful about what you might say.
>> When we organize a Bizango rally,
>> We don't wish for you to start talking about our
>> songs and dances, the morning after.

After they have sung this song, Legba, a Voodoo spirit, the guardian of gates and crossroads, is invoked. He is called to open the gates so that the people might be able to leave the temple. He is supposed to protect them as they walk through the streets at night.

> Ouvè, ouvè
> Mdi ouvè chemin
> Papa Legba, o
> Societe an la ki rantré.
>
> Open, open
> We say, open the gates
> Papa Legba
> The society is ready to leave the temple.

When the society is out walking in the streets, there is a specific order that members follow. Leading the band is the *sentinelle* (guard), then follows at distance the major *(lansé)* with a rope in his hands, and behind him walks a *porteur* (carrier) who carries a small coffin *(sèkey madoulè)*. The *porteur* is accompanied by two to four flag carriers, who are usually women. Then comes the crowd and finally the leader of the band with his bodyguards. The coffin contains the common funds of the society. Once a month, the faithful are called to contribute to those funds.

If the society meets a passerby, it is the duty of the *sentinelle* to stop that person. The major comes to pass the rope around his neck and the flag carriers come around him to identify him for the crowd. The *sentinelle* puts his hands on him and waits for the leader of the band to come. When the entire crowd is present there, the leader asks him to see his passport or starts asking questions to find out if he has any friend or relative who belongs to the Bizango society or if he belongs to another friendly secret society or Voodoo group. If he proclaims himself a Voodooist, the leader starts shaking hands with him to find out about his Voodoo knowledge.

The Bizango handshake is a ritual and a means of communication. Bizango members refer to it as a secret language. The preliminary phase of the Bizango handshake begins this way. First the group leader puts his index finger in the upper palm of the right hand of the other person, pushes his index finger on the person's skin so that he might be aware of the sign. This is a greeting sign by which people reveal their identity to each other. Second, they shift from right to left hand and to right hand again in a way that only a degree-holder Voodooist can decodify.

Some of the members of the Bizango secret society carry at night a machete on their waist to defend themselves if they meet a competing band. It is more a ritual than anything else since a band has power only over a certain delimited domain (a village, a rural or urban district) and the society would not try to move in someone else's domain. While walking at night in the streets, the Bizango people sing this following song.

> Li minuit o li lè pou malé
> Banm pasé
> Li minuit o li lè pou malé
> Map volé
> Mgin devan Baron pou mal dansé
> Li minuit o li lè pou malé.

> It is midnight, it is time for us to leave
> let us go
> It is midnight, it is time for us to leave
> Let us fly
> We have to go to the cemetery and dance for Baron Samedi.
> It is midnight, let us go.

The members of the Bizango society receive during their formation a training in tactics of guerrilla warfare. This is to prepare them for eventual defense of their land against mulatto and black elite. When they are walking at night, the *sentinelle* can alert the rest of the group at any time if he decides to do so for some reasons. To do that, he uses his whistle and the people immediately lie down on both sides of the road or the street. This is to avoid the driver and passengers of a passing automobile from being able to identify or see the members of the group. He routinely does that when a car or truck is coming their way.

The Bizango secret society begins its rallies after 11:00 p.m. and returns to the temple at about 3:00 a.m. The evening rallies are a kind of festive celebration in which the people eat, drink, dance, and have a good time together. Evening rallies are part of the rural carnival bands *(rara)* which circulate at night in the countryside during the lent period.

FROM MAROON COMMUNITIES TO BIZANGO SECRET SOCIETY

Maroon communities in colonial Haiti were formed and functioned on the base of secrecy. Secrecy was important to keep French colonists from knowing where these communities were located, who the maroons were, and what political and economic systems they used to survive (Debbash, 1961). Newly arrived maroons were evidently forced to take an oath not to reveal the secret of the community and consequently had to pledge allegiance to the group and obedience to the leaders.

Secrecy was further necessary to facilitate evening raids on the plantations. Passwords were needed for communication between accomplice plantation slaves and maroons. These passwords were not different from those used among colonial Voodooists. Voodoo provided a base of solidarity between slaves and maroons in that they were all Voodoo believers (Laguerre, 1973b, 1974a, 1974b). The function of passwords and handshakes was to help distinguish friends from slave spies. Secret languages, still used today among Voodooists, were a means to differentiate maroons and Voodooists from outsiders. Passwords, handshakes, and secret languages were means developed to strengthen a spirit of solidarity among maroons and slaves so that they could fight in their own domains against the brutality of the slave system.

Maroon communities were not homogeneous. Subgroups existed and were formed on the base of tribal language spoken by their members and also with people revolving around Voodoo priests and medicine men. Religion was, indeed, a factor of cohesion and group integration in maroon communities (Laguerre, 1973b). Maroon priests played a very important leadership role during the wars for the independence of Haiti. Postindependence secret societies emerged out of subgroups centered on the leadership of cult leaders.

The Bizango society emerged out of maroon communities. It is not totally a postindependence creation. Maroonage offered proper means for a restructuration of groups of slaves who had fled from the plantations and provided the mechanism by which secret societies could function in colonial Haiti.

After independence, the migration of maroons to cities and valleys, taking over white people's properties gave rise to the development and maintenance of secret societies. This time, the new maroons must be able to fight back in the eventual return of the French, but they also stood in opposition to the black and mulatto elite, who failed to provide enough lands to the peasants or were trying to take lands from them. It was a custom, after independence, for presidents to give large portions of so-called government land to army officers (Nau & Telhomme, 1930). It has been common throughout the history of Haiti for politicians to dispossess peasants of their lands. With the agrarian reform initiated by Jean Jacques Dessalines, the first ruler of Haiti (1804–1806), peasants were given lands for their economic subsistence. Over the years, the lands have been divided and passed from a generation to another without individuals having ownership papers. Influential politicians often try to steal the lands from the peasants. At times they have been successful in so doing; at other times, they have not been because of the stiff resistance offered by secret society groups.

After independence, secret societies comprised of both male and female members functioned to keep hold of their lands. The *lakou*[2] system was in the process of formation and membership in a secret society was a force to resist against outsiders' invasion on one's land and domain. Secret societies created a solidarity in villages and *lakous* against outsiders, and they defined the power boundaries of villages.

Networks of secret societies became well known when peasants hit the Haitian governmental system through the *Piquets* and *Kakos* revolts (Pierre-Charles, 1967). Their association came out of secrecy because of historic urges to organize group resistance. During the U.S. occupation of Haiti (1915–1934), groups of secret society people pledged their allegiance to the self-proclaimed revolutionary leader, Charlemagne Péralte, and fought against the U.S. marines.

After the U.S. occupation of Haiti ended, secret societies continued to function as the hard-core section of some Voodoo temples, charged with protecting their zones against the interferences of neighboring secret societies as well as the Voodoo temple and congregation to which they belong. The Voodoo temple is a separate institution to which a secret society may be connected. The Voodoo priest is a kind of public relations man between the outside world and the members of the secret society. Of all the members of a secret society, he is the only one who might be known in that capacity by the general public.

CONCLUSION

The Bizango secret society is a retention of Haiti's colonial heritage and stands as an integrated unit in the Haitian social structure. The integration of individuals into such a unit is done through a ritual of rebirth (ritual of initiation) that every

---

[2]*Lakou* is a creole word derived from the French "la cour." (Laguerre, 1978) Lakou means "a residential compound in which the residents are linked to each other through ritual, affinal, consanguineal, and fictional kinship ties" (Laguerre, 1976a; 1976b).

member had to pass through, through making an oath of allegiance to the group and through sharing secret languages (handshakes, passwords). The Bizango secret society stands as the conscience of certain districts in Haiti in that it protects the residents against exploitation by outsiders.

The study of secret societies is one way to understand the makeup of Haitian society. They are widespread on the island. If those secret societies could establish linkages making them nodes in a complex network, they would stand as a strong underground government capable of competing with the Haitian government. However, because of local competition, they have not been able to form such a network of relationships.

References

Courlander, H. *The Drum and the Hoe.* Berkeley: University of California Press, 1960.

Debbasch, Y. Le Marronage: Essai sur la désertion de l'esclave antillais. *L'Année Sociologique,* 1961, 3e serie, 1–112.

Débien, G. Le Marronage aux Antilles Francaises au XVIIIe siècle. *Caribbean Studies,* 1966, 6 (3), 3–43.

Fouchard, J. *Les Marrons de la Liberté.* Paris: Editions de l'Ecole, 1962.

Hobsbawn, E. J. *Primitive Rebels. Studies in archaic forms of social movements in the 19th and 20th centuries.* Manchester, Eng: University Press, 1959.

Laguerre, M. S. *Nativism in Haiti: The politics of Voodoo.* M.A. thesis (Sociology/Anthropology). Chicago: Roosevelt University, 1973a.

Laguerre, M. S. The place of Voodoo in the social structure of Haiti. *Caribbean Quarterly,* 1973, 19 (3), 36–50.(b)

Laguerre, M. S. An ecological approach to Voodoo. *Freeing the Spirit,* 1974, 3 (1), 3–12.(a)

Laguerre, M. S. Voodoo as religious and political ideology. *Freeing the Spirit,* 1974, 3 (1), 23–28.(b)

Laguerre, M. S. Belair, Port-au-Prince: From slave and maroon settlement to contemporary black ghetto. In N. E. Whitten (Ed.), *Afro-American ethno-history in Latin America and the Caribbean* (Vol. 1). Washington D.C.: American Anthropological Association/Latin American Group, 1976, pp. 26–38.(a)

Laguerre, M. S. *The black ghetto as an internal colony: Socioeconomic adaptation of a Haitian urban community.* Ph.D. dissertation (Social Anthropology). Champaign-Urbana: University of Illinois, 1976.(b)

Laguerre, M. S. Ticouloute and His Kinfolk: The Study of a Haitian Extended Family. In D. B. Shimkin (Ed.) *The Extended Family in Black Societies.* The Hague: Mouton, 1978, pp. 407–445.

Mackenzie, N. I. *Secret societies.* New York: Holt, Rinehart and Winston, 1967.

Manigat, L. The relationship between marronage and slave revolts and revolution in St. Domingue-Haiti. In V. Rubin & A. Tuden (Eds.), *Comparative Perspectives on Slavery in New World Plantation Societies.* New York: The New York Academy of Sciences, 1977.

Metraux, A. *Voodoo in Haiti.* New York: Schocken, 1972.

Moreau de Saint-Méry, L. F. E. *Description topographique, physique, civile, politique et historique de la partie française de l'Isle de Saint-Domingue.* Paris: Larose, 1958.

Nau, M., & Telhomme, N. *Code Domanial 1804–1930.* Port-au-Prince: Maurice Telhomme, 1930.

Peters, C. E. Société Mandingue. *Revue de la Faculté d'Ethnologie,* 1965, 10, 47–50.

Pierre-Charles, G. *L'economie haitienne et sa voie de développement.* Paris: Larose, 1967.

Price, R. (Ed.), *Maroon societies. Rebel slave communities in the Americas.* Garden City, N.Y.: Doubleday, 1973.

Simmel, G. *The Sociology of Georg Simmel.* New York: Free Press, 1950.

7

The Management of Secrecy: The Klu Klux Klan's Successful Secret

Richard T. Schaefer
Western Illinois University

In the United States there has been institutionalization of two countervailing mechanisms—public disclosure and secrecy. Publicity has its roots in the distrust of the aristocracy that marked the founding of the American Republic. Secrecy, at least at the governmental level, stems in part from a fear of conspiracy within as well as concern for subversion by infiltration or exposure of national defense secrets. At the individual level secrecy has its source in many less laudable traditions—hyperpatriotism, xenophobia, isolationism, fundamentalism, and populism (Shils, 1956). Interestingly, social scientists are the chief beneficiaries of the twin traditions of public disclosure and secrecy. It allows the researcher to observe without any negative sanctions for prying into private affairs, since they invoke their professional respect for privacy in order to maintain a measure of objectivity (Merton, 1968).

The significance of secrecy and attempts to uncover other's secrecy have been repeatedly stated in contemporary discussions of government affairs. However, the current interest should not be taken as representative of past periods in governmental history. For example in 1929, Secretary of State Henry L. Stimson closed down the only cryptanalytic (code-breaking) effort declaring, "Gentlemen do not read other's mail" (Dulles, 1963). Much more recently, the House Committee on Armed Services convened a Special Subcommittee on Intelligence (1972) to investigate the classification of government documents. The hearings disclosed a complex procedure for downgrading and declassifying of documents bearing such labels as "top secret," "secret," "confidential," "restricted data," "national security information," and "warning notice." Even with elaborate regulations, nearly 400,000 people were cleared by the armed forces to peruse documents with the highest classification, that of "top secret." For some observers the issue was one of too much information being restricted in its dissemination. While for others, national security was being jeopardized by unauthorized "leaks" that needed to be sealed by quasi-authorized "plumbers."

This recent publicity given to secrecy, has ignored the vital role secrecy plays in social life. Simmel writing in 1908 noted the varied functions secrecy performs. It can function to uphold the highest values as in the individual who conceals his or her own contributions to avoid expressions of appreciation. Secrecy can also be utilized to hide acts seen by society as immoral or unethical. The latter recognizes the not uncommon phenomenon of people not hesitating to do "evil" as long as they do not appear "evil" (Simmel, 1950; Hazelrigg, 1969).

Ignorance of the outsider is the purpose of the maintenance of secrecy by the possessor of knowledge (Moore & Tumin, 1949). Secrecy has been the subject of social inquiry in several areas. Weber recognized that "every bureaucracy seeks to increase the superiority of the professionally informed by keeping their knowledge and intentions secret" (Gerth & Mills, 1958). In no other area of social behavior has the preservation of secrecy accompanied by ignorance been as systematically studied as in the area of secret societies. Professional researchers and lay people alike have been attracted to what Shils (1956) termed the "fascination of secrecy." Secrecy permits the powers of revolutionary movements to be greatly exaggerated by the aristocracy. Occasional assassinations give lip service to the continuing belief in a sinister plot hidden away in some corner of society. From Freemasons to the Mau Mau, the Carbonari to the Cosa Nostra, the rituals and purposes of secret societies have been consistently, often unsuccessfully, monitored. This study examines the purposes secrecy has served for the Ku Klux Klan during its more than one hundred years of existence.

THE KU KLUX KLAN IN HISTORICAL PERSPECTIVE

Although founded in 1867, the Klan cannot be regarded as a single, century-old organization. True for over a hundred years there have been organizations using that name and similar nomenclature. However one cannot accurately view it as a continuous secret society (Degler, 1965). There are three distinct periods of Klan activity (Schaefer, 1971, 1979). Following the Civil War, the Klan was created to meet the threat posed by the newly freed slaves. Convinced that it had succeeded in preserving the antebellum South, the hooded knights vanished.

Another war, World War I, brought the Ku Klux Klan back to deal with a host of changes in the "American way" including immigration of aliens to the United States and migration from the rural South to the Northern cities by blacks. William Joseph Simmons, as this century's first imperial wizard, took the ritualistic elements of the Reconstruction Klan and expanded them to create an autocratic hierarchy of officials, an elaborate ritual, and a detailed array of regalia. The hierarchy listed such officers of the klavern (a local chapter) as the kludd (chaplain), kligrapp (secretary), klarago, klexter, and nighthawk (guards). Such an obsession with ritual and titles prompted the historian Richard Hofstadter (1969) to note that the Klan set up a secret organization that in some ways flattered its opponents, e.g., the priestly garments of Roman Catholicism and the secret cells of the Communist party. All this ritual and use of impressive titles was not without purpose. The status-exalting nomenclature and rituals helped the Klansmen to set themselves apart from the mass of humanity and to become what appeared to be an indispensable part of the Invisible Empire (Lowe, 1967; Mikell, 1966). As one author (Rice, 1962) suggested, "When a man joins the Ku Klux Klan, a sensation seems to come over him as definite as falling in love. He simply drops out of society and enters a new world."

Simmel (1950; Hazelrigg, 1969) noted the "aristocratic motive" that was served by secret society membership and outsiders' ignorance. Secrecy often preserved a privileged position by limiting the access to knowledge that might be used to undercut power and privilege (Moore & Tumin, 1949). However, sometimes in secret societies and specifically with the Klan, secrecy itself becomes a sign of privilege—the privilege of access to the Invisible Empire and its secrets. Clearly much of the secrecy maintained by the Klan throughout its history protected relatively useless knowledge—a trait characteristic of many secrecy systems, including those associated with many government bureaucracies (Lowry, 1972).

Despite these "benefits," the Klan had fewer than 5,000 members when Simmons turned to the services of professional publicists, Edward Young Clarke and Elizabeth Tyler, in 1920.

Their staff utilized financial incentives to recruit new members by devoting 80 per cent of the $10 initiation fee to sponsors of the new Klansmen. By such techniques, membership climbed to 100,000 within 16 months (House Un-American Activities Committee, 1967). Ironically (but as will be stressed later not unwelcomed), this secret society received a healthy boost through the publicity of an extensive series in the New York *World* in September 1921 "exposing" Klan activities. Carried in 18 newspapers and publicized throughout the press, the articles appeared to do more to arouse people's curiosity than their opposition (Chalmers, 1965).

As with all secret societies, the size of the Ku Klux Klan has been the subject of both study and speculation. Secret societies such as the Ku Klux Klan have few detached observers—people either reject it out of hand or are its steadfast friends. It is interesting to realize that both the Klan's opponents *and* friends have something to gain by exaggerating its size. In the case of the Ku Klux Klan, the use of secrecy not only allows the organization to *stop* the flow of information but also to *force* information on the public (Wilsnack, 1977). The bigger the organization, so the logic goes, the bigger the threat it poses or the more significant the force it symbolizes. For example, currently the FBI estimates the Klan at 2,200. However the NAACP's estimate is in the tens of thousands. One Klan group claims 300,000 (McNulty, 1976a, 1976b). As a secret society its membership is closed to public scrutiny. Efforts by the Klan to maintain its privacy were the subject of legal action. In 1928, the Supreme Court in *Bryant* v. *Zimmerman* upheld a New York statute designed to force the Ku Klux Klan to disclose its membership. Curiously just 30 years later, the antithesis of the Klan, the NAACP, also resisted efforts to disclose publically its membership. In this instance however the Supreme Court in *NAACP* v. *State of Alabama* ruled that the

> ... inviolability of privacy in group association may in many circumstances be indispensable to preservation of freedom of association, particularly where a group espouses dissident beliefs.

The court in these two decisions ruled that secret membership was to be protected when pursuing acceptable goals as defined by the Constitution but was inappropriate when the organization was engaged in unlawful activities (Rourke, 1961). Expectedly, estimates vary as to the size of the Klan throughout its history. Table 1 reflects the different calculations of this secret society's size.

The Klan steadily weakened in the 1930s and although not officially dissolved until 1944, it ceased to be a significant organization long before that. Today's Ku Klux Klan is marked by fragmentation and the failure of Klan leaders to agree on a common course of action in response to Klan selected issues. In reality, it is several organizations. A recent estimate of the FBI (Federal Bureau of Investigation, 1970; Williams, 1976) placed the number of different Klan organizations at 18 with a membership of 2,200 in 1972, an estimate still cited in 1976 (McNulty, 1976a). Typical of secret organizations, the Klan has experienced what Gist (1940) termed "schismatic differentation"—secession of disgruntled and dissatisfied members who form new Klan groups.

One of the important reasons for this type of person to belong to such a secret society as the Klan is the feeling of superiority that becoming a citizen of the Invisible Empire affords him. Although this was touched upon earlier, it is now a more important reason since many of the other reasons (e.g., the prestige that comes with belonging to the Klan) are absent. Vander Zanden's (1960) principal thesis is that Klansmen are men who have been generally thwarted from obtaining societal goals. Instead of blaming themselves, they turn to scapegoats and speak of plots, conspiracy, and corruption. Thayer (1967) argues that the typical Klansman "feels trapped and sees no way out except by lashing out viciously at the Negro below him and the white power structure above him." The regalia and emotional symbolism lift them out of the frustrating lives they lead. A former Klansman says,

> Take for instance, you make a man a security guard and pin a little old bar or something on him, he thinks he's a big wheel and a deal and, therefore, he'll follow it till he spends all of his money every weekend for gas, run up and down the road right—just that he can get out there and strut with them bars on, think he's a big shot of some kind. If he go back and check his home, no doubt he wouldn't have no decent food in his house to eat (Lowe, 1967).

The transformation reaches the height of absurdity when Klansmen successfully recruit Roman Catholics and immigrants on the pretext they "will be accepted as members of the

Table 1
Klan Membership, 1868–1978

Date	Estimate	Estimator	Source
1868 Autumn	550,000	Imperial Wizard Forrest	HUAC, 1967
1871	550,000	Anti-Defamation League	ADL, 1965
1871	500,000	George Thayer	Thayer, 1967
1871	500,000	Robert M. Mikell	Mikell, 1966
1920	5,000	Anti-Defamation League	ADL, 1965
1920	1,000–2,000	Gustavus Myers	Myers, 1943
1921 Summer	85,000	David Chalmers	Chalmers, 1965
1921	100,000	Clarke and Taylor	HUAC, 1967
1921 October	700,000	Gustavus Myers	Myers, 1943
1922	1,200,000	Imperial Wizard Simmons	Myers, 1943
1924	over 2,000,000	David Chalmers	Chalmers, 1965
1924	3–5 million	HUAC	HUAC, 1967
1924	4½ million	Anti-Defamation League	ADL, 1965
1925	8,904,871	"authoritative source"	Myers, 1943
1925	4–5 million	Anti-Defamation League	ADL, 1965
1925	5 million	George Thayer	Thayer, 1967
1926	350,000	Anti-Defamation League	ADL, 1965
1926	slightly more than 2 million	Gustavus Myers	Myers, 1943
1926	5 million	Judge, Indiana US District Court	Myers, 1943
1927	350,000	George Thayer	Thayer, 1967
1927	321,000	Gustavus Myers	Myers, 1943

Date	Number	Source	Citation
1928	150,000	Gustavus Myers	Myers, 1943
1928	200–300,000	HUAC	HUAC, 1967
1928	350,000	Robert M. Mikell	Mikell, 1966
1929	82,602	Gustavus Myers	Myers, 1943
1930	34,694	Gustavus Myers	Myers, 1943
World War II	10,000	Imperial Wizard Colescott	HUAC, 1967
1961 February	35,000–50,000 (UKA:[a] 15,000–20,000)	Anti-Defamation League	Bakst, 1961
1963 late	(UKA: 8,000–9,000)	HUAC	HUAC, 1967
1964 October	8,500 active 50,000 work closely (WK:[a] 6,000)	US News and World Report	October 19, 1964
1964 Fall	10,000 hard core 25,000–35,000 like-minded (UKA: 26,000–33,000)	HUAC	HUAC, 1967
1965 May	51,000 (UKA: 40,000)	Anti-Defamation League	ADL, 1965
1965 October		Anti-Defamation League	ADL, 1966
1966 January	20,000	Anti-Defamation League	ADL, 1967
1966 July	29,500 (UKA: over 20,000)	Anti-Defamation League	ADL, 1966
1966 December	40,000	National Jewish Post	December 23, 1966
1967 January	50,000 (UKA: 44,300)	Anti-Defamation League	ADL, 1967
1967 January	16,810 (UKA: 15,025)	HUAC	HUAC, 1967

Table 1 (continued)

Date	Estimate	Estimator	Source
1967 May	50–100,000 (UKA: 35,000)	George Thayer	Thayer, 1967
1967 October	55,000	Anti-Defamation League	ADL, 1967
1969 September	6,500	*Time*	October 3, 1969
1970	2,200	FBI	Williams, 1976
1972	(UKA: 3,200)	FBI	*Miami Herald*, September 16, 1974
1974	(UKA: 1,700)	FBI	*Miami Herald*, September 16, 1974
1975	2,200	FBI	*Newsweek*, November 24, 1977
	1,500–1,700 hard core		*Chicago Tribune*, July 19, 1975
1975	6,500	Anti-Defamation League	*Chicago Tribune*, November 27, 1977
1976	2,200	FBI	Williams, 1976
1976	tens of thousands	NAACP	*Chicago Tribune*, September 6, 1976
1977	8,000	Anti-Defamation League	*Chicago Tribune*, November 27, 1977
1978	6,500–8,000	Anti-Defamation League	*Chicago Tribune*, September 24, 1978

[a] UKA refers to the United Klans of America; WK refers to the White Knights (Mississippi).

'white' community and thus will enjoy all the benefits available thereof" (*The Pittsburgh Courier,* March 2, 1957).

Although the contemporary Klan is significantly smaller and less powerful than its predecessor, it continues to rely on both secrecy and publicity. Both are essential to the success of its operation. HUAC based on its 1966 hearing concluded:

> Committee investigation reveals that secrecy has enabled a relatively few Klansmen to operate outside the law as vigilante groups to "deal with" those whom the particular Klan group or Klan leader opposes. It has made it possible for a few organized Klansmen, whose strength in numbers is minute compared to total population, to obtain influence and power in local communities (House Un-American Activities Committee, 1967).

This veil of secrecy is most closely guarded with the "action" groups that operate extralegally and violently against those who dare to work for civil rights.

The various Klan organizations openly admit their dependence on secrecy. A 1966 directive from the White Knights of the Ku Klux Klan in Mississippi labeled secrecy the group's greatest asset (House Un-American Activities Committee, 1967). The Ku Klux Klan's management would be an example of what Warren (1974) refers to as private-life secrecy that includes concealment of attributes or actions that, if discovered, might bring harm to the group. Private-life secrecy is to be contrasted with public-life secrecy associated with the CIA or FBI purportedly performed "in the public interest." However in all honesty, the Klan depends equally on publicity. For example, in 1965 one klavern permitted the filming of its initiation ritual as a part of the CBS television news documentary "The Invisible Empire: The Ku Klux Klan." This represented only one of the more recent self-exposures by Klan organizations of their allegedly supersecret ritual. In fact, several "secret" rituals are copyrighted and can be examined at the Library of Congress (Gist, 1940).

Also the Klan receives what in some circles would be favorable publicity from its violent attacks on civil rights workers was accompanied by a brief growth in its membership. (See Table 1.) According to one FBI estimate, between 1963 and 1970 the Klan was responsible for 250 violent acts annually of bombings, arson, and murders (McNulty, 1976a). Congressional investigations by the House Un-American Activities Committee in 1966 also helped to publicise the organization's purposes.

Other recent attention-getting events were the burning of Pontiac, Michigan, school buses by Klansmen in 1971, the disclosure in 1975 that one of the few female jockies, Mary Bacon, is a long-time member of the Ku Klux Klan, the 1975 appearance before the Senate Committee on Intelligence (1975) of Gary Rowe, an FBI operative who participated in Klan violence for six years, and the open activity of the Klan on a U.S. marine base in 1977. The Rowe incident is especially perplexing since apparently Rowe's discoveries were not always heeded by law enforcement, officials and even more recently he has come forward to support some of the Klan principles (Rowe, 1976). The use of secrecy to uncover secret organizations was obvious in Rowe's appearance before the committee. He appeared wearing a mask.

One advantage to membership in a secret society, as noted above, is that it permits the individual the freedom to do certain things that society as a whole would not condone. Klan violence is obviously an example of this expression of one's suppressed desires. However, secrecy can be manipulated by outsiders to undermine a secret society. Observers of government intelligence have quipped that most of the Klan's funds come from undercover agents. Both the various Klan organizations and the FBI either refuse to confirm or even to respond to such allegations. However, the FBI did admit in 1976 that previously it had created a new Klan group boasting 200 members to disrupt the regular Klan organization. Reportedly the FBI-organized Klan group was "phased out when it had 'done its ultimate damage to the regular Klan'" (Senate Committee on Intelligence, 1976). Obviously, today as in the past the Ku Klux Klan continues to rely on both secrecy and publicity.

MANAGING SECRECY

The Ku Klux Klan, as with most secret societies, incorporates many of the characteristics enumerated by Georg Simmel (1950). He noted in secret societies the following,

1. The importance of reciprocal *confidence* among its members to provide protection.
2. *Silence* is encouraged to the point of frequently requiring new initiates to abstain from speaking out at all to nonmembers for several weeks.
3. *Written communication,* when it occurs, to be governed by intricate norms.

4. Secrecy may well not only be a tool but the very purpose of the organization, as in a society that guards from outsiders some theoretical, mystical, or religious *knowledge.*
5. The division of labor through a *hierarchy* is absolute.
6. The growth of *ritual* derives from secret societies generally not stemming from a historical precedent but built up from their own basis.
7. Ironically, secrecy permits a measure of *freedom* not found outside society.

This should not be taken as an exhaustive list. Simmel himself notes that some additional features of secret societies are merely modifications of features found elsewhere. In fact Weber (Gerth & Mills, 1958) and Merton (1968) have both noted the fundamental importance of secrecy to the functioning of bureaucracies. Therefore, it is appropriate that among Simmel's characteristics of secret societies are two readily associated with bureaucracies—written communication and hierarchy.

Secrecy for the Klan member ultimately serves the function of what social psychologists have termed the "deindividuation" phenomenon. This refers to the situation in a group where members do not relate to one another as individuals *qua* individuals. Antisocial behavior has been found to increase when anonymity (as for example achieved by wearing a mask) is guaranteed and by a group presence. Demasking laws have served to mitigate somewhat the deindividuation among Klansmen. Nonetheless secrecy encourages rather than discourages people from doing behavior judged improper by society (Diener et al., 1976; Festinger et al., 1972).

The importance of confidence, silence, and written communication to the various Klan organizations is apparent. The Klan's knowledge and ritual as reflected in such documents as "The Seven Symbols of the Klan" and the many oaths also play an important role even if only as window-dressing to make Klan activities appear more exalted. The hierarchy moves from the new initiate to the klexter (outer guard), the exalted cyclops (a klavern president), and finally to the imperial wizard himself. Membership in the Invisible Empire grants one the freedom to defy societal laws, "alien" laws as described by the Klan. Annan (1967) in examining the entire history of the Klan concludes that "every criminal or man who wanted to pursue a vendetta wore a hood" and gained freedom through secrecy.

But absolute secrecy makes it difficult to gain members. Thus the Klan had to make itself known and perhaps intriguing to nonmembers. Mystical ritual is not enough, of course. The various Klan groups had to appeal to a sentiment that was popular in a certain segment of the population. For those who did and do join they become part of an organization that depends on the total allegiance of the initiate. Simmel (1950) termed this process *Entselbstung* or deselfing. This leveling of individuality or deselfing occurs frequently, but in secret societies it becomes absolute. The shedding of one's self is graphically and emphatically illustrated by the wearing of masks. This is often done for the purpose of secrecy, but it also is one aspect in the suppression of individuality. More recently this process has received significant attention as it occurs in "total institutions" such as the military, prisons, boarding schools, and mental institutions. Upon entrance, the individual is stripped of outside supports and the self is frequently mortified in a way to guarantee commitment of the new institutional arrangement (Goffman, 1963). In a group such as the Ku Klux Klan, support for the organization and the willingness to maintain secrecy must be absolute.

Klan initiates, despite their feelings of superiority over non-Klan members, still seek to legitimize themselves to outsiders. Once again, this requires to some extent the lifting the veil of secrecy. Not only has the Ku Klux Klan during all its historical phases sought to appeal to larger society, but to change it as well. This makes the Klan an example of what Lyman (1970) calls a "conformative" as opposed to an "alienative" secret society. Conformative in that the Klan is basically a patriotic organization in close accord with the central values of society (Gist, 1940). Even its racist doctrine is supported by a significant segment of the population. Similarly the Klan would be "expressive" rather than "instrumental" employing Lyman's use of the terms, since it seeks to bring about change or, in some instances, to prevent unwanted social reform. The analogy of a veil of secrecy is rather appropriate since the Klan and its members either lift the veil or replace it depending on what functionally serves the interests of the organization and its members.

ROLES OF SECRECY

Secrecy constitutes a process that can perform functions as have just been outlined. However the secrets themselves can be distinguished by the relationship of the informed individual to those ignorant of the knowledge. Goffman (1959; Ottenberg,

1972) in discussing discrepant roles has outlined certain characteristic types of secrets that are applicable to the Ku Klux Klan.

Of the six types, strategic, entrusted, latent, and inside secrets would seem to most typify the use of secrecy of the Klan throughout its different periods. Strategic secrets refer to plans or capacities that are concealed from nonmembers in order to prevent interference. Coupled with strategic secrets are entrusted secrets where an outsider such as law enforcement official has the knowledge but does not disclose it since it may be disruptive of Klan activities. Latent secrets involve information uncollected that if released would undermine the image of the organization. Everything from the actual size of membership to the possibility of alien (e.g., Roman Catholic, FBI) members is considered so potentially destructive that even informed Klan members rarely have access to such information. Inside secrets refers to information that marks an individual from others. Such information is a major factor in conveying to Klansmen the sense of exclusiveness they inevitably acquire upon entry into the Invisible Empire.

Less appropriate to the Ku Klux Klan throughout all periods would be Goffman's so-called dark secrets. Not unlike latent secrets, dark secrets also involves information potentially destructive to the Klan image. During the fading of the 1920s Klan, dark secrets were evident. Goffman (1959) defines these as "facts about a team which it knows and conceals and which are incompatible with the image the team is attempting to present." Obviously the sexual and financial improprieties by top Klan officials constituted dark secrets that were eventually uncovered. Free secrets, "somebody else's secret known to oneself that one could" be disclosed without discrediting the image, are least applicable of the six. Most antisocial behavior committed in the name of the Klan, such as physical acts or intimidations are seen as perfectly appropriate to obtain the desired goal.

In summary, the types of secrets function to minimize possible disruption to the organization as in the case of entrusted, dark, and latent secrets. Entrusted secrets also along with strategic secrets expedite the Klan's carrying out of activity that non-Klan people would judge inappropriate. Finally inside secrets serve to give membership a significance virtually unrelated to whether organizational goals are fulfilled or not.

Governmental secrecy has consistently been a topic of interest, but little scholarly study has been made of secrecy in interpersonal behavior. The Ku Klux Klan offers a case example of an organization that has managed secrecy to serve the group's ends while still encouraging publicity about its functions. In examining the three periods of Klan activity—Reconstruction, the 1920s, and post-World War II—it is apparent that the Klan has deliberately allowed its allegedly secret oaths and regalia to be leaked to outsiders. However, Klan activities and the importance individuals derive from membership could not be maintained without secrecy. The functions and roles of secrecy in the Ku Klux Klan are analyzed relying on the descriptive and theoretical constructs of Simmel and Goffman.

CONCLUSIONS

The mystic rituals and status-exalting titles serve the purpose of instilling in the membership of the Ku Klux Klan a sense of authority and potency otherwise lacking in their lives outside the Klan. In order to attract new members and financial support, the Klan uses secrecy to tantalize potential joiners and to exaggerate the power it wields. Klan symbols such as the burning cross have been used and undoubtedly will continue to be used by people unassociated with any Klan organization. The use of such symbols by isolated individuals only serves to imply the presence of a massive clandestine organization despite a current nationwide membership of little over 2,000. Simmel (1950) himself noted at a time when the Klan was dormant, secrecy creates both a barrier and a tempting challenge to break through it. The nature of secrecy allows the Klan to capitalize on covert operations, which are illegal, as well as to publicize an image to an extent unjustified by its real size.

References

Anti-Defamation League of B'nai B'rith. The Ku Klux Klans. *The Facts,* May 1965, *16,* 321–336.

Anti-Defamation League of B'nai B'rith. Trend report—Ku Klux Klans. *The Facts,* July 1966.

Anti-Defamation League of B'nai B'rith. ADL Press release. *The Facts,* October 1967.

Annan, D. The Ku Klux Klan. In N. MacKenzie (Ed.), *Secret Societies.* New York: Holt, Rinehart and Winston, 1967.

Bakst, J. The Ku Klux Klan: Nothing ahead but trouble. The *ADL Bulletin,* February 1961, 3, 8.

Chalmers, D. *Hooded Americanism.* Chicago: Quadrangle Books, 1965.

Degler, Carol N. Century of the Klan: A Review Article. *Journal of Social History,* 1965, *31,* 435–443.

Diener, E., Fraser, S. C., Beaman, A., and Kelem, R. T. Effects of deindividuation variables on stealing among Halloween trick-or-treaters. *Journal of Personality and Social Psychology,* 1976, *33,* 178–183.

Dulles, A. *The craft of intelligence.* New York: Harper and Row, 1963.

Federal Bureau of Investigation, *Annual Report, 1969–1970.* Washington: Government Printing Office, 1970.

Festinger, L., Pepitone, A., and Newcomb, T. Some consequences of deindividuation in a group. *Journal of Abnormal and Social Psychology, 47,* Supplement 1972, 382–389.

Gerth, H. H., & Mills, C. W. *From Max Weber: Essays in sociology.* New York: Oxford University Press, 1958.

Gist, N. P. Secret societies: A study of fraternalism in the United States. *University of Missouri studies: A quarterly of research,* 1940, *15,* 9–184.

Goffman, E. *The presentation of self in everyday life.* Garden City, N.Y.: Doubleday, 1959.

Goffman, E. *Asylums.* Garden City, N.Y.: Doubleday, 1963.

Hazelrigg, L. E. A reexamination of Simmel's 'The secret and the secret society': Nine propositions. *Social Forces,* 1969, 323–330.

Hofstadter, R. The paranoid style in American politics. In Barry McLaughlin (Ed.), *Studies in social movements.* New York: Free Press, 1969.

House Committee on Armed Services (Special Subcommittee on Intelligence), *Hearings on the proper classification and handling of gov-*

ernment information involving the national security, March and May 1972, Washington: U.S. Government Printing Office.

House Un-American Activities Committee, *Hearings October 1965 to January 1966,* Washington: U.S. Government Printing Office.

House Un-American Activities Committee, *The present day Ku Klux Klan movement,* December 11, 1967, Washington: U.S. Government Printing Office.

Lowe, D. *The Ku Klux Klan: The invisible empire.* New York: Norton, 1967.

Lowry, R. P. Toward a sociology of secrecy and security systems. *Social Problems,* 1972, *19,* 4, 437–450.

Lyman, S. *The Asian in the West.* Reno: Desert Research Institute, 1970.

McNulty, T. Klan—From confederacy to conspiracy. Chicago *Tribune,* September 6, 1976, 6. (a)

McNulty, T. Good ol' boys in a bad old scene—White robes and burning crosses. Chicago *Tribune,* September 6, 1976, 1, 6. (b)

Merton, R. K. *Social theory and social structure.* Rev. Ed. New York: Free Press, 1968.

Mikell, R. M. *They say blood on my hands.* Huntsville, Alabama: Publishers Enterprise, 1966.

Moore, W. C., & Tumin, M. M. Some social functions of ignorance. *American Sociological Review,* 1949, *14,* 787–795.

Myers, G. *History of bigotry in the United States.* New York: Random House, 1943.

Ottenberg, S. *Secrecy in social relations.* Paper presented at the meeting of the American Anthropological Association, Toronto, 1972.

The Pittsburgh Courier, Terror on the Loose: Inside The Ku Klux Klan, March 2, 1957, Magazine, 5.

Rice. A. *The Ku Klux Klan in American politics.* Washington: Public Affairs Press, 1962.

Rourke, F. E. *Secrecy and publicity: Dilemmas of democracy.* Baltimore: Johns Hopkins Press, 1961.

Rowe, G., Jr. *My undercover years with the Ku Klux Klan.* New York: Bantam, 1976.

Schaefer, R. T. The Ku Klux Klan: Continuity and change. *Phylon,* 1971, *32,* 143–157.

Schaefer, R. T. *Racial and ethnic groups.* Boston: Little Brown, 1979.

Senate Committee on Intelligence (Select Committee to Study Governmental Operations With Respect to Intelligence Activities), Hearings, Federal Bureau of Investigation, November and December 1975, Washington: U.S. Government Printing Office.

Senate Committee on Intelligence (Select Committee to Study Governmental Operations With Respect to Intelligence Activities), Final Report, Book III, 1976, Washington: U.S. Government Printing Office.

Shils, E. A. *The torment of secrecy.* New York: Free Press, 1956.

Simmel, G. *The sociology of Georg Simmel.* Trans., Kurt H. Wolff. New York: Free Press, 1950.

Thayer, G. *The farther shores of politics.* New York: Simon and Schuster, 1967.

Vander Zanden, J. W. The Klan revival. *American Journal of Sociology,* 1960, *65,* 456–462.

Warren, C. A. *Identity and community in the gay world.* New York: Wiley, 1974.

Williams, Dennis A. The South: The Klan Also Rises. *Newsweek,* 1976, *87,* 33–34.

Wilsnack, R. W., *Information control: A conceptual framework for sociological analysis.* Paper presented at the meeting of the American Sociological Association, Chicago, September 1977.

8

The Dynamics of Military Conspiracy

Kenneth Fidel
De Paul University

For the most part, social scientific interest in military revolt has focused on the societal preconditions for insurrection and the aftereffects of power seizure. Until recently there has been little concern for variations in military organization or the internal dynamics of coup-oriented groups. Yet we now know that to a great extent the success or failure of military revolt and, in the case of a successful revolt, the postcoup political culture is very much effected by the history and dynamics of coup oriented groups. For this reason, it is important to have some understanding of the internal dynamics of military groups and organizations whose goal is the overthrow of the existent regime. This essay discusses one type of military coterie—a conspiratorial group composed primarily of middle and junior ranking officers in a large, bureaucratically structured military organization. Our primary concern is the dynamics of conspiracy and, more specifically, the issues and problems created by secrecy. The discussion is based on materials from a case study of the conspiratorial group that carried out the 1960 Turkish military revolt and observations made of other military conspiracies. (Fidel, 1971, 1975)

CONSPIRATORIAL GROUPS

Three polar concepts provide the parameters that distinguish conspiratorial groups composed of middle and junior level officers from other politicized military groups. These are: (1) access to channels of political communication—lack of access to political communication; (2) legitimacy—illegitimacy; (3) secret—public. Conspiratorial organizations can be defined in terms of the extremes of each of these conceptual dichotomies.

First, although conspiratorial groups attempt to influence or change the political culture, their members often lack access to legitimate channels through which political influence is exerted. There is little or no contact with individuals or groups capable of exerting formal or informal political influence, and efforts to establish such contacts are minimal. As a result, unless exposed, conspiratorial groups may be invisible to both political and military leadership. Lack of contact with legitimate or informal political personages also limits the strategies available to conspiratorial military groups. Unable to influence the political culture through existent channels of political communication, conspiratorial groups are limited to strategies of displacement or supplantment. Second, conspiratorial groups are illegitimate in two senses of the term: The men participating are legally barred from active political participation; and the modes of organization and political involvement are illegal, and participation would be severely sanctioned if discovered. Third, conspiratorial groups are secret societies. The membership share knowledge that is barred to the general population. However, conspiratorial military groups differ from the associational form that Simmel describes in that membership is limited to individuals who share a single occupation and institutional identity (Simmel, 1950). Consequently, patterns of sociation also differ from those Simmel describes as characteristic of secret societies.

The characteristics that differentiate conspiratorial groups from other politicized military groups also create internal tensions, dilemmas, and problems of organizational cohesion and maintenance that must be dealt with if the group is to survive and achieve its objectives. The manner in which these are handled vitally effect the life history and character of conspiratorial groups and, in the case of a successful *coup d'état,* partially determine the course of postrevolutionary events.

THE SCHOOL SYSTEM AND POLITICIZATION

Conspiratorial activities are not common to all segments of a military organization nor even necessarily to those most typically affected by the social and political preconditions for revolt—middle and junior ranking officers stationed in urban regions. Conspiratorial involvement is most likely to be located or initiated within the military school system or among members of a class cohort stationed in and around the political center. In particular, those schools providing advanced training for upwardly mobile officers are the seedbeds of conspiratorial group organizations. While the conditions of life at any post, in which officers are thrown into close and intimate contact, are conducive to group formation and the nurturance of discontent, the status position and career lines of officers attending advanced military schools or regularly stationed in political centers exacerbate alienating conditions and make conspiratorial group formation more likely to occur among these men and in the school or postschool environment.

The military career orients the individual to a nationalist perspective and that sense of nationalism is heightened within the school environment. Curriculum at military schools invariably include history courses that trace national political development and emphasize the role of the military in bringing about social change. There is a consideration of present social issues and conflicts that cause students to reflect on present developments and their personal role in shaping contemporary and future events. In effect, the public servant role of the military is made salient and nationalist values are stressed.

Heightened personal concern with national issues is less a manifest function of the curriculum than a latent function stemming from informal discussions among faculty and students and from personal introspection. While the formal curriculum is not, in and of itself, an impetus to conspiratorial activity, the atmosphere created by juxtaposition of nationalist concern and the outward manifestation of societal problems immediately outside the military compound make for simple recognition of national issues, such as contrasts in living standards between different sectors of the population or political repression. A recognition that might not occur in a less nationalist-charged atmosphere or a location physically isolated from the extremes of affluence and poverty or the locus of political activities and unrest. For these reasons, conspiratorial activity is more likely to occur in urban schools than those located in outlying areas of the nation.

However, differential location is not the only explanation of why conspiratorial activity occurs in some schools but not in others. School faculty may act as catalysts to conspiratorial activity through presentation of course materials and informal discussions outside the classroom. There are a number of instances in which an influential military instructor conceived and organized an insurrectionary conspiratorial group. (Fidel, 1971)

The military school also provides a suitable physical setting for conspiratorial group formation. The grounds are sealed off from civilian intrusion and provide ideal conditions for secret meetings. Moreover, school cohort groups are in continual interaction. The daily round of activities provide ample opportunity for students to speak privately with one another and ascertain individual feelings and beliefs. Thus it is possible to identify those within the cohort who share similar beliefs and aspirations, diagnoses of national ills, and suggested therapies for those ills. Finally, the shared school experience provides a basis for friendship and mutual trust that permits free discussion of potentially treasonous topics and interpersonal reliance in dangerous or delicate situations.

The variety of schools at which conspiratorial activity has emerged suggests that the phenomenon is not the product of any particular class or cohort group but inheres in the student status. For those attending a military academy it is a period of military socialization likely to have a profound, if temporary, effect on self-perception as an agent of social change. Attendance at other schools, such as a staff college or war school, is indicative of upward mobility and a future role in military decision-making. This may lead to a sense of personal and national destiny through radically altering the course of national history; making for personal ambitions that cannot be fulfilled through legitimate participation in political affairs.

Conditions that obtain at military school may also provide the student with an unrealistic view of national politics: National goals may be escalated out of proportion to what is realistically possible for the nation to achieve. Social problems and the culpability of government, political, and military leaders may be exaggerated. And standards of personal and political morality that are unreasonable within the current political culture may be used to evaluate people and parties. Political unrealism easily leads to political alienation and an absolutist view of politics (Janowitz, 1960).

Political absolutism stemming from alienation is transformed into conspiratorial activity by the very factors that make for unrealistic appraisals of political conditions—isolation from ongoing political processes and the absence of channels for direct political involvement. Those most susceptible to political alienation and absolutism are upwardly mobile middle-ranking and junior-ranking officers presently or recently in the highly charged nationalist atmosphere of military schools and living in urban areas. These men are also most aware of political events and most frustrated by inability to influence them. Given these conditions, conspiratorial involvement employing strategies aimed at displacing or supplanting the government become the only viable forms of political activity.

THE DILEMMAS OF SECRECY

Illegitimacy of conspiratorial organization and activity imposes the need for secrecy that, in turn, imposes limitations on every facet of organizational existence including recruitment, organizational structure, and planning. Secrecy also hinders the formation of conspiratorial groups and, once formed, makes continued organizational maintenance imperative lest dissolution or factionalization expose all members, past as well as present, to official sanctioning. Political compromise, while often unavailable in conspiratorial group interaction with the regime, is a primary technique for obtaining the internal cohesion and solidarity requisite for continued organizational maintenance and for preventing exposure or betrayal. However, conspiratorial group solidarity may be transitory, lasting only so long as cohesion is dictated by fear of exposure and potential sanctions.

Secrecy also provides a dilemma for recruitment. To be politically effective, conspiratorial groups must recruit as widely as possible. Open recruitment, however, increases the possibility of exposure. Moreover, it is precisely those who may be most useful to conspiratorial groups that are least likely to be interested in conspiratorial activity and most likely to betray group existence. Those most prone to joining secret, illegitimate groups may also be the officers with the least potential for effective political activity.

Another dilemma of secrecy is its effect on conspiratorial organization. To implement important political change, a viable political organization must be developed. Such an organization requires large numbers acting in a coordinated manner. Furthermore, there must be interaction between members and communication between affiliated groups. Without freedom of communication, neither coordinated action nor effective implementation of strategies of involvement are possible. Yet the requisite of maintaining secrecy makes free communication between groups and members impossible. Lines of communication must be guarded and protected lest nonmembers become aware of the organization's existence and betray it (Aubert, 1965). As a result, conspiratorial group effectiveness is limited by inability to sustain an uninterrupted flow of information within the organization. Group meetings present a similar problem, a large number of officers gathering at a house or public place invariably arouse suspicion. Consequently, the size of gatherings is limited and meetings may be held outside of cities or in secluded areas. In which case, large numbers of officers seen traveling to an out-of-the-way place are also cause for suspicion.

The need to remain invisible also affects implementation of plans and strategies. Overt political activity cannot be identifiable as an act of the conspiratorial group, lest such a connection lead to an investigation and exposure. Only at the point at which definitive political action is taken, such as the point of revolution, can the veil of secrecy be lifted and conspiratorial activities linked to the organization.

Yet another dilemma associated with illegitimacy and the need to maintain secrecy is the problem of internal social control and sanctioning processes. While close internal control is requisite within illegitimate organizations, the ability of any member to expose the group makes such control superfluous and ineffectual. Sanctioning a member risks alienating him and provoking betrayal. Consequently, although internal social control is necessary it is also impossible to maintain. This does not mean that sanctions are unavailable. The most brutal sanctions, political murder or the threat of assassination, are viable techniques of internal control. However, the use of brutal sanctioning techniques is also likely to cause disgruntled members to attempt avoiding punishment by exposing the group prior to imposition of sanctions. Ostracism is also available as a sanction, however its use is limited to those individuals whose dedication to revolutionary goals and depth of personal involvement in conspiratorial activities preclude betrayal.

Restrictions that secrecy imposes on conspiratorial groups both maintain existence and hinder achievement of goals. Organizational maintenance resulting from protective measures obtains at the cost of impaired organizational functioning. The resultant extension of organizational life is problematic in that extended longevity increases the likelihood of betrayal and exposure. Secrecy in conjuction with extended organizational longevity also create organizational problems that in other circumstances might be inconsequential but under the conditions of conspiratorial group life are critical. While cohesiveness is a requisite for conspiratorial groups, over time, anticohesive factors may emerge. Interpersonal enmity, distrust, and competition that did not exist at the time of group formation may emerge as a result of extended organizational longevity and inability to attain group goals. Over time, issues and problems that were previously unperceived may threaten internal cohesion and solidarity. Thus, the very techniques that maintain conspiratorial organizations may also cause their demise.

EQUALITY

Sharing conspiratorial secrets make conspiratorial group members equals. Equal in the sense that illegitimate activity, if exposed, would lead to a common fate. Equality is also rooted in shared knowledge that is denied to other members of the community. Given equality of knowledge and fate, equality of status follows.

As Simmel perceptively pointed out, egalitarianism in secret societies is a function of separation from the larger society and can continue only as long as members are able to mask their public identities or seclude themselves (Simmel, 1950). While this is possible in a heterogeneous group, it is impossible in homogeneous military conspiratorial groups. Although certain aspects of identity lose salience in conspiratorial groups, institutional identity cannot be hidden. Every participant is known to other members as both an individual and an officer of a given rank and status. The source of knowledge is threefold. First, every officer wears his rank on his uniform. Second, within the military community, personal status and reputation quickly disseminates throughout the professional officer corps. And third, the need to maintain secrecy limits membership and recruitment to those who are known and trusted.

Given knowledge of institutional status and position, it is impossible to avoid impingement of rank upon egalitarian practices. Both level of participation and military rank establish status within conspiratorial groups, destroying even the potential for egalitarianism. Once admitted to the inner circles of conspiratorial groups, high ranking officers invariably assume important roles in group decision-making. In a similar fashion, bureaucratic position also impinges upon egalitarianism. Conspirators occupying key positions within the military organization are, by dint of their institutional function, more important and powerful within conspiratorial organizations than others occupying less important posts. While conspiratorial activities provide an alternative source of status and power within the group, it does not confer institutional rank and position on the individual. Consequently, tension exists between claims to status and authority rooted in conspiratorial participation and claims rooted in military status and position.

Men whose leadership status stem solely from participation are constrained to maintain their position within the organization through often nonessential activities such as meeting attendance, intragroup communication, and recruitment. Performing nonessential functions and lacking institutional power, these men often find their leadership roles tenuous. Unable to serve a critical operational function within the group, participatory leaders tend to be primarily concerned with ideological issues and questions of postrevolutionary government. They may advocate revolution rather than reconciliation and prolonged military rule rather than immediate elections. Exposition of these political positions continually lead to clashes with senior officers and men whose views are less absolutist. These debates tend to become major anticohesive issues within the group and may even threaten the continued existence of the conspiracy.

Within conspiratorial military groups, competitive claims to status and authority stem from a poorly defined relationship between the organization and the military institution. If the group views itself as an adjunct of the military institution, and such factors as exclusive membership and an ideology rooted in military definitions of political issues favor this view, then status rooted in institutional rank and position is consonant with the membership's world view. On the other hand, when the group defines itself as distinct from the military institution, a view buttressed by alienation from the political stance of institutional leaders, then conspiratorial group status and authority stemming only from participation is legitimate. Resolution of tensions stemming from competing claims to conspiratorial leadership is dependent on clarification of the relationship between conspiratorial involvement and military affiliation. This is a function of such factors as government and military reaction to the conspirators, the strength of professional identification, and the course of events.

Legitimacy represents another aspect of the dilemma imposed by the absence of a clearly defined relationship to the military institution. Severing ties with the military denies the very social status that military conspirators view as their legitimate entree to politics—that of apolitical, nationalist oriented, public servants whose foray into politics is inspired solely by objective and impersonal criteria. On the other hand, submission to military authority ultimately places conspirators under the authority of the chief of staff; thus acknowledging that conspiratorial political activity is essentially illegitimate and unwarranted. Neither position is fully tenable and tensions resulting from competing claims to authority remain irreconcilable and a fact of conspiratorial group existence.

Egalitarianism is also destroyed by the development of organization. Increasing group membership requires the establishment of an organization to coordinate group activities. The very characteristics of organization are inimicable to egalitarianism: Hierarchical structure places some men in decision-making positions while excluding the bulk of membership; transmission of decisions to the membership establishes command functions; and the need to protect the organizaion from exposure limits information and activities to a select few men. Furthermore, there is no reason to believe that the so-called Iron Law of Oligarchy does not obtain as a result of leadership participation in spheres of political interaction that are closed to most members (Michels, 1959). Organization leaders may develop personal interests that differ from those of the membership. Although the total membership share the risks of conspiratorial participation, the emergence of conspiratorial organization may result in unequal distribution of benefits.

The development of differential interests, resulting from establishment of organization and unequal distribution of power and authority, may also lead to internal differences rooted in divergent personal goals and approaches to goal attainment. While this may lead to organizational factionalization, there are also pressures for organizational maintenance that preserve the group despite lack of internal cohesion. The illegitimate nature of the group and need to guard against exposure have already been mentioned. Another is belief that at the crucial moment a leader or coterie sharing a particular viewpoint will be capable of subordinating opposing individuals and approaches, co-opting the total organization rather than some fraction of it. Consequently, the critical point in conspiratorial group life is not its inception but its climax—the point at which a definitive move is attempted and opposing factions, previously bound together, engage in a decisive confrontation determining the dominant political position. The outcome of this confrontation is, in part, a reflection of previous patterns of internal inequality but, more importantly, it is also the resolution of the question of inequality of fate that inheres in conspiratorial organization.

CONSPIRATORIAL GROUP RECRUITMENT

The illegitimate nature of conspiratorial group activity limits recruitment and the ultimate size of conspiratorial groups within the military. The need for secrecy imposes a filtering process on recruitment activity that allows only a select few to become aware of the existence of the conspiratorial organization.

The first filtering process is friendship, as it provides the only basis of trust that allows a conspirator to approach another person with an offer to join an illegal organization and participate in illegitimate and negatively sanctioned activities. Trust is a second filtering process. The officer solicited for group membership must be perceived as a person who will neither willingly nor unwillingly betray the group. Correlative with trust the potential recruit must also be esteemed for his good judgment as every member is also a potential recruiter. As indicated earlier, shared school experiences are likely to provide the types of interpersonal relationships requisite for conspiratorial group recruitment.

The common denominator of potential recruits is shared beliefs and a common outlook. Not in the positive sense of sharing a common vision but in the negative sense of being dissatisfied with the present situation. Complete congruence of belief is not requisite; few conspiratorial groups display a complete consensus. However, a minimal requirement is recognition of the importance of those issues that coalesce the conspiratorial group and willingness to provide a therapy for perceived ills.

Finally, propinquity serves as a filter through which selected individuals are recruited for group membership. Only those who are close at hand can be approached and examined as potential members. The necessity for secrecy and accurate judgment limits recruitment to those with whom face-to-face interaction is possible. This limits recruitment to men stationed in the same vicinity as the conspirators. The large number of men stationed at major military encampments in urban centers make recruitment there easier, as a large pool of potential members are available. Remote posts, where officers are isolated from the civilian population and the political culture, make for intense friendships potentially leading to the development of conspiratorial coteries. However, organizational size is limited and distance from the political center reduces the potential for effective political action.

Two distinct recruitment patterns characterize conspiratorial groups: One allows members to freely approach and recruit among friends and acquaintances. The second consists of group members nominating potential recruits, followed by a collective decision on suitability for membership. The latter represents selective recruitment. Recruitment selectivity is directly related to perceived illegitimacy; the most stringent recruitment techniques obtain when the climate of military opinion is unfavorable to revolution. When a favorable climate of opinion obtains, open recruitment may swell the ranks of conspiratorial organizations as restrictions on recruitment are eased.

Selective recruitment is also closely tied to the emergence of political strategies and tactics. Once the form of a general plan is agreed upon it may become necessary to recruit individuals occupying key institutional positions, the duties of which are requisite to goal attainment. The only alternative to recruitment of institutionally important individuals is to gain control of these positions through placement of group members.

Irrespective of the prevailing climate of military opinion, group leadership consensus is requisite to recruiting general officers. Their status precludes complete sharing of conspiratorial secrets and their access to government officials and agencies make them potentially dangerous. For involved officers, the risks are too great to entrust career and civil status to an outsider whose interests may be radically different from one's own.

Generals involved in conspiratorial organizations are not necessarily fully privy to the secrets of the groups that co-opt them. Instead, their contact with these groups may be limited, with core leaders viewing them as titular or figurehead leaders. Limitations on contact between general officers and conspiratorial groups serve other functions as well. Exclusion from the group's inner circle precludes preemption of all leadership roles by general officers. In effect, it is a technique used by middle-rank officers to preserve control over conspiratorial organizations.

Differential perception and interest provide yet another reason for excluding general officers from conspiratorial organizations. Having access to high military and government officials, many of whom may also be personal friends, general officers may be more interested in compromise than junior officers. In the event of a revolution, they may insist on saving or retaining old colleagues and friends that junior officers want removed. General officers may also want to occupy government positions that junior officers have already assigned to themselves or to others. Finally, in the event of internal dissent, they may betray the conspiratorial group to existent authorities.

Among groups that have an open recruitment policy, the conspiratorial network can grow to include several hundred men. Tactically, these groups may be too large, as many members can in no way assist in execution of a revolt and excess membership only increases the possibility of exposure. Yet there are a number of reasons for a policy of overrecruitment. In a climate of discontent and revolution, by accepting new members the conspiratorial organization is able to maintain itself as the revolutionary vanguard and prevent other groups from forming or revolution-oriented officers from joining other organizations. Expanded membership also increases revolutionary sentiment within the military, as new recruits become propagandists for the organization. Finally, by continuing to accept new recruits, the conspiratorial organization is able to stave off the possibility of disgruntled applicants exposing the group. In effect, the dysfunctional policy of overrecruitment helps maintain the revolutionary movement intact.

CONSPIRATORIAL GROUP ORGANIZATION

There are typical conspiratorial group organizational patterns that can be related to the size and longevity of the conspiracy. While the group is new and small it meets as a unit and decisions are reached through group discussion and consensus. However, with increasing size the group meetings become dangerous and organization becomes requisite for maintaining secrecy. The original organizational format can be democratic, with elected officials and the total membership apprised of major decisions and events; over time, however, a gap between members and leaders develops and important conspiratorial involvement becomes limited to group leaders, whose identity is often unknown to the general membership.

Over time, a cell system of organization may develop in which every cell, isolated from other cells and the larger organization, exists as a separate entity, thus protecting the total group from exposure of a single cell and individual members from exposure of the conspiratorial group or some segment of it. Cell group structure limits the dangers of illegitimate activity, thereby limiting not only the threat to individual members but the threat to the revolutionary movement as well (Aubert, 1965). In the event a cell is exposed, the organization may continue to operate through other cells even if the government suspects that a larger conspiracy exists.

The cell system has other functions as well. As recruitment is often based on personal friendship, individual cells tend to be composed of men who know and trust one another. This lessens the potential for internal disintegration resulting from personal animosity. Another function is to maintain the leadership position of early conspirators. New members are absorbed by the cell that recruits them and excluded from even attempting to assume decision-making positions within the larger organization. As a result, personal competition for leadership is limited to the cell, where previously established patterns of interpersonal relations determining leader-follower relations are likely to obtain.

Cell system organization also allows a greater degree of central committee control over group activities and individual participation. Cell leaders, who are in touch with organization leaders, receive orders that are then carried to the general membership. There is little opportunity for the membership to react to or oppose organizational policy, and where it exists dissent or disobedience is limited to small groups, some of which may be expendable.

LEADERSHIP

Outside public politics, conspiratorial groups are insusceptible to events occurring in the political milieu and irresponsible to any broader public. In these circumstances, the quality of leadership is critical to maintenance of group existence and development of strategies and tactics. Where there is a centralized organization, leadership is the determinant factor in devising and carrying out revolutionary plans. There are four bases of conspiratorial group leadership: participation, institutional position, rank, and popular support. Participation in conspiratorial group activity allows the individual to circulate among other conspirators, be present at group meetings, and help shape conspiratorial group decisions. In this instance, leadership is a function of having a voice in organizational affairs. As participation increases, so too does the circle of acquaintanceships within the group, knowledge of group secrets, and influence in decision-making processes. Those who are original members often assume leadership positions in the expanded organization. Having been present at the formative stage, these men are able to assume key roles and participate in crucial group decisions.

Institutional position may also affect both participation and leadership. Those who occupy important institutional positions automatically become important to the conspiratorial group. Access to important men, control of such bureaucratic functions as duty assignment and force deployment, and access to information increase their value to the conspiratorial group. These important men are immediately co-opted into the leadership cadre.

Closely associated with institutional position is rank and associated command. High-ranking officers may command large armed units which may be enlisted *in toto* for revolutionary purposes. Troop command, in conjuction with the respect and obedience due a ranking officer, automatically makes one a group spokesman. Finally, popular support serves to create a leadership role within a conspiratorial group. Regardless of rank, officers who command a large following must be given a voice and role in conspiratorial leadership. If satisfied with their level of participation, popular officers can help the group gain support among the officer corps. On the other hand, disgruntled popular officers may turn large numbers of men against the group or found their own, competing conspiracy.

LEADERSHIP TYPES

Although all conspiratorial group leaders are politicized, two types can be distinguished: those who are politically involved and those who are not politically involved. The politically involved view conspiratorial activity as having a broader political meaning and issues as essentially political and/or developmental in nature. Either they place their hopes in one of the existent political parties or they press for formation of a new party—a view often directly related to a position favoring military domination of politics. The politically uninvolved may be more concerned with status issues and favor supporting civilian political parties that recognize military needs. These men are politically available and may be courted and captured by either of the two politicized types. Consequently, conspiratorial participation may also be a time of political socialization for the uninvolved leader. The political outlook of group leaders only becomes crucial after a successful revolution, as only then can they determine the nation's political future. At that time, whether or not the leadership cadre is dominated by civilian-oriented officers becomes a critical variable in determining postrevolutionary national politics.

CONSPIRATORIAL GROUPS AND INTEREST GROUPS

Unless the conspiratorial group is acting as the arm of a specific political faction, group life and activity tends to be isolated from other continuing political processes. Despite this, conspiratorial military groups may be indirectly bound into the political culture and interactive with it. Although military men may be partially shielded from the realities of the social and political milieu, such as overt political repression, participants are likely to have personal and collective reactions to continuing processes and changes in the patterning of national and institutional existence. If the group continues in existence over a long period of time, it is unreasonable to assume that it can maintain complete secrecy and anonymity of membership. The very processes of organizational growth and maintenance create the conditions for the breakdown of secrecy systems. It is not at all unlikely that conspiracies become known to higher level military men, government officials, and political leaders. To the extent that these individuals view the conspiracy as a potentially viable force in institutional or national affairs and feel unable or unwilling to destroy the group, they are likely to take the group into account in planning and carrying out their own policies. Moreover, individuals and groups may even attempt to make contact with the conspiratorial leadership and co-opt the group to its own ends.

The basic problem of conspiratorial group interaction with outside leaders or groups is that of superordination and subordination. Group leaders may share some common goals with other political interests, although these communalities are not likely to be complete. Even if their shared goals completely agree, conspiratorial leaders are not necessarily willing to subordinate themselves to other individuals or causes. Thus, alliances, if any, may take the form of tacit understandings or temporary coordination and affiliation. To the extent that they remain secret, conspiratorial groups are at an advantage in their dealings with other interests; they may cooperate with them without at the same time becoming identified with or captured by them. The tenuous quality of political alliances potentially allows conspiratorial group leaders to deal with more than one political faction at a time; they are able to make and disavow alliances with relative ease. The question of conspiratorial group relationships to other political groups can be left ambiguous for long periods of time. Thus, the long term implications of interaction with other political groups are largely undeterminable until either the conspirators actually seize control of the government or other events change the nature of the political milieu.

IDEOLOGY

Conspiratorial coteries are not necessarily characterized by communalities of ideology among the membership. Sentiment leading to conspiratorial group formation and recruitment may be less a common approach to political and developmental issues than personal and status group alienation resulting from the impact of social and political trends. Moreover, the very processes of recruitment and organizational maintenance may serve to throw together men of heterogeneous belief, vision, and political attattchment—men who under other circumstances would be unlikely to engage in a common political endeavor. Consequently, conspiratorial group solidarity is often more rooted in opposition to the government and fear of exposure than agreement on goals, strategy, or tactics. This does not mean that the conspirators are necessarily nonideological or that no common base of political perception exists. All may share in a common nationalist orientation, ingrained through cultural and military socialization. However, a nationalist orientation, in and of itself, may not provide a clear definition of contemporary social issues or guidelines for ameliorating pressing social issues.

In groups whose membership is ideologically heterogeneous or who have a range of attachment to civilian interest groups and political parties, the character of the group and the political thrust of its activities are determined by the pre-coup processes, by the scramble for position at the time of power seizure, and by the continuing scramble during the period of indeterminance immediately after the coup. At that time, men who have succeeded in placing themselves in key organizational positions may emerge as the public spokesman of the group or, if there is a successful coup, as new government leaders. Within those contexts it is the ideological stance or the political and interest group affiliations of individuals that are salient rather than the character of the group as a whole.

STRATEGIES AND TACTICS

Given the conditions of their existence, there are but two strategies available to conspiratorial groups in their efforts to replace the government: displacement and supplantment. Displacement as a choice of strategy implies that the group has somehow been co-opted by other political interests and is working on their behalf. The tactics of displacement include acts that lead to the withdrawal of military support for the government or somehow create a situation in which the government fears an imminent revolt and abdicates in favor of some other party, in an effort to avoid internal strife (Finer, 1962). In either case, the tactics of displacement are potentially dangerous to the conspirators, as both require exposing the existence of the group and possibly the identity of its membership. Given the illegitimate nature of the group, this may lead to arrests and the destruction of the group even if the goal of displacement is achieved.

A more viable alternative is supplantment, in which the conspiratorial group overthrows the government and its members assume the role of governors (Finer, 1962). The tactics of supplantment consist of two stages: preparation and enactment. Preparation consists of placing group members in strategic positions from which they may carry out a military coup. What may be considered a strategic position varies with such factors as the size, dispersal, and technological level of the armed forces and the particular characteristics of the nation. Generally speaking, however, they are those bureaucratic offices that allow the incumbent control over such functions as personnel assignment, force deployment, operations, communications, intelligence, and access to important political persons and places.

The second stage, the coup, is likely to be a limited operation involving relatively few individuals and carried out swiftly. Typically, this entails seizure of important political officials and those places that symbolize government, such as the parliament or presidential palace. In carrying out a coup of this type the conspiratorial group faces a number of potential dangers. One danger is that the revolt may meet with armed resistance stemming either from opposition to the coup or from military leaders and units unaware that a revolt is in progress. Should armed conflict erupt, the group is faced with the danger of failure and its consequences, or widespread fighting over which it has little ability to exert control. In which case, even if the coup is eventually successful the conspirators may no longer be in a position to carry out their plans or in any way benefit from the situation. A second danger is that in the midst of the revolt, individuals either not involved in the conspiracy or tangential to it may insert themselves in key positions or publicly announce that having carried out the coup they are now in control of the government. To the extent that the conspirators have been successful in maintaining secrecy as to the existence of their organization and their individual identity, the public has no way of assessing the claims of individuals or groups at the time of revolt. At that critical time and in the period immediately thereafter, the conspiracy is unwittingly susceptible to a takeover by outside individuals or groups, and there is little that can be done to preclude it.

CONCLUSION

In discussing the dynamics of military conspiracy we have attempted to show that secrecy in combination with illegitimacy and isolation from decision-making processes create a series of dilemmas and organizational constraints that largely pattern the nature of conspiratorial group existence and determine the outcome of its endeavors. Thus, any analysis of military conspiracy must take into account not only the societal preconditions for unrest and the outcome of revolt but organizational structure and process variables as well. For to a great extent the translation of discontent into action and the end result of action are determined more by the dynamics of conspiracy than any other single factor.

The essay also implies that military conspiracies have a tenuous history subject not only to continuous threats to their existence but to ambiguities of direction, leadership, and ultimate political effect as well. Throughout the course of its life, a military conspiracy may undergo dramatic changes resulting from the membership's attempts to maintain organizational and political viability in the face of processes and events that might otherwise destroy it. Indeed, so indeterminate is its history, that the critical point is not its inception but the moment at which definitive action is taken. Only then can one judge whether or not the original purposes of the group are fulfilled. Finally, it should be apparent that while the discussion has focused on one type of conspiracy, the substantive issues and observations are generalizable to a wide range of illegitimate secret organizations that share many of the same conditions of existence.

References

Aubert, V. *The Hidden society.* Totawa, N.J.: The Bedminster Press, 1965.

Fidel, K. *Military Organization and Conspiracy in Turkey.* New Brunsick, N.J.: Studies in Comparative International Development, VI, 2, 1971.

Fidel, K. Militarism and development, in *Militarism in Developing Countries,* K. Fidel, Ed. New Brunswick, N.J.: Transaction Books, 1975.

Finer, S. E. *The man on horseback: The role of the military in politics.* New York: Praeger, 1962.

Janowitz, M. *The professional soldier: A social and political portrait.* Glencoe, Ill: Free Press, 1960.

Michels, R. *Political parties: A sociological study of the oligarchical tendencies of modern democracy.* New York: Dover, 1959.

Simmel, Georg, "The Secret Society," in *The sociology of Georg Simmel* translated and edited by K. Wolff. New York: Free Press, 1950.

Unit 4

Secrecy in Business

Introduction

Competition and conflict of any sort generate an environment within which secrecy thrives. The need to conceal results from conflict and competition over such valued and scare resources as wealth, power, and prestige. This is especially true in the realm of economic enterprise.

We are well aware of the extensive secrecy employed by modern corporations to protect their economic and political interests. But secrecy is employed by small-scale economic competitors as well.

The paper by Raoul R. Andersen on Newfoundland deep-sea trawler fishing, points to the economic benefits that the fishing captains gain by deceiving each other about the size of their catches. In their radio exchanges with each other, the skippers commonly underestimate the size of their catches, or, on the other hand, overstate the size. By concealing their large catches, skippers discourage other nearby captains from joining them at the fishing site and by overstating the catch size, they may attract rival captains from distant locations, thus forcing them to lose fishing time. When good fishing grounds are discovered, a skipper often maintains radio silence so as not to reveal his position to rivals.

Even their crews gain economic advantages from deception: They get higher earnings. The skipper who has a consistent record of successful catches will be able to keep an experienced crew with him while those captains who are less successful will be able to attract only less skilled hands.

The paper by Brian J. O'Connell discusses the strategy and tactics of modern corporate secrecy. Multinational corporations not only conceal business secrets from other business rivals, but also illegal, but quite common, policies they have adopted to expand business and enlarge profits. These secrets must be hidden from the public and from potential adversaries in the media and government.

Within private corporate bureaucracies there is much internal secrecy. Top managers maintain tight control over knowledge concerning overall corporation planning. On the other hand, top management may shield themselves from detailed knowledge concerning the operations of middle-level managers who may be using illegal or unethical means to further company concerns. Ironically, the top managers themselves, as a result of the pressure they put on lower-level managers for efficiency and profits, may be the ones who encourage that illegality in the first place. Such middle-level bureaucrats may cooperate in the process by restricting knowledge of these affairs to only their most trusted associates.

Not only does the hierarchical nature of corporate structure encourage secrecy but also the specialized subnetworks into which the corporation is divided. Such specialist teams (e.g. marketing experts, advertisers, scientists) may employ secrecy to protect divisional interests as well as to hide mistakes and inefficiency that would be quite embarrassing to experts who claim special technical expertise.

A great deal of corporation secrecy is maintained not by conscious design but by the mere fact that the corporation is so complex and has so many diverse operations that even the most persistent outsider finds it hard to learn much about the financial and other economic affairs of the business bureaucracy.

Security gained from such structural complexity is reinforced by such normal security operations as counterespionage units, employee surveillance, security classifications, and compartmentalization; such operations enable corporations (and banks, also) to conceal a great deal of information about their records, activities, and future operations. O'Connell gives the details of some of these secrets including foreign bribes, illegal political contributions, the corporations' hidden influence on policies of regulatory commissions, illegal or unethical financial transactions, and hidden information on stocks and bonds ownership.

Such bureaucratic secrecy often proves to be detrimental both to the corporations and the government. When corporations conceal or withhold vital economic data from government agencies, government economic planning is hindered. The secrecy employed by departments within corporations undermines the overall coordination and planning within the organization. In an atmosphere of secrecy, rumors replace more rational and open means of internal communication.

However, secrecy has promoted inefficiency in small-scale industries as well; for example, Andersen suggests that competition between Newfoundland fishing trawler skippers promotes inefficiency in the integration and use of expensive capital equipment and manpower.

Thus, while information control can give corporations or business organizations a competitive advantage over rivals and a means of avoiding government regulations, secrecy can also result in both disorder and inefficiency within corporations as well as contribute to a government's failure to adopt and carry-out rational economic plans at both the national and international levels.

9

Hunt and Conceal: Information Management in Newfoundland Deep-Sea Trawler Fishing[1]

Raoul R. Andersen
Memorial University of Newfoundland

INTRODUCTION

Soon after Newfoundland joined Canada in 1949, government and private enterprise sought to modernize the provincial fishery to exploit the American frozen fish market. Government also undertook to "rationalize" Newfoundland's coastal population by moving people from dispersed and isolated 'outport' communities to 'fishery growth centers', where they were to provide the labour for the developing industry and thereby obtain an improved living standard.[2]

Fleets of seven to twelve non-fisherman-owned, groundfishing, side and stern trawlers (ranging from about 120 to 200 feet in length) are vertically integrated with fish plants at four such growth centers on the Burin Peninsula of Newfoundland's south coast. This essay derives from investigations with units of these fleets in 1967 and 1968.

Twelve to eighteen men crew each vessel, all of which have some of the most modern navigational, fish detection, and communication gear available. The trawlers range on trips of about ten days or more over the fishing grounds of the Gulf of St.

---

[1] A revised and abridged version of an earlier publication (Andersen, 1972).
[2] This resettlement program received much criticism for poorly defined goals and methods, neglect of alternatives, and results contrary to those intended (Brox, 1969; Wadel, 1969)

Lawrence and Grand Banks in search of mainly cod, flounder, sole, redfish, and haddock.

At first glance, their fishing operations suggest achievement of the utmost level of rational integration and efficiency permitted by their technology. Management advises its skippers to catch only certain species, attempts to dispatch its vessels to certain areas of concentrated or productive fishing activity, monitors catch success and movements of each unit by information supplied in daily reports (called hails), plots this information on large navigational charts accessible to all company skippers before they sail, and determines their day and port of landing.

At sea, ship-to-ship marine transceivers enable the trawler skippers to exchange information about their position and catch, bottom features, movements and strategy of other vessels, and weather conditions. The transceivers are employed to keep management at processing plants informed of their catch and position through daily reports. This information is critical to synchronization of vessel production and shore operations, landings and departures, and other matters integral to the daily operations of a complex, vertically integrated industrial endeavour.

But close observation of information exchange by radio between skippers at sea, and between skippers and their shore-based plants, reveals that much of the information is purposely distorted and sometimes deceptive (unlike the two-way radio exchanges among Island Harbour fishermen as reported by Stiles; 1972). These fishing operations are not so efficient and integrated as surface appearances suggest. This essay offers an interpretation of the information management in these exchanges.[3]

CONCEALMENT IN TRANSACTIONS

If one spends some time in the wheelhouse of a Newfoundland trawler at sea, one is soon struck by the amount of time skippers spend listening and talking to other trawler skippers on their radio transceivers. They chatter about many topics, some serving primarily to sustain lonely, information-starved

---

[3]Neither the rest and entertainment nor the aesthetic rewards one might glean through the "art of lying" in radio exchanges will figure in this discussion. They should be considered in a more complete study of fisherman communication.

men through long, uneventful days, and others pertaining directly to fish. Their exchange of information about catch success, strategy, bottom features, and location of other vessels, appears full and unrestrained on first view. But once sensitized to the special way skippers conceive of their role in handling this information, one finds them all concerned with its management and concealment by means of a variety of strategies in transactions with other skippers and managers.[4]

SKIPPER–SKIPPER TRANSACTIONS

How often the management techniques discussed below are employed is a speculative matter, particularly since information about their use is difficult to obtain. But all skippers are familiar with these techniques, have used some on every trip, and anticipate their use in nearly all radio exchanges with and by other skippers. Exceptions, known as trust exchanges, will be explained later.

Skippers misrepresent fishing facts most commonly by underestimation of their catches. One may withhold 50 per cent and sometimes more of the actual catch in answer to direct questioning by other skippers. This technique is commonly reinforced with impression management ploys manifest in the expression "Fish are scarce!" which is repeated *ad nauseam*.

Skippers also employ "dramatic accentuation" portraying despair and resignation to ill fate and to an infinite, fruitless, and uncertain quest for fish. As one skipper said to another in a radio chat, "It's bad all over I guess. That's the way it seems anyway. Spent more time hung up on the bottom than towing since we started this trip. All the gear torn to hell. Only about 500 pounds the last tow, and 1,500 the tow before—and most of that was trash. I don't know where this is going to lead. Hope for the best, anyway. Over." The skipper quoted on this occasion was on his way to landing one of his best catches in 1967 —about 340,000 pounds—with the disadvantage of a relatively inexpert crew.

A skipper knowledgeable about bottom features and hazards in a certain area may purposely withhold this information to

[4]In this short exploration I have not attempted an exhaustive treatment of the techniques skippers employ, their circumstances of use, or the variation among skippers in preference for a given strategy or "style of competition" (Sutton-Smith & Roberts, 1964). Each of these matters has basic and practical implications for fishery organization and operations.

the detriment of another trawler master fishing nearby. One skipper, who was fishing where he recently had success, was suddenly faced with the arrival of another trawler from among his company fleet. The first skipper withheld information about bottom snags, and the other soon became "caught up and lost the whole works"; that is, it lost all its trawling gear. "He said he wouldn't stay there no more. He got out of it right away."

A master may also be lured to misfortune when, judging another skipper an expert about a particular bottom area, he openly seeks his aid in fishing it successfully. The expert may use this opportunity to deceive his inexperienced colleague. During a trip on the edge of the Great Bank, one skipper informed me he heard another tell his trusting peer to fish in 70 fathoms while he was taking good catches at only 50 fathoms. "Now there was a man out to hurt that man. He was out to hurt him. I *never* did anything like that!" But this same informant related the following maneuver he used with similar results.

Having explored the features of a rather deep fishing location on a previous trip, this skipper was now taking very good catches of fish. But he discovered in a radio exchange that two other trawlers in the same company fleet were coming to examine the possibilities of his location. They were about 15 miles away and unable to see him. He advised them that he was some 30 miles farther on, then hauled in his gear and steamed across the bank to meet them. "I stayed there half a day and there was no fish. Then we separated and I came back to the deep position. We got *our* good trip of fish that time."

Some feints are made by expressing plans to depart from one's present position. This may be particularly effective when attempted by one who is regarded an expert for the area, for it may be taken as sufficient evidence to others that the area has no fish. This technique has short-term distractive power, for skippers watch each other closely. As one skipper put it, "A man tells you where he is one day, and that he's not doing well, and the next day is in the same place—why, you *know* he's taking some fish." But the extra time bought may assure one a good catch or trip of fish.

Both overstatement of catch success and thinly disguised inconsistent facts are used in attempts to seduce each other away from distant positions. Overstatement is used in the medium of closed exchanges over special high frequency channels believed exclusive to one's company fleet. The aim is to have the other skipper lose fishing time while steaming to a new position where he expects to find better fishing. As one mate explained, "Get the other guy to risk that (lost time), and when he arrives, why the fish have gone, and he can't prove different." This technique might also be applied indirectly in skipper-plant exchanges over exclusive, long-range, single-side band transceivers, with the expectation that the information will get back to one's fleet counterparts.

Factors inherent in Newfoundland trawler fishing—namely, foul weather, great distances, and different landing times and places—all make for inability to corroborate and verify facts transmitted in these radio encounters. But concealment is at times exposed by discovery of unintended errors and inconsistencies ('clues') on one skipper's part. Such blunders help generate retribution.

Radio silence is a further technique of interest. It may be used when a trawler strikes good fishing to preserve exclusive exploitative or predatory rights as long as it is possible and advantageous.[5] When used, it is tantamount to annoucing "Top secret!", and prima facie evidence that the missing vessel may have struck good fishing. If pursued too long, it provokes intense curiosity among other skippers about one's position. It may attract other vessels to the suspected location and end one's exclusive "rights." On the other hand, skippers recognize that radio silence may be used like overstatement of catch success; it might reduce another skipper's catch if it induces him to stop fishing his location and steam elsewhere in search of suspected better fishing grounds.

SKIPPER–MANAGEMENT TRANSACTIONS

The operators of Newfoundland's several fish plant and trawler fleet companies regard each other as rivals for a scarce common property resource. Because of mounting costs and declining resource levels, some companies discussed the idea of establishing a central information pool on fish concentrations and movements to overcome the inefficient system of fragmentary pools of company information. But each has maintained exclusive control over the flow of information about fish obtained by its trawlers at sea, by using closed radio channels and frequently changed codes in their daily radio exchanges with

[5]By contrast, Orvar Löfgren reports of the trawler fishermen of Bua, Western Sweden, "Skippers may try to keep their positions secret but dare not refuse to answer direct calls from other boats" (personal communication).

Figure 9.1 Comparison of Catch Estimates

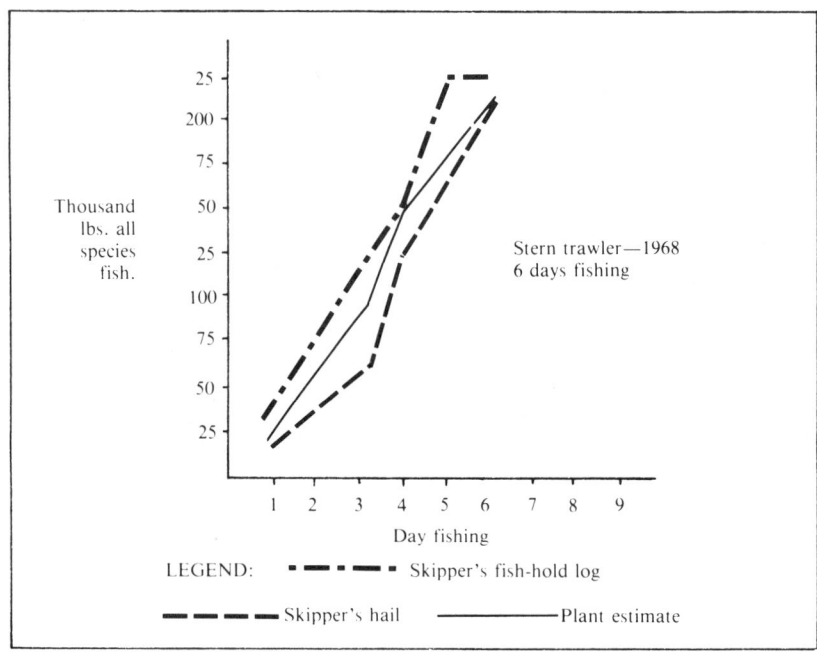

the vessels. Despite this secrecy, plants find that there is considerable uncertainty over the accuracy and value of information their skippers supply. One plant production manager who receives the skippers' daily radio reports observed that, "I never can be sure just how much a man has on his boat on a given day. You're only fairly certain of his total catch when he gives his last hail for the trip."

The manager's doubts about his information are substantiated by discrepancies apparent in a comparison of recorded daily hails, the manager's estimates of the actual catch by his "decoding" the hail, and the hold log kept by the skipper at approximately the same time.

Figure 9.1 illustrates such distortion in an actual six-day trip made by a stern trawler in 1968. Assuming the shipboard, fish-hold log is the most accurate, the daily hail appears to differ from "actual" catch by as much as 50,000 to 70,000 pounds.[6] But the plant operates as if the skipper regularly withheld about 25,000 pounds until his final hail. The discrepancy between the final hail and actual landings is usually negligible from the

---

[6]Some sharp discrepancies between hail and logged catch are due to the schooling characteristics of the diverse species sought. When hunting redfish and cod, for example, one meets a higher frequency of days with remarkably high and low catches than when fishing flounder.

plant standpoint. But if the weighed-out value is markedly below the skipper's final estimate, the trawlerman suspects the plant of fraud.[7]

Difficulties may arise when the plant orders a trawler to terminate fishing and land its catch before the skipper's projected final hail, when he brings his understanding of the plant's estimate of his catch into reasonable congruency with the facts. For example, one trawler made its fifth hail at 115,000 pounds; the plant estimated it to be 130,000 pounds, while the skipper logged 185,000 pounds. The trawler then struck very good fishing for about ten hours, and was then unexpectedly ordered to port to keep a plant processing line supplied with fish. The vessel landed nearly 220,000 pounds, whereas the plant anticipated only 150,000 pounds. This gross error distressed management considerably because of the ensuing confusion and delay in the systematic integration of this catch with other vessel landings and shore processing and manpower scheduling requirements. Such an event may involve rejection of considerable quantities of fish because of excessive delays in processing the oldest fish.[8]

Management grudgingly accepts this pattern of concealment because it has no easy way to verify the skipper's reports; but it regards it as deviant and tries to discourage it on two counts: (1) it creates problems for efficient integration of shore and sea operations; and (2) it means that much valuable information about the fish caught by individual skippers is always viewed as distorted—to what extent is always uncertain save for the final hail—and therefore it is of uncertain value if circulated to other skippers of the same company to achieve maximal fleet productivity. Skippers continue to distort information against management injunctions to cooperate for "the good of all," and despite the introduction of periodically revised codes initially exclusive to each fleet.

COOPERATIVE TRANSACTIONS

Sometimes skippers engage in both situationally restricted and prolonged trust exchanges with other skippers when at sea.

[7]In 1968, plants controlled the weighing-out and quality evaluation of all landed fish, save for inspections by the federal Department of Fisheries. Unionization in the 1970s has reduced management's control in these matters.

[8]Fishermen played no part in the decision to 'dump' fish, and it was often debatable from their standpoint. The fisherman suffered these decisions with little or no reward for labor and time invested. "Of the total landings by 120-foot trawlers, 12.7 per cent was classified as "rejected fish" of little or no value to the buyers. The figure for the 130-foot trawlers was 7.4 per cent" (Proskie, 1969).

These cooperative exchanges seem to occur when two or three Newfoundland trawler skippers for *any* company happen to be fishing the same area, probably at some distance from other vessels and concentrations, perhaps in visual and/or radar sight of each other and with transceivers turned low to limit signal range. They exchange information about bottom features and relevant fishing strategy and there *may* be some factual accounting of catch taken at this time. If the catch is good, there is an incentive both to limit information flow to those vessels at the site, and also to cooperate directly (through verbal exchange) or indirectly (through perceivable vessel movements directly over known benthic terrain), since known movements of individual boats over a fairly large area facilitate better tracking of fish movements. (Ground and dimersal species are thought to vacate areas fished when disturbed.)

Limited cooperation may occur when a skipper acts magnanimously toward another having a "run of bad luck." Such kindness is particularly likely to occur on the last trip before the Christmas holidays. Information is disclosed probably only when it cannot endanger the "donor's" trip. Sometimes clues are given in "riddles" posed by intentionally inconsistent factual statements (actions unknown to the donor's crew). But if the recipient fails to decipher the riddle, the donor may drop his philanthropic line without further concern. A lack of total congruency in skipper–crew interests is suggested here.

Many skippers have never met each other although they have often talked over their transceivers and fished side-by-side; others are neighbors or former shipmates. Some of the latter have long-standing friendships that they regularly or periodically activate at sea to establish trust exchanges. These two cases are illustrative:

The first involves two senior skippers in the same company who are neighbors and old shipmates. Today they exchange factual information via an auxiliary marine transceiver with channels absent in those used by other skippers in their company fleet. Prior to the use of their "crystal sets," the two formulated a secret grid-code navigational scheme (which had to be altered on one occasion when another skipper in their fleet discovered their arbitrary base reference point or "buoy"). They switch back and forth from "public" to collusive exchanges, discuss and map strategy together, and tend to integrate their hunting and catching operations (see Löfgren, 1972, for a similar case). They have rated first and second in their fleet for several years, and attract and hold crews with very high expertise. Both crews favour the way their skippers regularly cooperate or fish together and their joint success may be a key in the crews' loyalty to them.

The second case involves a pair of senior skippers of two different fleets. Each captains a modern stern trawler and appears to engage in honest radio exchanges with the other while in near radio range. To cope with the problem of competitors exploiting their information capital, and lacking the crystal set employed in the case cited above, one skipper slips the upper set of his false teeth from his palate toward the front of his mouth and garbles his speech while talking to the other. He apparently does not do this in radio exchanges with other skippers or his plant.[9] Each maintains a top productive position in his respective company fleet and is regarded as a 'big fish killer' by fishermen familiar with their skills. But because each works for a different plant and fishes different species, one skipper has a broader range of hunting alternatives than the other and they do not regularly work the same fishing grounds. Their cooperation is therefore more sporadic in contrast to the first case cited.

ANALYSIS

Each time the skipper uses the radio he engages in a decision-making situation. He must choose what information he should relate, and what he should believe. Put differently, he must select a communication line, or pattern of verbal and nonverbal acts vis-à-vis his listeners, and interpret the line his listeners take toward him (Goffman, 1967). We have seen that skippers employ and expect concealment in their radio transactions when discussion centers on catch particulars. This choice is channeled by certain constraints and incentives, some more or less characteristic of marine hunting generally.

The key factors to be considered here include: (1) an unequal distribution of values (scarce manpower expertise; trawlers of varying type, age, and capability; and the reputations of the fishermen) which is both derivative of and instrumental to differential success in fishing; (2) "bad breaks" caused by human or technological difficulties, which may force cessation of fishing (and lost time and earnings) unexpectedly; (3) limited

[9]Observations by my research assistant, John Cove, made during the summer 1968, while with one of the Burin Peninsula fleets.

knowledge and control over natural and cultural ecological factors—problems characteristic of common property resource exploitation; and (4) the special rights and obligations characterizing Newfoundland trawler skipper-crew, and skipper-management relationships, and comprehended, in large part, by fishermen status as "coadventurers" in a vertically integrated enterprise.

The following discussion develops the view that the first three factors are somewhat derivative and secondary consequences of the last. The central factor influencing the line taken by Newfoundland trawler skippers is the special coadventurer relationship between each skipper and his crew, wherein the major part of each individual's earnings come from the catch of his vessel alone. Further, the fact that this reward system operates in the framework of a vertically integrated industry where access to values (jobs, vessels, fish, and earnings) is "casual" and ultimately set by nonfisherman vessel and plant owners or their managers, adds additional incentive toward intervessel rivalry and deception.

UNEQUAL DISTRIBUTION OF VALUES

In the early years of the Newfoundland trawler fishery, particularly in the early 1950s, there was a serious scarcity of berths and an abundance of good hands willing to ship out. The number of former schooner skippers and fishermen from the old salt-banking fishery exceeded jobs available, and informants declare that "You couldn't even buy a job on a dragger (trawler) if you had the money!" Fleet owners recruited reliable former schooner skippers who knew the nearby deep-sea fishing grounds. They were instructed in ground-fishing techniques, and given command of imported side trawlers. They had the pick of men and quickly built highly efficient, hard-working, stable crews. For the first time in their lives, many found themselves fishing year round. Men dared not take any days off except for urgent reasons, for fear they would be replaced by others. Much hardship and deprivation were endured in favor of earnings far better than those they had known in the schooner fishery, and better than what could be got from other work alternatives.

These small fleets grew in size over the years and were modernized with a shift toward larger stern trawlers. During the period between 1956 and 1968, the number of trawlers in Newfoundland increased from 12 to 60. In this same period, fulltime fishermen (those engaged in the fishery for over ten months of the year) increased from about 230 to 710 in trawler centers, namely those in Fortune and Placentia Bays. As new vessels joined company fleets, skippers and mates with seniority tended to have first chance at them. When a skipper moved to a new trawler, his crew tended to follow, while other men, sometimes the skipper's former mate, assumed command of the older side trawlers, having to build their own crews and reputations as masters.

By the mid-1960s, the supply of older and experienced schooner skippers and fishermen had diminished, so that most new recruits today are comparatively inexperienced. The modern skipper often observes that "I take men I wouldn't have looked at ten years ago."

The consequence is an unequal distribution of individual fishermen (especially skippers) of repute, expert fishermen, and efficient trawlers. Within the same company fleet, one finds highly regarded skippers with the most modern and productive stern trawlers in their charge and expert and stable crews with correspondingly higher earnings; then there are other skippers, frequently as experienced, with recently obtained stern trawlers but relatively young and inefficient crews characterized by high turnover and lower earnings; and, finally, in some fleets, still other young masters charged with operating the oldest, least efficient side trawlers. The last experience serious crew recruitment problems, as modern fishermen tend to reject the old, uncomfortable, and unsafe working conditions and lower earnings. In some instances, these skippers have been forced to tie up in port for lengthy periods when an adequate crew could not be secured.

BAD BREAKS IN FISHING

Every fisherman must deal with bad breaks, that is, unpredictable accidents (Turnstall, 1968, 1969; Howden, 1968), and breakdowns of gear and vessel. Both interrupt fishing operations for varying periods of time. For example, engine bearings, generators, and winches may fail without warning, and force a return to port or costly delays at sea while repairs are made. Trawl gear may get hung up on the bottom and be damaged seriously, if not lost altogether; fishing must be stopped while repairs are made. Sometimes the gear becomes snarled on the propeller shaft, totally disabling the vessel, and another trawler is required to tow it into port.

There are many ways in which men may be seriously injured and require immediate medical attention and hospitalization: parting lines and breaking blocks, falls on slippery decks and cuts and fires.

Speaking impressionistically, older vessels crewed by men with less expertise probably suffer more bad breaks as compared to the newer vessels with more experienced and stable crews. Reduced earnings due to technical and human difficulties of this sort compound the disadvantages already imposed by fishing with a technologically less efficient unit and crew.

UNCERTAINTY IN HUNTING A COMMON PROPERTY RESOURCE

Trawler ground fishing is a hunting adaptation somewhere between the more passive forms of fishing represented by cod-trap and drift-net fishing and the more active forms such as whaling. In the latter, the fisherman searches for his quarry, makes direct visual contact, gives chase, sometimes even drives and surrounds it, and then captures it. Similarly, in trawler fishing, the skipper searches for, pursues to a lesser degree, and captures sometimes highly mobile species. He can detect his quarry by means of electronic detectors, but he must often follow hunches, and "shoot blind" after fish. Only when the trawl is retrieved are the results of his efforts known.

Each skipper comes to know various parts of the fishing grounds in more microscopic detail than the latest fishing charts available. And he develops an understanding about the behavior of each species he pursues. This includes occurrences and yield potentials at various bottom locations and redistributional patterns under varying rates of fishing intensity. Nevertheless, his information suffers from inaccuracies, a lack of systematic acquisition, and storage. Information retrieval is fragmentary and often impossible. Each skipper must "find out for himself" and treat any information given him with severe skepticism.

His information-getting problems are compounded by the unknown and unexpected impact of competitors exploiting the same resources. Canadian and foreign trawlers freely exploit the same common property resources beyond the three-mile international boundary (except for occasional violations of this limit). He has too little information about their movements and their impact on fish stocks at a given time. Thus, a bottom area thought to have recovered its stock through redistribution might be fished out again by these competitors. But this fact might only be known by fishing the area unsuccessfully.

The three factors just examined, namely, inequalities in the distribution of expertise, trawlers, and reputations; bad breaks; and information problems associated with the exploitation of a common property resource, do not in themselves explain information management by Newfoundland trawler skippers. On the contrary, one might argue, from the company fleet standpoint, that more cooperation in sharing information would mitigate the disadvantages set by these factors and improve the returns to *all* of a company's fishermen.

Instead, information management may increase the consequences of, for example, technological disadvantages imposed by trawler type; add to the frequency of costly mechanical and gear failures experienced by all fishing units (anyone may withhold information about bottom snags); and forces all units to engage in costly duplication of effort. Indeed, some skippers within the same company cooperate on a sustained basis against the background of the canalizing factors cited. For most skippers, however, information management is set in motion by the special complex of rights and obligations existing between them and their crews and owner-managers examined in the following section.

COADVENTURESHIP AND VERTICAL INTEGRATION

The important statuses in Newfoundland trawler fishing are defined by established formal and informal casual contracts including: (1) fleet management (fleet and plant owners and their managers) with the comprehensive right to manage all vessel affairs including provision of gear, determination of crew, departure and landing times and destinations, specific species to be sought, their handling on shipboard, prices paid for landed fish, and lay arrangements for all crew; (2) a skipper who commands vessel and crew fishing operations and in practice, recruits and selects most of the crew; (3) a working crew distributed among the following positions:

Deck: one mate, one bosun, and from six to eleven deckhands; a total complement of from eight to thirteen hands.
Galley: one cook.

Engine Room: two or three engineers (ranked as first, second, and third engineers).

These three basic statuses form a division of labor and authority, and as Barth (1966) observes for the Norwegian purse-seine herring fishery, "The various rights are distributed in such a way as to make possible a series of transactions over complementary prestations." The crew provides labor for those with the right to exercise authority; there are minimal contractual limitations on hours of work and days at sea, although the tasks to which the crew may be assigned are restricted by their geographical-functional positions. Their subordination is generally absolute within the limits of their contractual positions, and unrestricted in times of emergency.

Each crew member receives, for his labor at the end of each trip, a share of the vessel's landed catch value paid by the plant, and varying with position held and individual company lay arrangements, a guaranteed percentage, daily wage, and other bonuses. (Earnings are less deductions for food and other minor items, such as the Canadian pension plan, life insurance, cigarettes, and gloves and other rubber gear consumed during the trip. Earnings are generally not paid out to the fisherman for ten to twlve days after landing, i.e., the time required to complete another average fishing trip.) This reward system provides no direct means for the calculation of profits that might be gained from intrafleet cooperation.

The skipper is fully responsible for his vessel and crew, and the success of the fishing operations, although he regularly delegates considerable responsibility to various crew members, especially to the mate and bosun. Once at sea, he decides where, when, and how to fish, oversees the handling and storage of fish, and determines how best to bring his vessel safely to port again. In return, based upon his vessel's catch he receives two to four times the earnings of most crewmen.

Management, for its part, assumes all risks and decisions in the processing and marketing of landed fish passing their (and government's) inspection, provides for the reasonable needs of all fleet units without prejudice, guarantees payment of all hands according to a fixed, predetermined fish price and lay scale. In return, they reserve the right to determine the times of vessel departure, landing and destination, the right to all earnings in excess of costs incurred bringing the catch to market, and the ultimate right to determine appointments and removals from positions on specific vessels in their fleet. Thus the skipper earns his right to command a trawler by demonstrated expertise in fishing operations both prior to and following his appointment by management. Fishing operations are broadly conceived by management and include individual reliability and cooperation in response to management decisions and expectations, success in taking fish—measured in relation to the performance of other vessels of similar type in the fleet, handling men, and the vessel itself.

The skipper, like all other casually employed trawlermen holds tenure on a trip-by-trip basis in most cases, knows that management may order his dismissal at any time, and, inasmuch as he is a casual, unorganized worker, he has little recourse short of direct personal protest (Tunstall, 1969). Moreover, he believes that he is expendable and replaceable—even by his own mate.

Given this minimal set of rights and obligations, with the skipper and crew of each trawler joined together as coadventurers[10] in a continuing succession of relatively short-term (each vessel may make about 25 fishing trips during a 12-month period) bargaining relationships, the skipper works to maximize those factors that will ensure the best catch possible.

Fishing follows a repetitive routine. Over each 24-hour period the vessel may go through 10 or 12 or more complete cycles in shooting, towing, hauling, and repairing gear, and processing and storage. During the average 10-day fishing trip involving perhaps seven 24-hour fishing days, minutes lost through sluggishness, indecision, and oversight concerning shooting, hauling, and gear repair mean reduced catch. As in purse-seine herring fishing (Goodlad, 1972; Wadel, 1972; Barth, 1966), it behooves the skipper to create a working relationship and atmosphere wherein men act effectively without being told and respond cooperatively and quickly under necessary commands. It seems that the ideal skipper-crew relationship is one where crewmen remark of the skipper that "He's so quiet, you hardly know the man is up there" (in the wheelhouse); or "He hardly says a word" and orders rarely have to be given.

Success in trawling, unlike purse-seining, is based largely on the skipper and crew's persistent attention to complex gear and operating details throughout the duration of the trip. This con-

---

[10]In 1968 Newfoundland trawler fishermen were legally classified as "coadventurers," and not employees. They had no legal right to bargain as a union. This prohibitive legal technicality, long destructive of both labor *and* company interests, was successfully challenged in Newfoundland in 1971, and, subsequently, most of this province's trawler fishermen have unionized. Similar laws for example, in New Brunswick, persist elsewhere in eastern Canada, however.

trasts with Norwegian and Shetland purse-seine fishing where only a few hours of concentrated effort often means a successful trip.

It follows that trawler skippers are attentive to building a crew with expertise and compatibility necessary for optimal operating efficiency. In Newfoundland, Hull, and Grimsby fisheries, there is a close relationship between a successful skipper and the stability of his crew (Turnstall, n.d.). The conduct and performance of each man is always under scrutiny; men found unfit are discharged at trip's end, and others sought out. In return for his labor and expertise, each crewman looks to the skipper to provide the necessary conditions of crew and gear and above all, to find fish. Thus, skippers are recognized for their quality as "fish dogs," "big fish killers," or "high liners," and as crew makers. Men finding a skipper wanting are free to leave at trip's end without explanation, thereby sanctioning him for failing to meet his part in the bargain. While members of a crew sometimes acidly and enviously remark that "All the skipper does is drive the boat around," the implication being that they are mere passengers, they more accurately conceive themselves as carrying the skipper about in search of a mutual quest.

Given a general skill in bringing together a reasonably compatible and effective crew, each skipper's decisions are ultimately judged (by his crew and management) against his vessel's catch relative to others in the same fleet. What he does with information obtained about fish while on the fishing grounds reflects on his relationship with his crew. They expect him to act in *their* best interests, and both are joined in a continuing series of transactions in which all "keep their guard up." For the highly mobile fisherman making the occasional trip on various boats, the transactions taking place between skipper and crew tend to be consummated at trip's end; but to more or less committed regulars seeking steady good earnings and stable crew relationships, these transactions are never fully consummated. On every trip, the skipper-crew exchanges, fishing decisions, actions and radio performances test the validity of their complementary positional privileges and obligations as coadventurers.

The skipper has ready access to formal and informal information about each individual's performance through direct observation, his junior officers, the cook, and direct exchange with individuals in the semiprivacy of the wheelhouse. He performs his role mainly in and from the wheelhouse, and in the galley where he eats and chats with his men. The wheelhouse itself is accessible to all those not performing other duties. Day and night, nearly all crew members visit it to chat with the man on the helm, check the radar, listen to readily accessible radio exchanges between skippers on various channels, and audit the progress of their vessel's fishing efforts and those of others in the fleet and of English-speaking crews fishing nearby.

If we conceptualize this dramaturgically (Goffman, 1959), and conceive of the wheelhouse as a stage, the skipper performs simultaneously before three distinct audiences: his crew, skippers and men of other vessels, and the management. His is a complex game of impression management wherein he must overcommunicate to the crew his commitment to their good interests.[11] He must subtly do the same in mutually comprehensible expressions of helplessness to other skippers (most with whom he has no basis for establishing an enduring trust-exchange relationship to enable a continuing program and strategy of cooperative exchange acceptable to the crowd of each vessel). And finally, he must display resignation before the feeling that, "Fishermen are the biggest bunch of liars! Nobody ever tells the other guy the truth. And the skipper that does, well he won't last long out here. I never tells especially them (other skippers) anything but lies, or the plant anything (accurate) until we have *our* trip of fish and make our *last* hail."

While employing the information management techniques described earlier, he strives otherwise to convey an image of good will and skill to his audience on other vessels. He cannot openly help them by giving away information that might jeopardize his own crowd's (crew's) catch, but he does offer noncritical advice and information and never openly tries to "hurt the other fellow" by his actions. In doing so, the skipper advances his reputation among other fishermen.

He strives for an image of himself as a skillful fisherman and a "good skipper"—the sort who takes care of his men first but does not try to hurt others while doing so. It is understood that the interests of his crew have priority; when their joint capital

---

[11]One plant manager said of his relieving skipper; "He's the biggest liar of them all when he's out there!" The "relieving" or "shore skipper" may be under the greatest pressure to overcommunicate his commitment to crew interests while frequently also chanting management expectations for intervessel cooperation in the company fleet. He must quickly establish good, short-term work relationships with various crews and maintain acceptable vessel productivity to justify holding his scarce and much envied position.

has been invested and fish are located, maneuvers designed to keep others from encroaching and "stealing our fish" are legitimized and expected. Concealment here expresses a fundamental difference in the conception of relevant enterprise and role between the fisherman and fleet owner: for the fisherman, the individual crowd has primacy, while for management, the fleet-plant combination is primary. This difference also encompasses a discrepant view of correlated primary competitive boundaries: intrafleet unit as opposed to interfleet unit.

Primary enterprise among coadventurers, especially among skippers, generates basic distrust of all information tendered by other skippers. The skipper's problem is further complicated by his general inability to validate (apart from direct observation while fishing nearby) many critical facts supplied by others, and also by an absence of "systematic or stretch distortion" (Smith, 1966) in this information; that is, the error tends to be indeterminate. There is no applicable, reliable correction for error at a given time. He must seek clues presented by accidental inconsistencies in information, and operate on the assumption that "fish are scarce" or find out for himself.

I argued earlier that knowledge of ecological characteristics and associated fish particulars is unequally distributed among trawler skippers. Facing a highly competitive field in which rivals ferret and withhold information from each other, each skipper strives independently to increase his expertise about various areas. But before his men he must always act as if he knows what he is doing while covertly risking their pooled capital to fish areas about which he has little information. If his men sense that he has sacrificed an average trip's earnings fishing known areas, in favor of less-than-average earnings fishing an unknown bottom, they may leave and his reputation may suffer. (It may be that the top trawler skippers with highly expert and stable crews have more freedom in this regard and actually explain their intentions against greater prestations of trust; Barth, 1966). That he must take these risks at times is incentive for the gambling skipper to lure other vessels away from good fishing grounds on the pretext that better fishing is found elsewhere. The need for such risks also indicates a lack of perfect congruency in skipper and crew interests.

The vertical integration of Newfoundland trawlers tends to create what may be termed "primary information exhange spheres." These represent the skipper's main competitive field. Units in the same company fleet fish for the same species, although they are not always sufficiently near to enable regular radio exchange; they land at the same plants; skippers, mates, and others are linked to each other by the same company-framed and controlled seniority system relative to access to vacant and new captain and mate positions and new or better trawlers. (Many men suspect caprice, prejudice, and favoritism in the company execution of these seniority systems.) Each fleet unit is equipped with the same radio channels and transceivers and codes for daily reports in what ought to be (from the management standpoint) collusive or secret communications inside the fleet.

Each skipper seems mainly oriented and attentive to the primary information sphere. Inasmuch as the company objective is maximization of fleet productivity, and inasmuch as all useful information supplied management by individual skippers may be disseminated to each competing fleet unit, each skipper is compelled to avoid unrestricted dissemination of his information as it would violate his primary loyalties. On the other hand, he owes his position to the management and feels compelled to portray a cooperative line befitting management expectations. This contradiction is mitigated by management's reluctant acknowledgment that one needs secrecy at sea, and that the skipper is best situated to decide the risks of information disclosure. They grant him almost complete de facto autonomy in managing information, thus complementing his total responsibility for fishing success, while qualifying what the master reports via "traditional" corrections.

Facts exchanged help stage expectancies with regard to landing times at various company plants. They also provide a field for innovative and subtle tactics designed to buy some autonomy from management with regard to landing time (one giving a full weekend ashore is most desired), sailing time, and extra fishing time. Skippers may occasionally run the risk of some spoilage in order to gain recognition for an outstandingly high catch (Cove, n.d.).

As indicated earlier, management tends to operate on the assumption that skippers usually underestimate to the extent of about 25,000 pounds. Skippers know and cultivate this expectation, a stretch distortion in information that they manage to have confirmed only in the final landed catch, if not the vessel log (although it too sometimes suffers from "impression management" designed to create an image of regularity in skipper control over fishing operations). Against this distortion, individual skippers at times subtly reveal and withhold information to better their catch, while trying to make another vessel land first. It is likely that with reduced catch levels due to overfished and depleted fish stocks, the time required to make a trip of fish today restricts the extent to which a skipper can manipulate the facts and time in this way.

But the primary information exchange sphere draws the attention of all hands aboard the trawler. There are some important consequences for skippers in this fact: His information management may demonstrate to his crowd an exclusive commitment to their interests over those of other vessels and management, but his crew constantly measures his success and actions against what they think other skippers are doing. Thus, while a skipper may wish to concern himself only with attaining the maximum possible catch no matter what other boats are doing, he is also aware that his men "are more interested in what the other guy is doing than he is. They (his crew) are always coming up to the wheelhouse to find out how so and so is doing." At times, this fact may cause the skipper to compromise his best strategy in order to maintain his status vis-à-vis other skippers in the eyes of his men. The crew's relativistic orientation toward their skipper's action and catch also suggests that one's success as a skipper, one's ability to build and keep a good crew, depends in large part on the position occupied in the catch statistics of his fleet and not simply on his absolute catch (cf. Barth, 1966, p. 10). If so, it becomes obvious why information management is sometimes used to cause other vessels, particularly in one's own fleet, to lose fishing time, and thus suffer reduced catch. Such use is intended not merely to protect one's store of information and exclusive fishing rights but also to maximize the skipper's status in relation to, and at the expense of, his peers in the same fleet.

CONCLUSION

Social behavior is now frequently viewed as an exchange of values, material and non-material (Homans, 1958; Barth, 1966). Pursuing their values, individuals and groups engage in information or cultural management (Goffman, 1959; Roberts, 1964; Paine, 1970). Further, every social role involves an entrepreneurial aspect relating to actions and activities by which persons take initiative and pursue some profit by manipulation of other persons and resources (Barth, 1963, p. 5–6). Likewise, we recognize that all kinds of workers develop information or impression management techniques while managing their roles; instances are recorded for both unorganized and organized occupations at all status levels. These ideas place much of our social science literature on the world of work, informal and formal organization, and, more recently, autonomous as opposed to controlled work organization spheres (Katz, 1967) in a different, economic light, and, perhaps, under more meaningful theoretical rubrics.

The present study has examined how trawler skippers *competitively* exploit common property resources, restrict the flow of important information, and thereby cause apparent inefficiencies in the "rational" integration and use of costly capital equipment and manpower. In other terms, this is an instance of intelligence failure or information pathology (Wilensky, 1967) in the operations and decisions of a large and complex organization.

Perhaps because fishing is often romantically conceived, the fisherman prevarication outlined is sometimes ascribed to a sea custom of undetermined origin—a supposed maritime penchant for "perpendicular lying" (Henningsen, 1965; Andersen, 1973). At other times, it is attributed to skipper individualism, or, as one writer said of small trawler skippers operating out of Hampton, Virginia, "Crusty and independent, they aren't inclined to cooperate" (Carlson, 1969). Such interpretations are poorly grounded sociologically. Seen from the fisherman's standpoint, this putative inefficiency has its underlying logic. As in many North Atlantic fisheries, the trawler fisherman regards another man's gain as his loss; fishing is conceived as a zero-sum game. "If we don't take it, somebody else will." Information management is the sine qua non of competitive commercial fishing. The single-unit, coadventurer relationship seems the key explanatory factor in Newfoundland trawler fishing. It is reinforced by ecologic uncertainties, inequalities in extractive requirements, and by the insecurity of tenure caused by labor arrangements.

Despite the high technology now used in modern fisheries, our evidence suggests it is not being used to full potential. The apparent inefficiencies in information management occur widely in world fisheries. This analysis leaves us with the implicit suggestion that cooperative information management on the intrafleet level is attainable by changing the reward system. Perhaps a clear redistributive mechanism that rewards fishermen for more cooperation could be designed. But what are the consequences? The answer is not obvious. Neither the bases for, nor functions of, competition in this or other fisheries have received sufficient study to permit quick or simple answers. And the state of our sociocultural knowledge of modern fishing industry uses of exploitative and communication technology is dim indeed when we understand that most of our limited knowledge was developed before the post-1976 era of extended coastal-state fisheries jurisdiction.[12]

---

[12] A fuller outline of social science research priorities in the modern Canadian fishery is given in a recent background study prepared for science policy (Andersen, 1978). The problems identified in this document are met widely in world fisheries.

References

Andersen, R. Hunt and deceive: Information management in deep sea trawler fishing, in *North Atlantic fishermen*. R. Andersen & C. Wadel, eds. St. John's: Memorial University of Newfoundland, Institute of Social and Economic Research Papers 5, 1972.

Andersen, R. Those fisherman lies. *Ethnos,* 1973, *1–4,* 153–164.

Andersen, R. The need for human sciences research in the Atlantic Coast fisheries. *Journal of the Fisheries Research Board of Canada,* 1978, *35,* 1031–1049.

Barth, F. *The role of the entrepreneur in social change in North Norway.* Bergen: Universitetsforlaget, 1963.

Barth, F. Models of social organization. *Royal Anthropological Institute Occasional Paper 23,* 1966.

Brox, O. *Maintenance of economic dualism in Newfoundland.* St. John's: Memorial University of Newfoundland, Institute of Social and Economic Research Studies 9, 1969.

Carlson, P. Aboard the *Dragnet. New York Times,* 1969, Vol. 49, No. 244, 1.

Cove, J. Personal communication, no date.

Goffman, E. *The presentation of self in everday life.* Garden City, N.Y.: Doubleday, 1959.

Goffman, E. *Interaction ritual.* Garden City, N.Y.: Doubleday, 1967.

Goodlad, C. A. Old and trusted, new and unknown: technological confrontation in the Shetland herring fishery, in *North Atlantic fishermen*. R. Andersen & C. Wadel, eds. St. John's: Memorial University of Newfoundland, Institute of Social and Economic Research Papers 5, 1972.

Henningsen, G. The art of perpendicular lying. *Journal of the Folklore Institute,* 1965, Vol. 2, No. 2, 180–219.

Howden, P. The Hull fishermen and worker's control. *Anarchy 86,* 1968, Vol. 8, No. 4, 97–113.

Homans, G. Behavior as social exchange. *American Sociological Review,* 1958, *63,* 597–606.

Katz, F. Explaining informal work groups in complex organizations, in *Readings in industrial sociology.* W. Faunce, ed. New York: Appleton-Century Crofts, 1967.

Löfgren, O. Resource management and family firms: Swedish West Coast fishermen, in *North Atlantic fishermen*. R. Andersen & C.

Wadel, eds. St. John's: Memorial University of Newfoundland, Institute of Social and Economic Research Papers 5, 1972.

Paine, R. Informal communication and information-management. *Canadian Review of Sociology and Anthropology,* 1970, 7, 172–188.

Proskie, J. *Cost and earnings of selected fishing enterprises, Atlantic Provinces, 1966.* Ottawa: Economics Branch, Fisheries Service, Dept. of Fisheries and Forestry, 1969.

Roberts, J. The self-management of cultures, in *Explorations in cultural anthropology.* W. H. Goodenough, ed. New York: McGraw-Hill, 1964.

Smith, A. G. (ed.) *Communication and culture.* New York: Holt, Rinehart & Winston, 1966.

Stiles, R. G. Fishermen, wives and radios: Aspects of communication in a Newfoundland fishing community, in *North Atlantic fishermen.* R. Andersen & C. Wadel, eds. St. John's: Memorial University of Newfoundland, Institute of Social and Economic Research Papers 5, 1972.

Sutton-Smith, B., & Roberts, J. M. Rubrics of competitive behavior. *Journal of Genetic Psychology,* 1964, *105,* 13–37.

Tunstall, J. *Fish: an antiquated industry.* Fabian Tract 380. London: Fabian Society, 1968.

Tunstall, J. *The fishermen.* London: MacGibbon & Kee, 1969.

Tunstall, J. Personal communication, no date.

Wadel, C. *Marginal adaptations and modernization in Newfoundland: strategies and implications of resettlement and redevelopment of outport fishing communities.* St. John's: Memorial University of Newfoundland, Institute of Social & Economic Research Studies 7, 1969.

Wadel, C. Capitalization and ownership: The persistence of fisherman-ownership in the Norwegian herring fishery, in *North Atlantic fishermen.* R. Andersen & C. Wadel, eds. St. John's: Memorial University of Newfoundland, Institute of Social and Economic Research Papers 5, 1972.

Wilensky, H. *Organizational intelligence.* New York: Basic Books, 1967.

10

Secrecy in Business: A Sociological View

Brian J. O'Connell
St. John's University

Recent stories of bribes by multinational companies, of accusations against large oil and gas companies for withholding supplies or price fixing, and of secret corporate gifts to political campaigns have spurred concern over corporate secrecy. Concern is not only focused on the revelations of information that had been kept secret purposely but also on the growing amount of esoteric information that is limited only to experts.

There are new circumstances that present varied opportunities for corporate secrecy. Business bureaucracies are splitting into more functionally specialized networks, each of which is staffed by highly trained specialists. Many new corporate ventures require the systematic application of the work of teams of specialists over a long period of time (Galbraith, 1967). The introduction of new product lines, the development of new energy resources, and the opening of new service organizations are examples of projects that require teams of scientists, marketing experts, lawyers, advertisers, accountants, and numerous other classes of experts.

This process gives enormous powers to the persons at the top of the planning process. They must have the resources to hire the appropriate classes of experts. Max Weber (Miller, 1963) pointed out in regard to the expert on specialized task teams that "normally the mechanism cannot be put into motion or arrested by him, but only from the very top." These top managers not only have access to the knowledge of the experts, but they determine the uses to which this knowledge is put.

This power of top managers serves many useful functions through the goods and services delivered. The questions of whether these top managers should be in the public domain or in the private corporation or whether the decision-making process should be open or secret will be addressed later. But at this point, three dysfunctions that result from the actions of these top managers can be specified.

1. These top managers can determine what types of research will be funded. This could result in a restriction of research and the advancement of knowledge to the short-range interests of corporate enterprise. This pattern need not be dysfunctional so long as universities, government funding agencies, and foundations maintain some degree of independence. Given the predominance of productive enterprise in our society, we must at least check that the top business managers do not have exclusive control of the growth of science.

2. Top managers may be able to shield themselves from detailed knowledge of the activities of middle-level bureaucrats who may use illegal or unethical means to advance the interests of the company. A classic case of this occurred on the U.S. Senate floor on November 23, 1971, when Senator John C. Stennis (Democrat, Mississippi) said, "You have to make up your mind that you are going to have an intelligence agency and protect it as such and shut your eyes some and take what is coming." It is unlikely that top managers in business would be as explicit in admitting such activity as Senator Stennis was about the covert actions of the CIA. But such a course of action may absolve the top managers of legal responsibility for all practical purposes, and their own eyes it may even absolve them from ethical responsibility.

3. The top manager may put such pressure on his or her middle managers for profit and efficiency that it may force these middle managers to use illegal or unethical means in order to keep their jobs. Or this pressure could keep scientists or experts from making the public aware of detrimental side effects or environmental or safety hazards connected with a product.

On the side of the experts or the middle managers hired by the top managers, two dysfunctions can occur:

1. In the complexity of the projects attempted by corporate enterprise, the experts or middle men can often successfully

hide their shortcomings or even their illegal activities from the top. This is the other side of the coin from the last dysfunction mentioned. In both cases, accountability for actions is lessened.
2. The person in the middle ranks may find himself or herself carried along with the tide of events, participating in illegal or unethical activities without being fully aware of the situation. Jeb Stuart Magruder said of his involvement in Watergate, "It's a question of slippage. I sort of slipped right into it. Each act you take leads you to the next act, and eventually you end up with a Watergate. (Terkel, 1973, p.67)." When Senator Baker asked John Porter why he didn't act on his own conscience and resist the tide of events, he said, "That question sounds good, but in practice we just don't do it. If you question too much, you find yourself out in left field, and that's true not just in government, but in business, too. It is much easier to say, I'll help out. It was simple, very simple (Roberts, 1973, p. 40)."

The experts or middle managers thus find themselves in situations that are bigger than they are. It may be argued how much responsibility each of these Watergare figures bore, but their responses show the compromising situations that similar middle-level personnel face. In a secretive atmosphere, persons can easily start rationalizing, become defensive, start coloring the truth (perhaps not knowing the full truth themselves), and end up telling bigger lies to cover the smaller lies.

SECRECY, POWER, AND COMPETITION

Knowledge control and secrecy are quite universally recognized as means by which power is gained and maintained in a society. Lowry (1972) notes that "secrecy maximizes the power potential of knowledge." Moore & Tumin (1948), show that ignorance resulting from secrecy is a preservative of privileged position by restricting access to knowledge and skills, by keeping people ignorant of alternative ways of doing things, and by avoidance of jealousies over unequal rewards. If actions of leaders are secret, it leaves them less accountable to the public.

Sociologists with different theoretical perspectives give more or less weight to the factor of secrecy insofar as it helps or hinders the efficiency of bureaucracies and the functioning of the competition system. Advocates of the elitist power system model attribute an essential function to secrecy. For Mills

(1959), the lack of visibility of the elite enables them to make key decisions without accountability, as attention is focused on lesser executives who operate within severe constraints established by the elites. Hunter (1953), uses the same model for community power structure.

The advocates of the pluralist power system model are less concerned about secrecy. Shils (1956), believes that "an effectively working pluralistic system will feel no need for complete publicity." There are "secrets which are functionally necessary for the safety of the society." He recognizes bounds to this secrecy, but he argues that a fair degree of publicity will be achieved by mutual adaptation of spheres of power and concessions that one sphere would make toward the others for the orderly functioning of society. Rourke (1975), similarly asserts that the essential right of the public to know is largely accomplished in the American system of democracy by the interplay of competing organizations.

Shils (1956) holds the position that corporations have the same right to privacy as persons in a society. "The first principle of individualist democracy is the partial autonomy of individuals and of corporate bodies or institutions." This autonomy includes privacy, and is essential to freedom. Shils admits there are situations when the "affairs of the corporate body shade off into the sphere of the legitimate concern of the public" in which it is difficult to get the right balance of privacy and publicity.

Shils distinguishes between privacy and secrecy. "Secrecy is privacy made compulsory." Very often, he admits that secrecy is the enemy of privacy in that it involves loyalty oaths and elaborate security checks. But Shils has a very restricted idea of secrecy, and all the examples in the part of the book where this definition occurs have to do with espionage and government security secrets. It is never clear that he applies the notion to the corporation.

Moore & Tumin (1948), although they are not as closely identified with the pluralist school as Shils and Rourke, still maintain that a certain amount of corporate secrecy is necessary to preserve fair competition by keeping the different sides of guard and by preventing the creation of overwhelming power combinations. Moore and Tumin also employ the analogy of the person, but in a slightly different context than Shils. They argue that just as friends are happily ignorant of some of each other's habits and thoughts, so too bureaucracy can flow more freely if some things remain unknown. Ignorance can preserve stereotypes, and all social behavior is directed toward stereotypes of social units. But they do not push this line of argumentation as forcefully or to the same practical extent as Shils presents his arguments for the privacy of the corporation.

Lewis Coser presents quite a different perspective on the function of secrecy. In his perspective (1956; 1963) conflict is most likely when adversaries cannot take each other's messages to be credible. Coser sought to identify situations where accommodation or conflict was more likely, for instance, between nations or between labor and management. Competition between companies shows aspects of accommodation (sharing in same market structure, playing by the same rules, etc.) and conflict (a struggle for the elimination of the opponent). While Coser did not address the corporate question directly, his treatment of the conflict process must make us ask at what point secrecy will force the participants in the competitive process to deceptive practices and to disobedience of the rules of the competitive game.

Lowry (1972), demonstrates that in secretive situations, rumor supplants rational communication and interaction. A rumored shortage of such products as coffee or sugar can cause a buying spree in which excess demand distorts the market. Nadel (1975) goes a step further to claim that excessive secrecy could destroy the very basis of the capatalist system. In the classical capitalist model, the investor seeks out high profit situations or areas where demand exceeds supply. But if reliable knowledge on the aspects of the competitive process is not readily available, the investor does not know where to put his capital. Nadel is especially concerned about certain industries where information is closely guarded among a small closed circle of corporations and government regulatory officials. Nadel argues that the government should mandate disclosure in some situations where it may be disadvantageous for particular corporations but will be socially beneficial. The right of eminent domain is a parallel exercise of government authority that is widely accepted.

There is another changing social situation that merits consideration in the study of economic competition. As corporate ventures become more complex, few corporations may have all the necessary expert skills available to compete. The demand for environmental impact statements, for instance, has been very difficult for small construction companies that do not have the legal and technical staffs to prepare such documents. As world markets open for many products, again only a few companies who have large marketing staffs, connections with foreign buyers, links to the transportation industry, and massive legal and financial staffs can participate. Only five companies shared 90 percent of the massive food exporting business (including the Soviet wheat sale), largely because no other companies were equipped to enter the market. Secrecy in the strict sense is not involved, but certain companies maintain an oligopoly on knowledge flow and knowledge skills.

INTERNAL AND EXTERNAL REGULATION OF BUSINESS

In the effort to get a healthy balance between corporate publicity and privacy, the government often acts as a balance wheel. It is often difficult to find the wisest way for government intervention, particularly with an ever-changing and growing corporate sector. Sometimes, boards of directors have difficulty getting the information they need to make decisions. This section will detail some of the problematical situations for which it is difficult to find solutions.

Lack of Uniform Accounting Procedures

In an age of partially owned subsidiaries, different depreciation laws in various countries, and incredibly complex tax laws, it is not surprising that corporations, especially the multinationals, have difficulty keeping their books. But the corporations can turn this into an excuse or a cover to hide their assets.

An example of the discrepancy between corporate and governmental statistics was the claim of the Anaconda Company against the Overseas Private Investment Corporation (OPIC) an arm of the U.S. State Department that insures the foreign investments of multinationals for its losses in the Chilean expropriation. Anaconda claimed losses of $171,000,000 but OPIC, allowed only a small part of the claim. This set off long legal battles.

During the week that John Hersey was allowed inside the White House to write a diary, he recorded a conversation of President Gerald R. Ford and many of his top economic advisers on Vice President Nelson A. Rockefeller's proposal for an excess profits tax on the oil companies (Hersey, 1975). Alan

Greenspan brought the conversation to an abrupt halt with his comment that "trying to audit through the profits system of the multinationals would lead you into a hopeless maze."

One of the reasons it is difficult to track profits is the vertical integration of many companies, which have different subsidiaries for obtaining raw materials, processing, transporting, and selling. The U.S. Justice Department has charged the companies that own the Alaska pipeline with overcharging on the pipeline operations and reducing the price of oil at the wellhead to avoid heavier taxes and royalties on the oil.

When parts of the vertical structure are in different countries, accounting is further complicated. This does not necessarily result from the intention of companies to be secretive or deceptive, it can simply be the result of a complex set of accounting standards to which the corporations must adapt. In what is known as triangle trade, however, companies sometimes place part of their operations in a tax haven like Liberia or the Bahamas, where they do not have to pay tax. Sometimes one division of a company sells to another division of the company in the Bahamas, and the Bahamian division resells at a large markup to a buyer in another country. In some cases, the product never actually touches the shores of the Bahamas. The picture gets even foggier when there are front companies whose ownership is hard to trace. The United Church of Christ accused Mobil and other large oil companies of using such companies to get oil into Rhodesia in violation of United States and United Nations trade restrictions. A number of investigators started a "paper chase" to trace the source of this oil. No charge of breaking any formal rules has been fully substantiated, but the situation at least shows some major loopholes in those rules.

In the case of the illegal contributions of Gulf, even the board of directors and the chief executive officers were not aware of the magnitude, and perhaps not even the fact of the illegal corporate gifts. One subsidiary, Gulf Petroleum S.A., was passing about $400,000 a year to a largely dormant subsidiary, Bahamas Exploration Ltd., which in turn gave this in cash to the chief Washington lobbyist of Gulf for distribution. It took a combination of Securities and Exchange Committee investigations, stock holders suits, and internal investigation by the chief executive officers to uncover the magnitude of the illegal dealings.

Different Cultural Values and Practices

Bribery of foreign government officials by multinationals has often been justified on the basis that these bribes are the common and expected way of doing business in some countries, and in some ways amount to a tax. Indeed payoffs to top officials were preconditions for doing business in some countries like Paraguay (Gwirtzman, 1975). Gwirtzman details the pattern in some countries where civil-service salaries are set very low with the assumption that public employees could supplement their salaries by payoffs.

While these practices may be commonplace in some countries, and even enjoy a certain amount of acceptance or tolerance, the very fact they are kept secret shows they are not fully accepted. It may be a sense of false moral pride to look at the less developed countries and assume their sense of morality is less developed than ours. A combination of government regulations and unified action by multinationals in refusing such preconditions, might produce a more open and more truly competitive climate for business.

The Sheer Volume of Paperwork

When the SCM corporation brought a $1.8 billion antitrust suit against Xerox for developing "patent thickets" that effectively kept other companies out of the office copier business it took four years to get through the preliminary proceedings. And when the trial opened in the U.S. District Court in Hartford, Connecticut in 1977, Xerox took over a floor of a Hartford hotel for a staff of 50 lawyers and secretaries and hauled in six trailer-trucks of documents for them to use. SCM mounted a similar effort and won only a partial victory in a 14-month jury trial. Years of appeals are in prospect.

This sheer volume of paper may appear to be the opposite of secrecy. But its practical effect can be the same. People can be so overwhelmed with data that they do not see the basic issue or fail to see the forest through the trees. The issues themselves are complicated, and there is no guarantee that there is a simple or easy answer to every problem. But the argument about complexity can be overdone. At some point adding more details and nuances can obscure the basic issue. After a few months of sitting on the board of Gulf, Sister Jane Skully, a nun who is president of Carlow College in Pittsburgh, said, "It troubles me that there are no easy answers" (Bender, 1975). The next year, Sister Jane Skully was influential in seeking the resignation of four top executives from Gulf, including the chief executive officer, after the revelation of $12 million dollars given to politicians here and abroad (Robertson, 1976). It was a case of top management not being fully aware of the operations of middle managers, and then hiding the full dimension of the illegal payments from the board. As mentioned earlier, the Securities and Exchange Commission, stockholder investigations, and internal investigations in the company were all necessary to reveal the full dimension of the payoffs. The directors had to break the "veil of politeness" as Robertson called it, to challenge the management, and in particular to challenge the chief executive officer who was influential in getting many directors appointed to the board. The Gulf case shows the difficulty of both internal and external regulation in a complex organization of a major company.

The Shuttle Between Regulatory Agencies and Regulated Companies

Regulatory commissions that monitor banks, insurance companies, utilities, and other services require members with a certain amount of sophisticated knowledge. Often this knowledge is attainable only by working in companies in the field. There has been a continuous shuttle of people from industry to regulatory commission, and back to industry. There is increasing pressure to get people with other perspectives on these commissions, but that might not serve the interest of the public if they do not understand the business sufficiently. Some "public members," however, might force a simplification of reporting and accounting procedures and prevent corporate executives from using the "you don't understand fully" argument when it is not necessary.

Who Supplies Credit?

Fears that the United States is starting to experience a shortage of new investment capital are arising in some quarters. Yet the flow of credit and capital is one of the least understood processes in our economic system, and it is one of the areas in which it is most difficult to get information.

There is a rapid increase in the number of cross-border loans. General Motors may book a short-term $25 million loan with Citibank, but Citibank may register it in the Bahamas. It means less taxes for Citibank. Carlos M. Canal, executive vice president of Bankers Trust Company says this cross-border lending may account for the statistics on lagging domestic loan demand (Crittenden, 1977).

Representative Fernand St. Germain, (Democrat, Rhode Island), chairman of the House Banking, Currency and Housing Subcommittee on Financial Institutions claims, "We're flying blind in this area ... We don't have a reporting system that enables us to track the impact of overseas lending on our domestic economy."

Ownership of stocks and bonds are rather closely guarded secrets. When some questions arose about the propriety of the actions of the banks' actions during the New York City fiscal crisis, the banks refused any information about their ownership of city securities to the New York *Times,* and gave only incomplete and vague data to the U.S. House Subcommittee on Commerce, Consumer and Monetary Affairs (Jensen, 1975).

On the neighborhood level, there is a similar lack of knowledge about credit flow. Recent legislation has opened up some information on the amount of mortgage money available in neighborhoods. A report of the New York State Banking Department showed that the savings banks in the state invested three out of every four dollars outside the state, while New York City based savings banks invested 85 per cent of their deposits outside the city (Spiegel & Moritz, 1977).

A city or a neighborhood without available credit is doomed. Yet the people of the city had little precise knowledge of how much mortgage money was actually being supplied. Much information remains hidden. There is still no effective way of matching deposits from a neighborhood with mortgages in a neighborhood. And there is still no way of tracking the mortgage lending policies of the mortgage associations who handle three-quarters of FHA mortgages, and which sell off mortgage portfolios usually containing about a million dollars of home mortgages to large commercial banks, insurance companies, or the semipublic Federal National Mortgage Association or General National Mortgage Association.

The New York Public Interest Group cumulated the available information on mortgage lending from the seven Brooklyn savings banks. With the exception of one small bank, these banks gave less than one-fifth of their mortgages in New York

City and an even smaller percentage in Brooklyn. Vincent Quinn, president of the Brooklyn Savings Bank, criticized the report because the data was "insufficient" (Freiberg & Rosenthal, 1976). Quinn may be correct, but there is no way the public can judge with certainty because all the facts are not published. Some may argue that the state has no role in forcing release of data or regulating in this situation. Society will have to decide how important the credit availability question is and the role the government should have in monitoring it.

Governmental Advertising Restrictions

The government, in cooperation with trade groups, has imposed advertising restrictions on doctors, lawyers, optometrists, and similar groups. The purpose of this is to ensure quality and prevent excessive competition. But there is an assumption that the consumer is ill-equipped to make a judgment on the quality of the services, or eyeglassess, or whatever the product. Forty-four states, for instance, have complete or partial restrictions on eyeglass price advertising.

While the consumer might have difficulty judging quality in some of these trade groups, license procedures already give trade groups and government some control over quality. The restrictions could be a weapon against discounting and for keeping new competitors out of the market and a way of supporting unnecessarily high price levels. With the decision in 1977 by the U.S. Supreme Court to allow lawyers to advertise, and the staff recommendation of the Federal Trade Commission to allow eyeglass price advertising, many of these trade group restrictions are likely to disappear.

POLICY CONSIDERATIONS

We have reached a position where our largest 100 companies control close to 50 per cent of the assets and profits of American companies; and 500 companies control close to 80 per cent. About 85 per cent of our exports are done by 250 companies. Howard Perlmutter has predicted that by 1985, 300 global companies will control 80 per cent of all productive assets in the non-Communist world (Barnet and Muller, 1974).

These trends often provoke sharply divided arguments. Those who fear this corporate concentration often call for the breakup of the large companies on the nationalization of corporations. Those on the other side argue for the maintenance of the current system lest we have further recession or corporate instability. Meanwhile, a middle-ground alternative is ignored. This alternative would maintain most of the present structure, but bring more openness into corporate relations either by the mutual agreement of companies or by government norm. This alternative would concentrate on reducing knowledge monopolies or oligopolies. It would check that secrecy would not undermine the competitive system, and that corporations would not have undue control over experts and the frontiers of scientific research. The remainder of the paper will focus on conditions where the general public and business people ought to monitor the control of knowledge.

1. The first condition occurs when a few companies dominate a particular market. Cartels and oligopolies are usually defined in reference to a group of companies that can effectively control the supply and price of a product. But companies can also dominate a market by controlling access to scientific data, to resource availability, or to cost-profit data. This refers to more than patent rights. The United States has a long tradition of trying to balance the rights of inventors with the value of an open market. The new situation is where a few companies control teams of experts to the point where it is virtually impossible for another company to break into a field and assemble the necessary expertise.

Even when there is no collusion, it is likely that the companies have a very good idea of their competitors' product changes, resources, and research plans. It is the government and the public who are excluded from this knowledge. Blair (1976) talks of the "observance of complex formulae and mechanisms" by which there is "parallel, noncompetitive behavior" among the large oil companies. The control of knowledge provides a middle ground between outright collusion and a free, competitive market.

2. The second condition where special public monitoring is necessary is when the state itself becomes a partner by subsidizing or insuring some part of the productive process. This process of subsidization is so complex that it exists largely out of the public limelight. It is often so complicated that only the largest companies with vast legal and clerical staff and statehouse or Washington lobbies can participate.

This can occur with cash subsidies (such as payments to the sugar beet and cane growers to protect that industry), payments to companies for manpower training, or help to medical schools to pay for the training of doctors. It may be in the form of tax subsidies, such as the investment tax credit and the oil depletion allowances. It may be an insurance subsidy like the FHA insurance on home mortgages, or the federal coverage of high risk theft insurance contracts of private insurance companies.

This is not an argument either for or against the role of the government in such subsidies. But a policy alternative is to keep these subsidies as publicized as possible so that the public, the corporations, and the government are aware of real costs. A simplification of such laws could prevent these subsidization programs from serving only those companies with large legal and lobbying activities.

3. Tax laws seem to defy attempts at simplification. Recent reform attempts have only made the tax laws more complex, and most commentators agree that it will be difficult for President Jimmy Carter to deliver on his promise of simplifying tax laws.

One goal of government should be to ensure that taxation procedures remain just and operational. If multinational profit figures are a "hopeless maze" as Alan Greenspan described them, how can there be just and reasonable taxation? Open disclosure and uniform accountancy laws are essential in the taxation process.

Senator Russell Long, (Democrat, Lousiana) who heads the Senate Finance Committee, figures the Congress can simplify tax procedures for 96 percent of taxpayers, but that taxes would remain complicated for the remaining 4 percent because these taxpayers "want it complicated" (Clymer, 1977). These taxpayers are often in businesses where special consideration is necessary. But Long's reflection is that "they get too much of the best of things" in the process. The Congress often has to vote on special tax provisions for various businesses where it is difficult to distinguish between the reasonable demands of specialized industries and the opening up of loopholes where businesses twist complicated aspects of the law to avoid proper taxation.

4. A fourth condition where control of knowledge ought to be monitored is the situation where limited resources are at stake. Energy is obviously a national concern. Calls for a national energy policy are coming from all quarters. Yet government and corporate estimates of available resources differ considerably. The oil companies argue their right to hold information

on this as trade secrets. Eleven natural gas companies refused a Federal Trade Commission subpoena for reserve and production data when there was a question of whether gas companies were holding back supplies to take undue advantage of pricing regulations. The nation has a special stake in these resources to justify some disclosure laws.

5. A final condition where increased monitoring of knowledge control is necessary is in the multinationals. Without some controls, these companies could be answerable to no one. Sometimes, the laws of the home country of the multinationals can accomplish this goal in some measure. But some governmental scale, corresponding to the international scale of business, is necessary. When the Flatbush Community Planning Board refuses to let a storm sewer go through that section of Brooklyn (a sewer that Bensonhurst desperately needs to relieve street flooding every time it rains), it is obvious that the local planning board is not the proper political scale or level to make the final judgment.

With the multinationals growing in scale, some corresponding political scale will be necessary. It may be an agency of the United Nations, but it is more likely at the start to be part of or similar to the International Monetary Fund. Proposals have been aired for some international licensing agency for multinationals with some control on uniform accountancy procedures. It would be self-defeating if this agency were invisible as the IMF has been. But increased responsibility can help create visibility. When the IMF insisted that Great Britain reduce government spending and reduce the growth in its currency supply as conditions for a much needed $3.9 billion loan to support the pound, the IMF became very visible in England. The cost of a well-functioning multinational business system may be the sacrifice of some corporate and national autonomy. But if the international agency would first concentrate on uniform accountancy procedures and an open business climate, it might smooth the way for an efficient competitive system and prevent the need for price or supply controls, or other stringent governmental regulations.

References

Barnet, R. J., & Müller, R. E. *Global reach.* New York: Simon & Schuster, 1974.

Bender, M. Ethics experts wax inconclusive on bribery abroad. *New York Times,* August 3, 1975, page C1.

Blair, J. M. *The control of oil.* New York: Pantheon, 1976.

Clymer, A. Senator Long on tax reform. *New York Times,* June 9, 1977, page D1.

Coser, L. A. *The functions of social conflict.* New York: Free Press, 1956.

Coser, L. A. The dysfunctions of military secrecy. *Social Problems,* 1963, *11,* 13–32.

Crittenden, A. Growing Bahamian loan activity by U.S. banks Causes Concern. New York *Times,* March 3, 1977, page A53.

Freiberg, P., & Rosenthal, D. Big banks accused of Brooklyn redlining. New York *Post,* December 26, 1976, page 2.

Galbraith, J. K. *The new industrial state.* Boston: Houghton Mifflin, 1967.

Gwirtzman, M. S. Is bribery defensible? New York *Times Sunday Magazine,* October 5, 1975, 100–110.

Hersey, J. The President. New York *Times Sunday Magazine,* April 20, 1975, 30–121.

Hunter, F. *Community power structure.* Chapel Hill: The University of North Carolina Press, 1953.

Jensen, M. C. City's crisis finds banks at center of controversy. New York *Times,* July 29, 1975, page A18.

Lowry, R. P. Toward a sociology of secrecy and security systems. *Social Problems,* 1972, *19,* 437–450.

Miller, S. M. *Max Weber.* New York: Thomas Y. Crowell, 1963.

Mills, C. W. *The power elite.* New York: Oxford University Press, 1959.

Moore, W. E., & Tumin, M. E. Some social functions of ignorance. *American Sociological Review,* 1948, *14,* 787–795.

Nadel, M. Corporate secrecy and political accountability. *Public Administration Review,* 1975, *35,* 14–23.

Roberts, S. V. Watergate Leaves Scars on Young Nixon Loyalist. New York *Times,* August 5, 1973, p. 40.

Robertson, W. The directors woke up too late at Gulf. *Fortune,* 1976, *93,* 126 ff.

Rourke, F. E. A symposium on administrative secrecy: A comparative perspective. *Public Administration Review,* 1975, *35,* 1–2.

Shils, E. A. *The torment of secrecy.* New York: Free Press, 1956.

Spiegal, C., & Moritz, O. State sees redlining in banks study. *New York Daily News,* May 11, 1977, page 3.

Terkel, S. *Reflections on a Course in Ethics. Harpers,* 1973, *247,* 59–72.

Unit 5

Bureaucratic Secrecy

Introduction

The secrecy/security systems used by large-scale political organizations (political bureaucracies), like those of corporations discussed in Unit IV, are developed in the belief that potential rivals or "enemies," either within or outside such mass organizations, could, if privy to certain covert information, prevent these bureaucracies from attaining their goals or fulfilling their missions. But information control is never, at best, totally successful. Thus secrets are leaked, resulting in political embarrassment, legal consequences, or economic disadvantages to the officials or personnel of such bureaucracies. Such leaks merely reinforce the attitudes of official distrust of more openness toward outsiders, thereby perpetuating the secrecy/security systems. The fear-distrust-secrecy-leaks-more distrust-more secrecy syndrome is, indeed, self-perpetuating.

In a rapidly changing political arena, the bureaucratic leadership may have great difficulty in determining who poses political threats as well as the nature of such threats to their secrecy/security systems. In highly competitive political situations, all organizations restrict information flow. To predict events in such a hostile political arena and thereby to be able to control that environment, organizations must learn as much as possible about the secrets of their rivals. Officials may place little trust in their overt intelligence-gathering activities because the security systems of their enemies conceal vital information. Overt intelligence operations must be supplemented with covert intelligence activities (espionage). But since knowledge about such covert operations must be kept secret from opponents, internal security must operate to guard against leaks.

In this unit, Patricia E. Erickson and James Flynn discuss the organizational strategies employed by a special police unit to control the activities of a political protest group by maintaining secrecy about the plans of the special unit but, at the same time, acquiring vital information about the protesters through espionage. Their report is based on their research concerning the police operations at the 1976 Republican National Convention at Kansas City, Missouri. It was at this convention that the local police faced the task of controlling a large political protest group. In handling this mass protest the police developed a paramilitary organization that monitored and controlled the activities of the protesters. Only a limited number of police officials were privy to the security plan until it was put into operation at the convention. The protesters themselves, unaware of the police operations because they were secret, found great difficulty in dealing or counteracting the police's secret tactics.

Through secret television and photographic surveillance, intelligence teams and undercover agents as well as community relations staff members, who maintained a liaison between demonstrators and police, the paramilitary unit was able to control protesters. The secrecy surrounding police motives, intentions, and strategies created confusion among the protesters, diverting much of their time and energy away from political protest itself to negotiating with the police.

Thus, the Kansas City police used their secret paramilitary operations as a means to gain control over potentially disruptive events and to contain them. The police employment of organizational secrecy for this purpose is similar to such strategies used by any organization that perceives the usefulness of secrecy as a device to attain its ends by making unpredictable environment more predictable and, thus, controllable.

The secrecy/security systems of our modern intelligence organizations operate for just this purpose. In the world arena, the political rivalries among nation-states generate an environment within which espionage becomes a vital means by which opponents acquire information allowing them to predict the actions of their rivals, enemies, yes, even allies and therefore have more control over their actions or at least to counteract any threats from any of these sources. By restricting the flow of strategic information to rivals and by attempting to obtain political or military secrets from its enemies, the modern state, through its intelligence operations, tries to understand, predict, control, and counteract the rapidly changing events within the international community of which it is a part.

While differing in their specific goals and functions, intelligence organizations share, according to Fred M. Kaiser, certain common characteristics. The conduct of members of the intelligence community is governed by certain common norms including obedience, discipline, dedication, and the defense of intelligence secrecy and internal security. There seems a greater emphasis on the norms of secrecy in the intelligence community than within the private corporation. However, the range of security devices is similar to those employed by large-scale business corporations or government bureaucracies, though more systematically employed: compartmentalization (rules that limit an intelligence employee's access to classified documents and information unless he or she can adequately establish "need-to-know"), security checks and elaborate clearance procedures, and the use of cryptonyms in documents to indicate personnel, projects, and locations. The effectiveness of such security systems is indicated by the fact that the U.S. intelligence community was able to keep even their illegal activities secret for several decades.

Security has also been enhanced by the strong allegiance and loyalty members develop for their respective intelligence agency. This strong communal identity is the result of many factors, including the sense that members have in the supreme importance of their mission in protecting national security. Moreover, most intelligence employees, unlike those in private industry, by nature of their profession have limited ties with the local communities in which they live. Thus, their social activity, their status, as well as their opportunities for career development, are all tied to the intelligence community almost exclusively. Their profession requires them to maintain strict anonymity about their job and total confidentiality about their job assignments. Thus, they must seek their emotional satisfaction from within the intelligence community itself, rather than outside it.

While business bureaucracies try to promote employee loyalty, this is even of more crucial concern to the intelligence community. Trainees are given elaborate and extensive indoctrination. Part of the selection and training process includes polygraph tests to determine the recruit's total honesty and to assure employers that no aspect of his or her private life is unknown to them.

A consideration of the above factors may suggest an explanation as to how, of all the large-scale bureaucracies, the intelligence agency, whatever its goals, has been able to maintain a sense of loyalty and common mission among its members quite similar to that of the secret society.

The success of bureaucratic secrecy/security systems may be deceptive. Often they plant the seeds of their own destruction. Ritchie P. Lowry's paper discusses the dysfunctional aspects of secrecy in a government agency, the Special Operations Research Office, the U.S. army think tank. Certain officials within this agency who were privy to secret information often leaked it to other officials to enhance their own position with the organization. Secrecy also operated to undermine proper and efficient functioning of the agency by promoting the protection of useless information (classified Top Secret and so forth) and by enabling employees to hide incompetent performances. The irrational use of secrecy classification by low level employees blocked the flow of useful information to various divisions within the organization as well as up and down the agency hierarchy. And because of secrecy requirements, agency policy, whether good or bad, was never given a systematic evaluation by appropriate officials.

However well bureaucratic secrecy enables mass organizations to gain control over the complex events in their national or international environments, a high price is paid for such security not only by the organizations themselves but by the citizens they serve and protect. Bureaucratic secrecy not only encourages deception and illegal acts for purposes of political expediency but also undermines efficient government by encouraging employees to cover up mistakes and officials to initiate programs that serve personal or political interests rather than that of the public. Secrecy also generates a citizen distrust of government that prevents the state from generating public support for even worthwhile programs.

11

Secrecy as an Organizational Control Strategy: Police Planning for a National Political Convention[1]

Patricia E. Erickson
University of Missouri—Kansas City

James Flynn
University of Kansas

More than 75 years ago Georg Simmel examined the role of secrecy in society (Wolff, 1950). For Simmel, secrecy was a phenomenon that merited careful analysis within the field of sociology because it permeated almost every dimension of social reality. Yet secrecy has rarely received attention within the field of complex organizations. Theoretical perspectives do not include it as a major construct useful for understanding organizational behavior. Research that examines its role in organizational settings is almost nonexistent. (For some exceptions, see Moore, 1962; Wilensky, 1967; Zander, 1977.) Recently there has emerged a renewed interest in the topic of secrecy. This interest is partially a result of the revelation of the covert activities of American governmental organizations. Predominately

---

[1] Partial support for this research was obtained through an L.E.A.A. grant, "Evaluation of the 1976 Republican National Convention," awarded to Midwest Research Institute. Patricia E. Erickson and James Flynn were employed as consultants to Midwest Research Institute during the grant period. An earlier version of this paper was presented at the 72nd annual meeting of the American Sociological Association.

written from a social problems orientation, these works explore issues involved in the general area of organizational deviance (Staw & Szwajkowski, 1975; Douglas & Johnson, 1977; Ermann & Lundman, 1978; Shrager & Short, 1978), and the special topic of secrecy (Lowry, 1972; Manning, 1977; Wilsnack, 1977; Draghici, 1977; Erickson & Kukuk, 1977). Secrecy is therefore likely to be examined in terms of a deviant form of organizational behavior; it is the illegal and inappropriate use of secrecy that is emphasized. Within the field of complex organizations, the role of secrecy is still ignored in both theory and research.

The intent of this paper is to examine the role of secrecy in complex organizations. The focus of the paper is on providing theoretical and empirical support for the prevalence and importance of secrecy as an organizational control strategy. Using data gathered at the 1976 Republican National Convention, secrecy will be received as an organizational process utilized to gain control over others; the others can be members of one's organization or segments of the environment.

A DISTRUST PERSPECTIVE

Traditionally, organizations have been viewed as units, subsystems, or parts that are more or less integrated toward the achievement of a set of goals. Usually such orientations have emphasized the harmonious arrangement of the parts either by arguing that such an arrangement is necessary for organizational effectiveness (Weber, 1947; Parsons, 1956; Price, 1968) or else prescribing harmony for organizational health (Likert, 1967; Argyris, 1972). Criticism of this view has come from diverse sources. Those whose work largely remains within this tradition have discussed problems with the goal orientation paradigm (Perrow, 1961; Simon, 1974; Warriner, 1965; Yuchtman & Seashore, 1967; Gross, 1969; Georgiou, 1973), the complex nature of member commitment (Homans, 1974; Blau, 1964; Warren, 1968; Etzioni, 1975), and the priority of other variables for explaining organizational effectiveness (Woodward, 1965; Perrow, 1967). Outside this tradition conflict theorists have emphasized power differentials, competition for scarce and desired resources, and the resulting conflict between individuals and groups in organizations (Coser, 1967; Dahrendorf, 1968; Corwin, 1970; Heydebrand, 1977). Frequently, however, the manifestation of conflict is seen as dissipating or reducing tension (for an alternative explanation see

Singelmann, 1978) and structural arrangements are often advocated for resolution of conflict before escalation threatens organizational stability (Lawrence & Lorsch, 1967).

Understanding the role of secrecy rests on viewing organizations from a somewhat different vantage point. Secrecy rests on a premise of distrust; at its core it represents judgments about others in terms of their lack of trustworthiness with certain information. Keeping secrets from others implies that one does not trust them to have information that one has; gathering information on others through covert means implies that one does not trust them to give one openly complete or accurate information. Largely the distrust view stems from fear. The fear stems from the possible reaction of others if certain information were known by them; that is, how this information would be utilized by them. This fear may take a variety of forms. One may fear public embarrassment, legal action, or in the case of trade secrets, fear that disclosure would result in other organizations gaining a competitive edge. It is distrusting the norm of "fair play."

The utilization of secrecy in organizations does not result in a harmonious arrangement of parts nor is it a mechanism for tension reduction; the possibility of discovery through disclosures, or leaks, is always present. Rather tension is below the surface and the image of harmony that may be observed can be disrupted at any moment. While secrecy may be grounded in a past history of empirical consequences (e.g., past embarrassment, legal action, unfair play) the use of secrecy tends to be reinforcing and self-perpetuating. Lowry's (1972) accounts are illustrative, suggesting that intelligence gathering can reach paranoia proportions; no one is to be trusted and every bit of information is judged to be valuable and hence classified as secret.

Yet it is also clear that all organizations do not engage in the same levels of secrecy and that its use by some organizations may be grounded in "accurate" assessments of what is valued information and who cannot be trusted. It is therefore important to examine the conditions that differentiate the extent to which organizations rely on secrecy and how organizations arrive at decisions on what information should be kept secret.

If secrecy rests on a distrust view of others, then others are perceived as potential enemies. But frequently organizations may have great difficulty deciding "Who are the enemies?" "How many are there?" "When will they act?" and "What do they want?" In other words, organizations lack information about the predictability of others who are to be potentially feared. For members of an organization the norms concerning presentation of self in organizational settings may be unclear or lacking; hence a narrow or restrictive image is given with much information about self kept private. In the environmental arena, organizations interacting in a turbulent field may find that environmental conditions change so rapidly and are so complex that little predictability about trustworthiness of others or valued information is possible. Friends of today may be the enemies of tomorrow; unimportant information can become critical information. Hence the entire environmental arena may become suspect and each bit of organizational information may be scrutinized for its potential use by others.

The reinforcing and self-perpetuating nature of secrecy follows from this discussion. If organizational members present restricted views of self, then bits of nonroutine information disclosed about self can serve to prove the rule of trusting no one. Revealing to an organizational confidant decisions about budgets, personnel reassignments, organizational restructuring only to have such information leaked to others results in the intensification of secrecy since "even friends cannot be trusted." Yet in such a structure, leaking information is highly probably since the acquisition of nonroutine information about others will almost certainly confer on one esteem when revealed to others. The same principle applies to the environmental arena; to engage in a cooperative strategy with another organization only to find that the information given to them has been "misused" results in the intensification of secrecy.

In a more inclusive context, norms of distrust based on fear are also self-perpetuating because in such structures others will also operate under these norms. For organizational members this means that others present a restrictive view of self; in the relevant environmental field other organizations present a restrictive image. These elements sustain the necessity for secrecy and the ultimate paradox in such structures is that when one claims to have revealed all information, that claim may not be trusted.

POLICE PLANNING FOR A NATIONAL POLITICAL CONVENTION

The intent in this section is to illustrate the relationship between environmental change and organizational secrecy by examining police planning for a national political convention. It will be argued that the changes introduced into the environment during the convention period were perceived by members of the police department as substantially altering the condition of their relevant environment. The environment was perceived to be potentially highly uncertain; segments of the environment were viewed as elements to distrust because of the potential action these elements could undertake during the convention period. In order to gain control over these anticipated changes, police engaged in an elaborate planning process and chose secrecy as a major strategy for dealing with an uncertain environment.

BACKGROUND

The data presented were collected as part of an evaluation research project conducted to access police security for the 1976 Republican National Convention. This was one of the special conditions attached to a $2.6 million grant from the Law Enforcement Assistance Administration (LEAA) to the Kansas City, Missouri, Police Department to help defray planning and operating costs incurred by metropolitan police departments in the security effort (Midwest Research Institute, 1977).

Those assigned to this security evaluation team were screened by the Kansas City, Missouri, Police Department (KCPD) and issued identification that allowed them access to police facilities, records and areas of activity before, during, and after the convention period. The performance of police departments involved in policing and security was evaluated in the most extensive study ever attempted during a national political convention. In contrast, the voluminous literature on Chicago 1968 and Miami 1972 were reconstructions done after the fact. In the case of the official report on Miami, the evaluation was done a year after the convention took place.

Four different types of data sources were utilized for this evaluation. First, members of the evaluation team served as on-site observers during the convention period. Observers were assigned specific areas of observation (e.g., the operation of the command posts, demonstration groups, criminal justice procedures). Twenty-eight on-site observers were utilized during the convention period, and their field notes were utilized as a major basis for the evaluation.

Second, members of the MRI evaluation team interviewed

commanders and staff of the Kansas City, Missouri, Police Department (KCPD) before, during and after the convention. Additional interviews were conducted with other metropolitan, state, and federal law enforcement agencies that interfaced with this police department during the convention.

Third, the written records of the police department relevant to security were reviewed and analyzed. These records included the documents developed during the planning process, special reports, and minutes of meetings.

Fourth, a chronology to the convention was constructed by utilizing the logs kept by KCPD during the convention, analyzing video tapes of media coverage of the convention by the three networks and abstracting newspaper articles relevant to the convention.

The following discussion of secrecy will rely on newspaper accounts, formal documents and field notes.

ANTICIPATED ENVIRONMENTAL UNCERTAINITY

The great majority of work done by officers of a police department involves a response to the actions and reactions of individuals and small ad hoc groups whose behavior requires immediate on the spot action. Recent typical discussions of police organization and administration (More, 1975; Gourley, 1970) describe police departments as structures that are organized to deal with individual incidents.

The added responsibility of dealing with a national political convention introduces changes into the environment of a police department and more significantly introduces changes in the nature and intensity of environmental uncertainty. On the surface, the environmental changes reflect a need for police departments to deal with large crowds made up of demonstrators, spectators, delegates, media personnel, political partisans, observers, and other law enforcement agencies. These environmental elements make a political convention different in kind from other types of conventions a police department handles in the normal course of their work. In the case of Kansas City, other conventions attracted corwds at least as large as those present for the 1976 Republican National Convention. In July 1976, a month before the Republican National Convention assembled, the national convention of Shriners drew between 65,000 and 75,000 people to Kansas City. The annual convention of the Future Farmers of America involves 50,000 or more.

While these conventions introduce changes into the environment, they did not introduce changes in the nature and intensity of environmental uncertainty.

There is one noteworthy difference between the normal convention and a political convention that can explain why a police department would perceive its environment during a political convention as different in terms of the nature and intensity of uncertainty. Politics involves organized groups in conflict, or at least in competition for control of the economic, administrative, legislative, or social institutions. As long as that conflict is contained within the organization of the political party, the police can treat a political convention much like any other. But the events of Chicago 1968 and Miami 1972 brought opposition groups of political activists into action outside the formal party structure. Demonstrators gathered at the location of the major political conventions in order to display their opposition to the prevailing governmental policies. The party convention of the incumbent President became the primary target of demonstrations.

For the police these situations were confusing. Instead of dealing with individual actions they were suddenly dealing with group actions, often large-scale groups. And while these groups may not have been as tightly organized as civil authorities, they were unified in terms of their goals and methods to the extent that they became a functioning group. The police response to these groups resulted in retrospective charges of a "police riot" in Chicago and "police state tactics" in Miami.

Essentially then, the environment of the police department changes in terms of the nature and intensity of uncertainty because of the possibility of oppositional group activity that could disrupt the activities of the local community in which the convention is being held and the political processes that are occurring in the community. The responsibility for controlling this political activity lies primarily with the local police department.

In the case of the 1976 Republican National Convention, officials of the police department clearly recognized that a national political convention could change the nature and intensity of uncertainty in their environment. Soon after Kansas City was chosen as the site for the convention, officials of the police department sought financial support from the federal government and manpower assistance for other local law enforcement agencies (The Kansas City *Times,* November 12, 1975). These types of support were viewed as necessary for an effective handling of security during this political convention. The need for these kinds of support was linked specifically to the potential for oppositional group activity. Three months after Kansas City was chosen as the site for the convention, the chief of police warned citizens of the community that terrorists might infiltrate Kansas City during the convention using tactics reminiscent of the 1968 and 1972 political conventions. In the same speech, the chief of police warned that the current Senate Intelligence hearings into allegedly illegal activities of the FBI might inhibit the FBI's work in investigating the very revolutionaries who might be drawn to Kansas City (The Kansas City *Times,* December 4, 1975). A week later, the chief of police spoke of "radical troublemakers" he feared would descend on the city during the convention period (The Kansas City *Times,* December 10, 1975). A month later, when federal financial assistance was problematic, the chief of police again reiterated the importance of federal financial support arguing that "Since 1972 demonstrators have moved from the practice of dissent to violence." (The Kansas City *Times,* January 15, 1976). A week later suburban police departments met with the Kansas City, Missouri, police chief to discuss the manner in which their departments could be of assistance during the convention (The Kansas City *Star,* January 27, 1976). Two months later, final congressional approval was given for a $2.6 million grant to be given to the police department for security planning and implementation (The Kansas City *Times,* April 2, 1976).

Yet while public statements made by police officials made claims to the possibility of a volatile, disruptive, and violent environment during the convention, intelligence information gathered by the Law Enforcement Intelligence Unit (LEIU) of the police department during the preconvention planning period revealed a somewhat different picture about the type of environment that the police could expect during the convention.

The KCPD Law Enforcement Intelligence Unit in September 1975 began gathering information of potential use in planning and operations during the 1976 Republican National Convention. A formal national network of police intelligence units, federal agencies, local law enforcement agencies, and newspaper clippings were used as information sources. Hundreds of intelligence reports and newspaper articles were processed during the preconvention planning period. In constrast the public statements issued by the KCPD chief of police about the potential for terrorism at the convention, the KCPD Law Enforcement Intelligence Unit has little indication of major demonstrator group activity or terrorism. Originally, the LEIU commander was to meet weekly for briefings with the KCPD convention planning task force. Because little information was being developed on demonstrator group or terrorist activity, these meetings became sporadic. To compensate, the convention planning task force collected information from some of the same sources as the LEIU, but still did not produce any information of potential terrorist or demonstrator activity (The Kansas City, Missouri, Police Department, 1976a).

On the surface it would appear that the intelligence information gathered should have acted as a mechanism to reduce concerns of the police department about the possibility of a disruptive, volatile convention. Yet it is apparent that while intelligence information indicated that no evidence had been found about such plans, public statements made by the police chief stressed the possibility of such activities. In examining the public statements made, it is important to note that the evidence used by the police chief were cases and generalizations about the past occurrence of such events. These "historical accounts" emphasized the unpredictable and unanticipated occurrence of such activities. Chicago 1968 was not anticipated; police in Miami 1972 did not know how large or volatile demonstrations would be. The example of terrorism only serves to reinforce the unpredictable nature of such events. Current intelligence information was received as an insufficient measure of events which might occur in the future because of the perception that disruptive elements cannot be totally predicted. In fact, the lack of intelligence information seemed to heighten concern; instead of viewing such information as valid, police began to wonder whether they had not been able to gather all relevant information. Indeed just prior to the convention, rumors surfaced among several members of the police department indicating that the "Legionnaire's Disease" was a precessor of a large-scale plan to be implemented in Kansas City.[2]

[2]What came to be known as the "Legionnaire's Disease" occured in Philadelphia shortly before the convention. At the time of the convention, no cause for the illnesses and deaths had been found. Water contamination was a possibility being investigated, as was food poisoning, gas, etc. The police often expressed an anxiety about what might happen in Kansas City because it was the Bicentennial year; they felt that some underground group must be planning something. The "mysterious" illnesses and deaths in Philadelphia were viewed with extreme caution by some police—they wondered whether this might be a precursor to a large-scale plan to be implemented in Kansas City.

Hence the recent history of protest activities served to create a set of distrust norms about the certain elements in the environment. These elements were viewed as unpredictable; information gathered through rational techniques (intelligence) was viewed as an insufficient measure about the future moves of such elements. In a sense, the police department planned a "what if" strategy and organized for the convention in such a way as to be prepared for the possibility of volatile, disruptive elements in the environment.

A PARAMILITARY ORGANIZATIONAL STRUCTURE

Nine months prior to the convention, members of the police department began to prepare for the event. Involved in the planning process were meetings with local, state, and federal law enforcement agencies to coordinate their convention efforts, setting up facilities and equipment to be used during the convention period and training and assignment of the KCPD personnel for the convention period. Planning was undertaken primarily by six members of the police department designated as the Convention Planning Task Force.

A major outcome of the planning process was the development of a 300-page security plan to be implemented during the convention period (The Kansas City, Missouri, Police Department 1976b). The security plan specified in detail the organizational structure of the police department for the convention period. This structure was significantly different from the normal organization of this police department. See Figures 11.1 and 11.2. The new organizational structure did not replace the normal organizational structure but existed in addition to normal police operations.

This new organizational structure was centralized and coordinated through the establishment of a Convention Command Post. The Convention Planning Task Force designed the philosophy and mission of the Convention Planning Task Force as a coordinating body or minipolice department with the major responsibility for policing and security of the 1976 Republican National Convention (The Midwest Research Institute, 1977). The Command Post physically housed the commander of convention security, the operations staff, and the primary functional commanders represented in the convention organizational structure. In addition to this Central Command Post, two additional smaller units were established inside and outside the convention arena.

Embedded within this new organizational structure was an intensification of the use of secrecy. The security plan itself was kept secret from most members of the police department until two weeks before the convention. A limited number of copies were printed, each copy was numbered, and each police officer who received a copy was advised to keep it in a secure area. The underlying assumption was that early revelation of security plans would pose a risk of those plans being revelaed to certain segments of the environment; in this case, other police officers were viewed as potentially untrustworthy. Assigning numbers to each copy distributed served as an additional guarantee against disclosing plans since "lost" copies could be traced to the guilty party.

While the security plan as a whole was viewed as information to be kept secret from certain segments of the environment, the police department relied on several different types of secret strategies to control potentially disruptive elements. These secret strategies can be illustrated by a brief examination of the equipment and facilities of the Command Post and the special functional assignments of personnel for the convention period.

The Central Command Post was located in a building that originally was a Shrine temple. Access to the Command Post was limited to those individuals who had special police clearance. The layout of the Command Post is illustrated in Figure 11.3 Included among its features are a large conference area for briefings and coordination meetings. A room just off the conference area was set up as a communication center to handle all convention-related communications and closed-circuit television equipment. The closed-circuit television monitors included remote controls to change angle, direction, and zoom of four cameras located on or overlooking the convention arena. The large office area contained a set of closed-circuit television monitors, commercial television to monitor convention arena activities, telephone message switching instruments, and incident files. Next door was a room equipped with large city-area maps, motorcade movement charts, a radio speaker, closed-circuit television monitors, commercial television, and an intercom to the dispatchers. The intelligence center was contained as a secure area and was the focal point for all intelligence reaching the Command Post. See Figure 11.4. The room was equipped with charts and bulletin boards and a computer terminal tied to such data bases as NCIC.

Certain personnel in the police department were given specific assignments relative to oppositional group activity. Pho-

Figure 11.1 Kansas City, Missouri, Police Department Organizational Structure

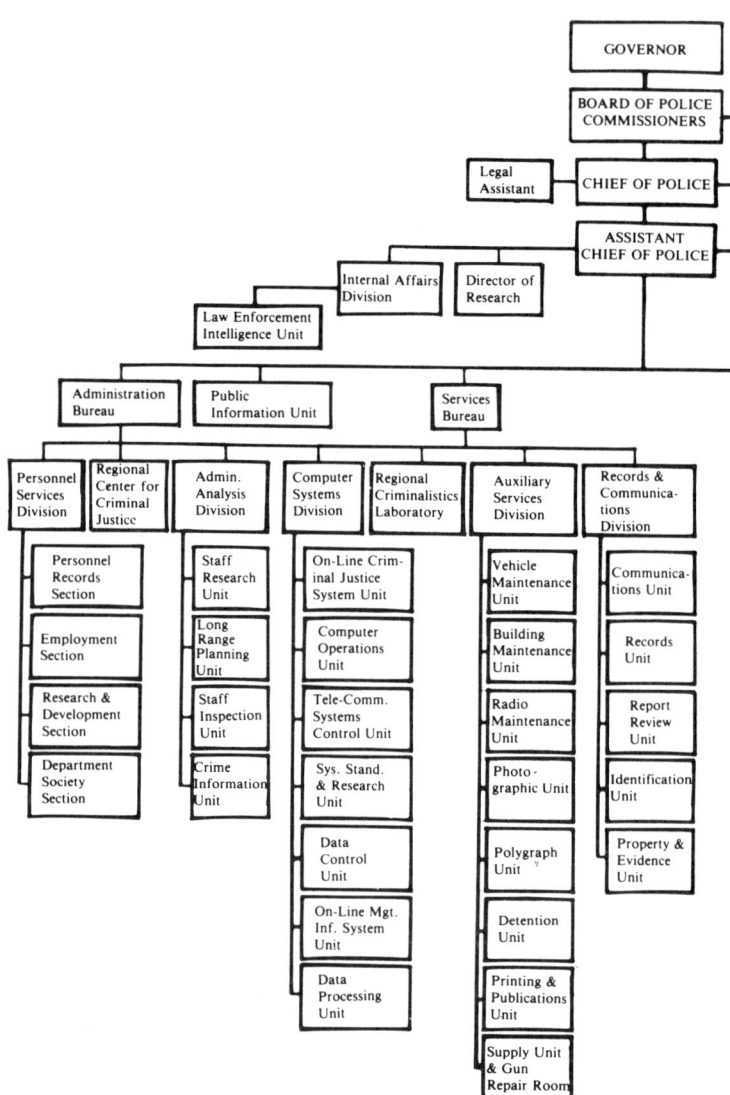

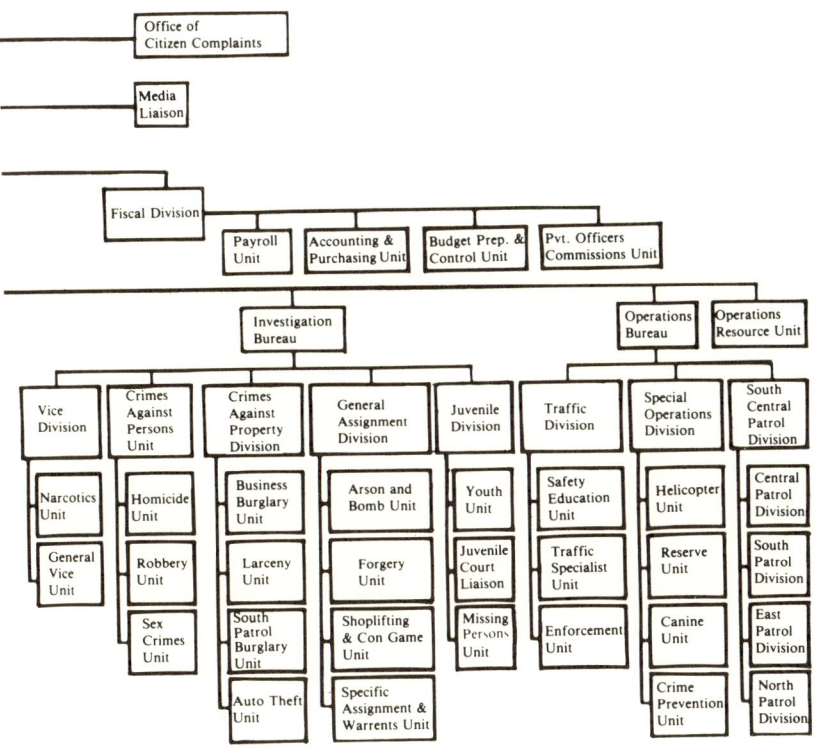

Figure 11.2 Organizational Chart for Police Security/Republican National Convention

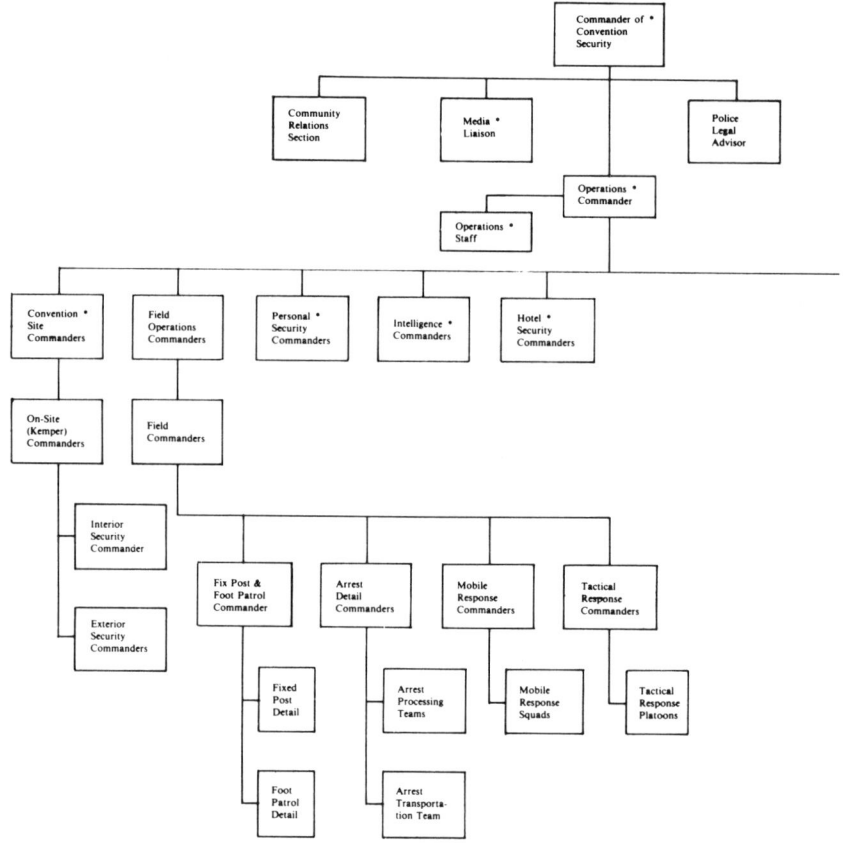

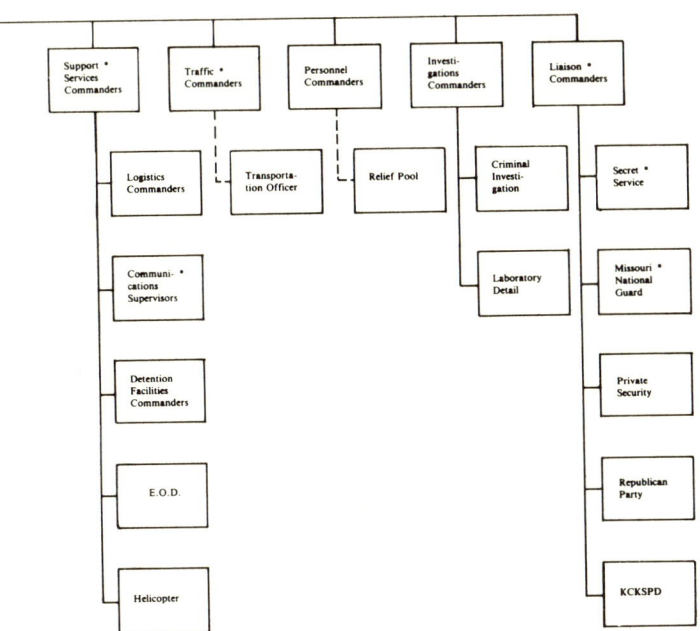

Figure 11.3   Command Post

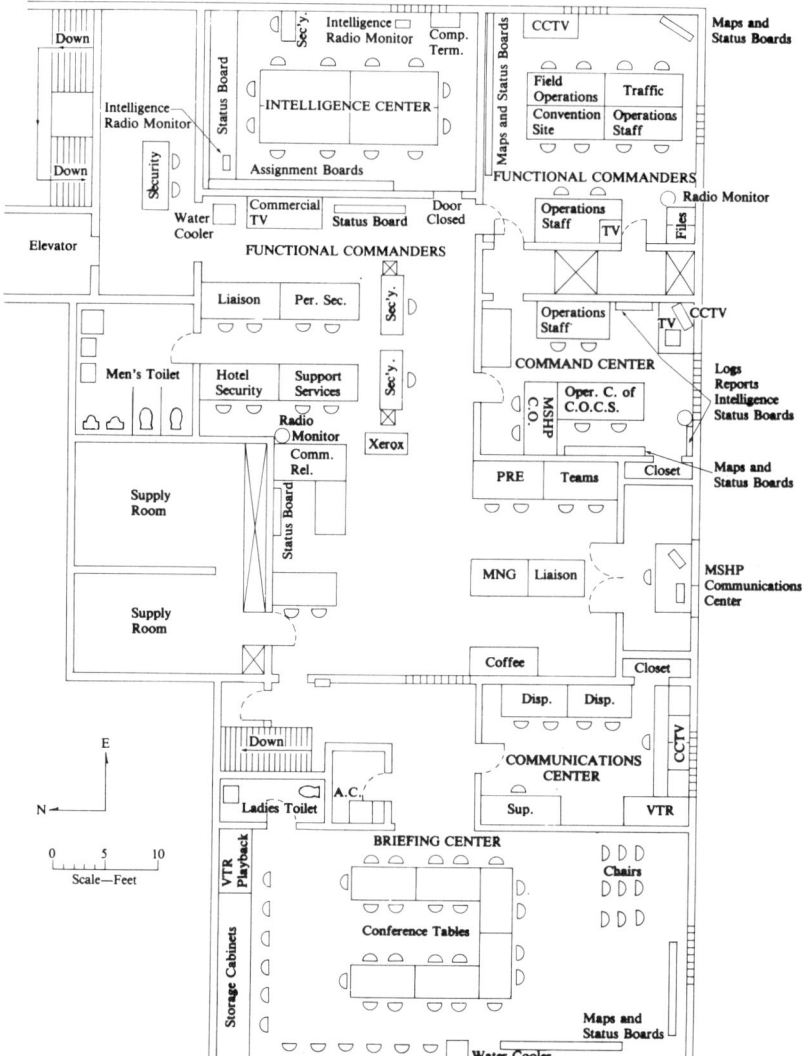

Figure 11.4 KCPD Intelligence Center

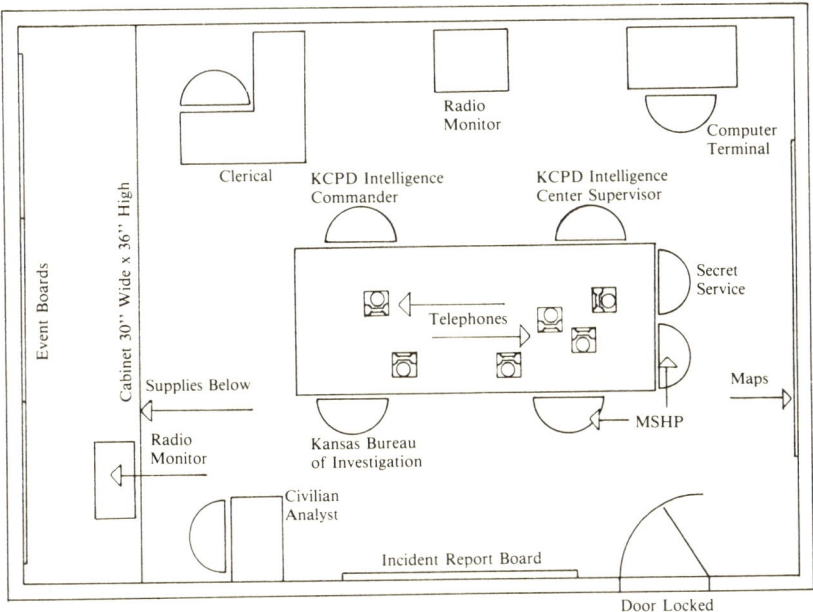

tography Recording Event (PRE) teams were assigned to photograph and videotape major activities and events of the convention. Working in two-man teams, and dressed in civilian clothing, they largely photographed and videotaped the activities of demonstration groups. The intelligence unit, of course, gathered both strategic and tactical information on groups that were perceived to have a known intent to disrupt the convention. However, the intelligence unit also comprised a field intelligence staff, which consisted of Mobile Intelligence Supervisory teams, Scout Car teams, Hotel Intelligence teams, and undercover personnel. The intelligence field personnel operated on a private radio frequency that was not dispatched through the convention communications center.

A Community Relations Staff (CRS) was also utilized for the convention as a mechanism for maintaining liaison with demonstrators and other groups. Finally the function of field operations during the convention was to respond to confrontations. A mobile response element responded to small group demonstrations or confrontations. The tactical response unit comprised five platoons and their major responsibility was to respond to large demonstration situations.

This elaborate planning and restructuring of the police department for the convention period was reflective of police perception about the nature and intensity of uncertainty in their environment. Based on the events of the last two national conventions, police expected demonstrators to be organized into groups and chose the employment of semimilitary tactics to deal with this possibility. As Drummond points out, "the paramilitary characteristics of police remains because police are uniformed so as to be readily identifiable" and because the police "return to a military form of organization during circumstances of emergency" (Drummond, 1976). In other words, the police culture is one with paramilitary values that responds to emergency situations (the perception of an uncertain environment) by organizing along military lines. In these situations, elements of the environment are viewed as untrustworthy and embedded within the paramilitary structure was an intense reliance on secrecy as a major strategy for control.

IMPLICATIONS

In this paper, secrecy has been viewed as an organizational strategy utilized to gain control over others. In the illustration given, the changes in the nature and intensity of the environment posed by a national political convention resulted in the restructuring of a police department along paramilitary lines. Members of the police department perceived segments of the environment as elements to distrust because of the potential disruptive set of actions these elements could undertake during the convention. These elements were perceived as organized into groups calling for a paramilitary response on the part of police. Secrecy became a major organizational planning strategy utilized by this police department to gain control over oppositional group activity.

While this illustration of secrecy may be viewed as an atypical organizational example, the use of organizational secrecy as a strategy for control appears to be fairly common as witnessed by popular news accounts of its use in government and corporate structures. If we extrapolate from the case just given to a set of generalizable conditions, the rationale for the rise and increased reliance on organizational secrecy becomes clear. Secrecy becomes a strategy for control when elements of the environment are perceived to be organized in such a fashion as to potentially subvert one's aims. In such settings, the use of overt power plays is not chosen as a control strategy either because the rules forbid it and these rules can be enforced (e.g., governmental interference) or too much risk taking (the option of failure) is at stake. In the case of the 1976 political convention, the memory of Chicago was of extreme importance for police planning strategies. To organize along lines of anticipating individual incidents and not anticipate group action, led to confrontation. The effect, in the case of Chicago, was a loss of control for police both during the time of confrontation and in terms of their organizational image thereafter. The police action was reactive; it was in response to events not anticipated. The confusion and brutalization during the convention and the moralistic judgments leveled at this police department afterward served as the guiding factor for police planning during the 1976 Republican Convention. This does not mean that police planning for the 1976 convention should not be moralistically judged by those whose concern centers on issues such as the actions of social control agents and the increasing reliance on secrecy by these agents. The use of the undercover agent, PRE-teams, and electronic surveillance equipment can certainly be judged as important issues for those concerned with First Amendment rights and protection of privacy. In fact, perhaps a major point that should be considered in looking at the future of organizations in industrial or postindustrial societies, is the extent to which sophistication at control may make certain styles of control outdated. Technological advancements (e.g., surveillance equipment) and the increasing knowledge base of organizational practitioners (e.g., simulation games, manipulation strategies) may lead to a reliance on strategies of control that cannot be detected by examining an organizational chart or analyzing the set of organizational inducements. The visible action an organization undertakes may only be the "tip of the iceberg"; underneath this manifest world may lie a world of action in need of further sociological investigation.

References

Argyris, C. *The applicability of organizational sociology.* Cambridge, England; University Press, 1972.

Blau, P. *Exchange and power in social life.* New York: Wiley, 1964.

Corwin, R. *Militant professionalism.* New York: Appleton-Century-Crofts, 1970.

Coser, L. *Continuities in the study of social conflict.* New York: Free Press, 1967.

Dahrendorf, R. *Essays in the theory of society.* Stanford, Calif.: Stanford University Press, 1968.

Douglas, J., & Johnson, J. *Official Deviance: Readings in malfeasance, misfeasance and other forms of corruption.* Philadelphia: Lippincott, 1977.

Draghici, S. *Secret services before the fifteenth century A.D.* Paper presented at the 77th annual meeting of the American Sociological Association, Chicago, 1977.

Drummond, D. *The police culture.* Beverly Hills, Calif.: Sage Publications, 1976.

Erickson, P., & Kukuk, C. *Organizational secrecy and environmental control: Police operations at the 1976 Republican National Convention.* Paper presented at the 77th annual meeting of the American Sociological Association, Chicago, 1977.

Ermann, M., & Lundman, R. *Corporate and governmental deviance: Problems of organizational behavior in contemporary society.* New York: Oxford University Press, 1978.

Etzioni, A. *A comparative analysis of complex organizations.* New York: Free Press, 1975.

Georgiou, P. The goal paradigm and notes toward a counter paradigm. *Administrative Science Quarterly.* September 1973, *18,* 291–310.

Gourley, G. D. *Effective Municipal Police Organization.* Beverly Hills: Glencoe Press, 1970.

Gross, E. The definition of organizational goals. *British Journal of Sociology.* September 1969, *20,* 277–294.

Heydebrand, W. Organizational contradictions in public bureaucracies: Toward a Marxian theory of organizations. *The Sociological Quarterly,* Fall, 1977, *18,* 83–107.

Homans, G. *Social behavior: Its elementary forms.* New York: Harcourt Brace Jovanovich, 1974.

Kansas City Missouri Police Department. *Planning Log for the 1976 Republican National Convention.* 1976.(a)

Kansas City Missouri Police Department. *Security Plan for Policing and Security at the 1976 Republican National Convention.* 1976.(b)

Kansas City *Star.* January 27, 1976; March 3, 1976.

Kansas City *Times,* November, 12, 1975; December 4, 1975; December 10, 1975. January 15, 1976; April 2, 1976.

Lawrence, P. and Torsch, J. *Organization and Environment: Managing Differentiation and Integration:* Boston: Harvard University Press, 1967.

Likert, R. *The human organization: Its management and values.* New York: McGraw-Hill, 1967.

Lowry, R. Toward a sociology of secrecy and security systems. *Social Problems,* October 1972, *19,* 437–450.

Manning, P. *Notes on watching.* Paper presented at the 77th annual meeting of the American Sociological Association, Chicago, 1977.

Midwest Research Institute. *Protecting the political process: An evaluation of the policing and security at the 1976 Republican National convention, Kansas City, Missouri, August 9–20, 1976.* Final Report for the Law Enforcement Assistance Administration. Submitted by the Board of Police Commissioners of Kansas City, Missouri, 1977.

Moore, W. *The conduct of the corporation.* New York: Random House, 1962.

More, H. U. *Principles and Procedures in The Justice System.* New York: Wiley Press, 1975.

Parsons, T. Suggestons for a sociological approach to the theory of organizations. *Administrative Science Quarterly,* June 1956, *1,* 63–85.

Perrow, C. The analysis of goals in complex organizations. *American Sociological Review,* December 1961, *26,* 864–866.

Perrow, C. A framework for the comparative analysis of organizations. *American Sociological Review,* April, 1967, *32,* 194–208.

Price, J. *Organizational effectiveness: An inventory of propositions.* Homewood, Ill.: Richard D. Irwin, 1968.

Schrager, L., & Short, J., Jr. Toward a sociology of organizational crime. *Social Problems,* April 1978, *25,* 407–419.

Simon, H. On the concept of organizational goal. *Administrative Science Quarterly,* June 1974, *9,* 1–22.

Singelmann, P. *Intraorganizational coercion and interorganizational structure: Theoretical considerations and a case study.* Paper presented at the 78th annual meeting of the American Sociological Association, San Francisco, 1978.

Staw, B., & Szwajkowski, E. The scarcity-munificence component of organizational environments and the commission of illegal acts. *Administrative Science Quarterly,* April 1975, *20,* 345–355.

Warren, D. Power, visibility and conformity in formal organizations. *American Sociological Review,* December 1968, *33,* 951–970.

Warriner, C. The problem of organizational purpose. *Sociological Quarterly,* Spring 1965, *6,* 139–146.

Weber, M. *The theory of social and economic organization.* Translated by A. M. Henderson and T. Parsons. New York: Free Press, 1947.

Wilensky, H. *Organizational intelligence.* New York: Basic Books, 1967.

Wilsnack, R. *Information control: A conceptual framework for sociological analysis.* Paper presented at the 77th annual meeting of the American Sociological Association, 1977.

Wolff, K. *The sociology of Georg Simmel.* New York: Free Press, 1950.

Woodward, J. *Industrial organization: Theory and practice.* London: Oxford University Press, 1965.

Yuchtman, E, & Seashore, S. A system resource approach to organizational effectiveness. *American Sociological Review,* December 1967, *32,* 891–903.

Zander, A. *Groups at work.* San Francisco: Jossey-Bass, 1977.

12

Secrecy, Intelligence, and Community: The U.S. Intelligence Community

*Fred M. Kaiser**
Congressional Research Service

The expression "intelligence community" has been adopted by political practitioners, journalists, and public policy analysts to specify a network of U.S. government agencies that conduct intelligence for national and internal security purposes.[1] Although this particular usage of community violates certain standard criteria of the concept, the notion of an intelligence community-qua-community can be adapted to other defi-

---

*The author is an analyst in American Government at the Congressional Research Service. The views expressed in this paper are my own and are not attributable to any other source. I am indebted to a number of individuals for their advice and suggestions. Stan Bach, Joseph Bensman, Douglas Lea, Robert Lilly, Marty Marger, and Harold Relyea commented on an earlier draft which was presented at the 1976 American Sociological Association annual meeting.

[1] The approximately 25 U.S. intelligence units include such prominent, major entities, as the Central Intelligence Agency (CIA), Defense Intelligence Agency (DIA), National Security Agency (NSA), military intelligence units, and the Federal Bureau of Investigation (FBI), as well as numerous intelligence units within other federal agencies—Civil Service Commission Bureau of Personnel Investigations; Department of Defense Investigative Service; Department of Justice Criminal Division, Drug Enforcement Administration (DEA), Immigration and Naturalization Service (INS); Department of State Bureau of Intelligence Research, Passport Office, Bureau of Security and Consular Affairs; Department of the Treasury Bureau of Alcohol, Tobacco and Firearms, Internal Revenue Service, Secret Service, and U.S. Customs Service; Department of Energy; U.S. Coast Guard; and U.S. Postal Service. Sources include, inter alia, Donner (1971); Hougan (1974); Kirkpatrick (1973); Ransom (1970); Ungar (1976); U.S. Congress, Senate, Select Committee to Study Governmental Operations with Respect to Intelligence Activities (referred to as Senate elect committee on intelligence hereinafter) (1976), Book IV; Wise & Ross (1967); and Wilensky (1967).

nitions, especially to those evolving from Max Weber's conceptualization based on sentiment—i.e., a sense of solidarity and significance among the membership (Clark, 1973). This study examines the U.S. intelligence community from this perspective, as a "community of profession" (Goode, 1957) exhibiting a high degree of solidarity and sense of significance. In this context, secrecy, which is a concomitant of intelligence activities, manifests multiple dimensions and serves as a critical determinant of community sentiment. The multidimensionality of secrecy is evident in the norms, communal identity, social and professional structure of the membership, and organizational controls of the intelligence community.

This research effort concentrates on the U.S. intelligence community, although the analytical framework, assessments, and conclusions may apply to varying degrees to the intelligence communities of other nations. The Soviet Union KGB, South Korean Central Intelligence Agency, and British Secret Service, among others, are likely to manifest equal or more intense community sentiment among their respective memberships, depending, in part, on the degree of secrecy surrounding those structures.

The focal point of the U.S. intelligence community is due, of course, to the recent public exposure of many intelligence operations, activities, and structures through examinations by the press, congressional committees, a presidential commission, and the agencies themselves. Those investigations revealed that intelligence community activities have incorporated abuses of authority, illegalities, and unethical conduct, including assassination plots against foreign leaders, drug testing on unwitting subjects, infiltration of domestic dissident groups, military surveillance of civilians, surreptitious entry, domestic counterintelligence programs, and other covert operations (Colby, 1974; Ross, 1975). Senate select committee on intelligence, 1975 and 1976; U.S. Congress, House, Select Committee on Intelligence, 1975; U.S. President's Commission on CIA Activities Within the U.S., 1975; Wise, 1975).

In light of these activities and the expansion and proliferation of intelligence units, it is important to analyze the intelligence community from novel perspectives, e.g., in terms of community sentiment, as in this case. By this approach, certain salient characteristics, such as secrecy, and their refinements can be explored and associated with the development of community sentiment as well as with particular operations and activities. As a result any explanation about intelligence community behavior should be more comprehensive and reliable than is currently available. The remainder of this paper is divided into three sections: (1) definition and characteristics; (2) contributing factors and conditions; and (3) conclusions and implications.

DEFINITION AND CHARACTERISTICS

Definition

As suggested above, community is not defined in terms of ecological traits, social activity, or social structure, but in terms of prevailing attitudes with an emphasis on a sense of solidarity and significance. The analysis of community by David Clark (1973), which isolates these two sentiments as the essential elements, provides the following interpretation: "The strength of community within any given group is determined by the degree to which its members experience both a sense of solidarity and a sense of significance within it."

Professional community, adopted from Goode's (1957) seminal interpretation, is defined in this context as a collectivity associated with a given profession, which has been entered in pursuit of common objectives and interests and whose members are governed by a pervasive set of norms and mores, thus producing a population whose sense of significance and solidarity is intimately allied with the grouping. Goode (1957) lists eight characteristics of a community of profession: shared sense of identity; terminal or continuing status within the community; common values; consensual role definitions; common language internally; community power over members; reasonably clear boundaries; community control over recruitment selection; and adult socialization of membership and successors.

The professional community may acquire certain reinforcing attributes of a "symbolic" community (Hunter, 1974) and may be compatible with a broader status community, defined as a "consensual community, in which the individual chooses to organize his major life interests within a framework of institutions, culture, practices, and social relations that are consistent with his adherence to a set of values..." (Bensman, 1972; Stub, 1972; Martindale, 1960).

The fundamental hypothesis to be determined here is that individuals who engage in the intelligence function (McDougal et al., 1973) sense a high degree of significance and solidarity within the collectivity—that there is an intelligence community-qua-community. Others have implied something akin to an intelligence community as understood here. Marchetti & Marks (1974) discuss a "clandestine mentality" within the "cult of intelligence" but do so in descriptive bureaucratic and operational terms. Garry Wills (1976) provides an intuitive grasp of some of the characteristics of an intelligence community, especially the norms and ethos. The common reference to the CIA, for instance, as "the Company" (Agee, 1975) might, at first, appear to underestimate the pervasive and controlling influence of the community over its membership, unless one considers the CIA as the prototype of future companies that generically possess community characteristics. However, former agents who subscribe to a "Company" notion (See McGarvey, 1972, and Turner, 1970, who discuss the CIA and the FBI, respectively) implicitly identify community characteristics. A particularly revealing interpretation of the pervasive ethos of even "the Company" designation is provided by Miles Copeland (1974), a former officer with the CIA and its predecessor, the Office of Strategic Services:

> To those deep inside the intelligence establishments, both East and West, it often seemed that the term "the company" should apply to all of them considered together (p. 278).

Although neither Clark's (1973) nor Goode's (1957) analysis provides a distinction between community and other types of groupings (e.g., mass movements, organized interests, total institutions) and appear to allow these other types to be classified as communities, the use of the concept here is more precise. Community signifies a way of life, not merely a limited occupational organization, interest group, or amorphous mass movement. Community does not refer to total institutions, which have some similar properties, but which are involuntary associations, lack a pervasive and accepted value structure, and often physically confine the population to restricted environments. It may be that within these other groupings, community sentiment exists. Nonetheless, distinctions among them must be made and it should be clear that other types of collectivities do not necessarily produce community sentiment.

Clark's reexamination of community is abbreviated; and Goode's analysis of professional community focuses on collectivities other than an intelligence community and lacks a full exploration of the contributing factors associated with the development of such communities. In consequence, some elaboration of community is required for an understanding of its utility as an explanatory concept in this contest. That conceptual refinement can proceed along with a description of the characteristics of the intelligence community.

Characteristics

A highly developed sense of solidarity and sense of significance are not spontaneous manifestations of individuals within a grouping, of course, but instead are developed and associated with other characteristics. In the case of the intelligence community, the other characteristics are well-structured norms and mores, common objectives and interests, and the communal identity of the membership. The characteristics are necessarily interrelated and mutually reinforcing.

Norms Internal norms and mores appear to be critical to the development of a sense of solidarity and significance within the community. A system of informal rules of conduct and standards of behavior are essential to governing behavior among individuals and to establishing supportive, reinforcing relationships among the membership. Norms and mores also help to designate priorities and hierarchy of values on which evaluations and judgments about behavior can be made.

In the context of the intelligence community, several important mores and associated norms apparently predominate—obedience, discipline, dedication, and most critically, defense of secrecy and internal security (Wills, 1976; Copeland, 1974; Marchetti & Marks, 1974).

The perception that a breach of secrecy might jeopardize national security, an important operation, the life of a colleague (and, by extrapolation, an agent's own), an agent's career, or the interests of the community corroborates the importance of secrecy as the commanding norm. The fact that illicit activities within the intelligence agencies went unexposed for decades testified to the importance of this norm. The norm of secrecy was epitomized by the security surrounding the CIA testing of chemical and biological agents on unwitting subjects beginning in the early 1950s and resulting in the suicide of at least one subject in 1953. The final report of the Senate select committee on intelligence (1976) reviewed the arrangements:

There were no attempts to secure approval for the most controversial aspects of these programs from the executive branch or Congress. The nature and extent of the programs were closely held secrets; even DCI (Director of Central Intelligence) McCone was not briefed on all the details of the program involving the surreptitious administration of LSD until 1963. It was deemed imperative that these programs be concealed from the American people. As the CIA's Inspector General wrote in 1957:

> Precautions must be taken not only to protect operations from exposure to enemy forces but also to conceal these activities from the American public in general. The knowledge that the Agency is engaging in unethical and illicit activities would have serious repercussions in political and diplomatic circles and would be detrimental to the accomplishment of its mission (Book I, p. 394).

Secrecy of operations and security of intelligence files and materials are maintained through a number of devices, including frequent security checks and elaborate clearance procedures. Another procedure is the need to know principle, which has been institutionalized through limitations on access to information and documents, including the use of cryptonyms in documents to indicate personnel, projects, and locations (Copeland, 1974). The secrecy norm underlying the use of cryptonyms and its implication is revealed by Miles Copeland (1974), a former CIA officer:

> I suppose that if I had been allowed the time, I could eventually have 'broken the code'; but only the officer who works full-time on each case has the time—and more often than not, he doesn't *want* to know. Richard Helms, when he was Director of Central Intelligence, refrained from learning the names of more than a handful of top agents whose cases were of such importance that he personally had to keep up with them (p. 171).

Such codes and cryptonyms epitomize the common language that characterizes professional communities (Goode, 1957) and reinforce the intelligence community sentiment by connoting an exclusive knowledgeability. One observer of the intelligence community perceived that "its members share a common privilege of knowing special codes and secrets which set them apart and make them 'superior'." (Interview)

The norm of secrecy extends to other CIA operations and to other agencies as well. An example is the existence for four years (1969–1973) of a Special Service Staff within the Internal Revenue Service, an intelligence unit unacknowledged until after its termination. The revelation of FBI covert operations, including the harassment of Martin Luther King, Jr. and COINTELPRO and continued illegal burglaries, are further illustrations of a common theme. As noted above, secrecy, confidentiality, and internal security are rationalized and justified for a variety of reasons. However, the extent of that secrecy and its implications for responsibility and control extend beyond the anticipated restrictions, limiting access of immediate superiors in the organization as well as colleagues. This dominant norm of secrecy, in turn, closely relates to the objectives and interests of the membership of the intelligence community.

Objectives and Interests Reinforcing and shared objectives and interests among the membership help to generate a sense of solidarity and significance. Allegiance, loyalty, commitment, and priorities are partial byproducts of objectives and interests held in common. The intelligence community appears to possess a variety of such common objectives and interests, ranging from broad demands of national security to the career goals of the individual member.

One of these shared goals, according to Allen Dulles (1963), the director of the CIA during its formative years, has been the "contribution to national security" (1963). Based on a reading of Dulles's recollections, this objective had been nearly universally shared among intelligence operatives and had superseded other considerations:

> In my ten years with the Agency I only recall one case of many hundreds where a man who had joined the Agency felt some scruples about the activities he was asked to carry on. In this case he was given the option of either an honorable resignation or a transfer to some other branch of work (p. 195).

An identical sentiment was evident more than a decade later, according to the investigation by the Senate select committee on intelligence (1976) of the FBI's mail-opening program, in the testimony of one of the responsible officials:

> It was my assumption that what we were doing was justified by what we had to do ... the greater good, the national security (Book II, p. 14).

Another instance of the national security objective in tandem with the interests of an intelligence agency provoked an operative to disobey a presidential directive. In this case, a CIA scientist secured and maintained a quantity of an extremely lethal shellfish toxin, despite a 1969 order by President Nixon to the National Security Council to dispose of existing stocks of bacteriological weapons (Senate select committee on intelligence, 1976). A further illustration of the theme involves Richard Helms, then deputy director for plans (CIA) and eventual director of the CIA, and his support for the continued CIA drug-testing program. Helms wrote the following to the deputy director of central intelligence (Senate select committee on intelligence, 1976):

> While I share your uneasiness and distaste for any program which tends to intrude upon an individual's private and legal prerogatives, I believe it is necessary that the Agency maintain a central role in this activity, keep current on enemy capabilities the manipulation of human behavior, and maintain an offensive capability (Book I, p. 394).

The nebulous and often undirected objective of protection of national security permits substantial administrative discretion within the intelligence community and aids the development of community sentiment. One of the clearest examples is the information classification system, which is based on executive orders but, in reality, implemented with extensive independence by the individual agencies, bureaus and officials. The present classification system's supposedly controlling phrase, i.e., "national security," lacks statutory definition and, according to President Nixon's Executive Order 11652, which still governs the process, refers collectively to "national defense *or* foreign relations of the United States." (Emphasis added) Moreover, the classification system, as it operates currently, is perhaps the ultimate illustration of the institutionalization of secrecy in the intelligence community, reducing, if not eliminating, access to intelligence products from opposing viewpoints; conferring substantial discretion and controlling influence for its propagation to the community itself as opposed to responsible elected officials in government; partially isolating the intelligence community from the normal channels of political accountability; and aiding the community's interests in influencing official and public opinion through judicious leaks and disclosures (Cox, 1975, and Sigal, 1975).

The objective of national security, the far-reaching interests of the community, and the interests of the membership in maintaining the dominant norms have been widely shared foundations for a variety of intelligence activities and operations. Even the recent revelations, which have relied on intelligence community leads, testimony, and records, do not necessarily obviate the conclusion of consensual interests and objectives. The initial leads for the press and congressional investigators would have come from personnel who found an unresponsive or unsympathetic structure within the intelligence community. Furthermore, some observers have speculated that former CIA director William Colby, who headed the agency during the recent congressional investigation, was removed for being "a reckless spiller of beans," as one Congressman perceived the action (Stern, 1975).

The commonality of interests and objectives are in part determined by certain characteristics of the recruitment, selection, and training processes of the intelligence community, factors discussed in a later section. These common objectives, as well as the norms of the community, are complemented by the communal identity of the membership.

Communal Identity William Goode (1957, p. 195) recognizes that "the elite of any profession are usually conscious of a communal identity." As this identity extends and becomes commonplace among the general community population, its sense of solidarity should increase. This appears to be the case with the intelligence community, the other characteristics and conditions of which encourage an identification with the professional community and virtually exclude identification with any other potentially competing community or even reference group.

The separate existence of the membership; highly confidential activities; supreme importance of the missions of the various agencies (e.g., national security), at least, in the self-perception of the membership; and selective recruitment processes tend to support a communal identity for the membership. Corroboration comes from the public appeals of the various agencies that emphasize the patriotism and importance of the career as an intelligence officer. Allen Dulles (1963), the former director of the CIA, presented a revealing portrayal in *The Craft of Intelligence* of this selectivity, the professional demands on the membership, and the subsequent separate and common indentification with the intelligence community:

> What all these men [intelligence officers] had in common was an awareness of the conflict that exists in the world today, a convic-

tion that the United States is involved in this conflict, that the peace and well-being of the world are endangered, and that it is worth trying to do something about these things.

What moved them is a more complicated thing than pure patriotism and a deeper thing than a mere longing for excitement. There is in the intelligence officer, whether he operates at home or abroad, a certain 'front-line' mentality, a 'first-line-of-defense' mentality. His awareness is sharpened because in his daily work he is almost continually confronted with evidences of the enemy in action. If the sense of adventure plays some role here, as it surely does, it is adventure with a large measure of concern for the public safety.

With this motivation, an alert, inquisitive and patriotic individual with an adequate education can be molded into a good intelligence officer. It is this complex 'motivational' aspect of a man which the intelligence service must probe in the prospective employee. Education, talent and the highest security clearances will not make him an intelligence officer if he does not have this motivation (p. 175).

None of these characteristics of community operates independently of others or substantiates the sense of solidarity or significance alone. The mutually reinforcing relationship among these ingredients is in part a result of their dependency on common factors and conditions.

CONTRIBUTING FACTORS AND CONDITIONS

With regard to the intelligence community, it appears that the members' sense of significance (e.g., professional achievement, career development, peer prestige, even social activity) is almost exclusively a function of the community. Furthermore, a sense of solidarity is held with equivalent intensity by a population that has little competition for its loyalty, allegiance, or commitment from other entities in the society.

A series of contributing factors and conditions are associated with the development of an intelligence community. Geographic location, one standard determinant of community, is relatively impermanent and is consequently of little significance in this case. Nonetheless, other factors more than compensate, including a lack of competition with other sources of influence over the lives of members, secrecy of intelligence operations, anonymity of membership, confidentiality of materials, elaborate socialization experiences, control of rewards and sanctions by the authority figures in the community, and a receptive clientele. These factors mutually support each other as well as the community characteristics.

Most individuals experience socialization, rewards and sanctions, prestige and status from a variety of sources (e.g., family, peers, occupation, profession, career, territorial community, voluntary associations). For intelligence community members that sharing is not as great and, in fact, is extremely confined. The secrecy surrounding intelligence production prevents some agents from revealing their duties, assignments, or profession to even their immediate families. Local, civic, service, or political organization involvement is precluded for most members of the intelligence community in order to maintain anonymity or confidentiality. Even those who are not agents but serve as analysts must maintain a high degree of confidentiality and isolation from neighbors and find that professional societies (e.g., academic organizations) may be excluded from their participation. The periodic change in location and assignment for agents also prevents an identification with a particular territory or local organization. Mobility, secrecy, confidentiality, anonymity, and isolation are inherent features of the intelligence community, features that exclude other sources of influence in the lives of the population.

Prestige and status for the member appear to be defined by his particular agency, assignment, and level of responsibility and confined to the internal community, since location is impermanent, occupation confidential, and profession secret. Therefore, the emotive rewards associated with individual prestige and status are not provided by sources external to the community.

One of the most reliable assertions of the community control is provided by Arthur Cox (1975), formerly affiliated with the CIA and the White House:

> (Former CIA Director) Allen Dulles used to emphasize to his staff that successful CIA employees had a passion for anonymity, getting their satisfaction from a job well done in a very closed community, but never from public recognition (p. 144).

Closely allied with the control of emotive rewards by the community is the commanding influence over material rewards and sanctions by the same community. The rewards/sanctions determined by the authority figures in the community include not only the usual monetary, tangible rewards but also the no less real but intangible assignment, its nature and location. The leadership also has impressive legal sanctions at its disposal by which to maintain the norms and mores of the community, to preserve its isolation and confidentiality, and indirectly its internal cohesion and solidarity. As with emotive rewards and sanctions, the control of material rewards and sanctions reflects multiple dimensions and manifestations of secrecy.

Intelligence agencies and their leadership elements have substantial authorities in this regard. Covert and confidential funding techniques preclude normal congressional authorization, appropriation, and oversight as well as General Accounting Office investigations; classified directives govern the activities and even the establishment of agencies, as with NSA; statutory exemptions for the CIA, FBI, and NSA from the competitive service exclude them from Civil Service Commission examination of their personnel policies; and periodic security clearances and internal personnel investigations are largely the domain of the agencies themselves. Epitomizing the nebulous and broad authority granted the intelligence community leadership is that of the director of the CIA, who, according to the 1947 National Security Act, is "responsible for protecting intelligence sources and methods from unauthorized disclosure." Consequently, even former agents may find that their revelations are subject to prior censorship (Marchetti & Marks, 1974) or publishable only abroad (Agee, 1975).

As impressive as the internal rewards and sanctions are the elaborate and extensive socialization processes of the intelligence community that continue throughout a member's career. Adult socialization is critical to intelligence community maintenance, because its behavioral demands exceed even those of other professional communities in contrast to the demands of the lay world (Goode, 1957, p. 196). Copeland (1974) has commented on the initial socialization experiences with the CIA and their continued influence:

> The most impressive part of this initial CIA indoctrination is the attitude toward loyalty, security, precision, attention to detail, and healthy suspicion that it manages to implant in the minds of the trainees. 'Because of my indoctrination,' writes Patrick McGarvey in his *CIA: The Myth and the Madness,* 'I still get a visceral twinge—and have qualms of conscience about writing this book.' Although one cannot detect any signs of reticence in

Pat McGarvey's book, I know what he means. The fact is that this aspect of the indoctrination has been designed by some of the nation's best psychologists, employing the most modern techniques of 'motivational research.' Certainly it achieves its purpose ... Also, the psychologists believe their course imparts a strong sense of mission, which is lacking in other branches of government (pp. 263–264).

Copeland (1974) then briefly describes the major indoctrination programs, including more than 400 courses that can be "adapted for a wide variety of trainees."

Part of the socialization process, which is most intensive at the time of appointment to an intelligence agency, includes polygraph tests (Copeland, 1974; McGarvey, 1972). During this procedure, the recruit must reveal intimate and personal details of his life in order to determine his credibility and, according to Copeland (1974, p. 165), "whether or not the employee is a security risk ... [determined by] the extent to which he feels shame about something in his past." The experience not only ensures total honesty and loss of privacy, but also functions as assurance of complete obedience and intense commitment to the intelligence community on the part of the member.

A final factor that contributes to the development and maintenance of an intelligence community is the actual recruitment process. It is likely that the community recruits and selects a receptive and responsive clientele, although there may be heterogeneity in terms of objective socioeconomic characteristics. In fact, Allen Dulles (1963) responded to critics of a homogeneous "elitist" orientation in the CIA, a criticism later recalled by Wise and Ross (1967). Dulles's defense follows:

> The charge has been leveled against CIA that it recruits almost exclusively from the so-called Ivy League colleges in the East with an overtone that possibly we have too many 'softies' and possibly too many 'liberals' for the tough job the CIA has to do. It is quite true that we have a considerable number of graduates from Eastern colleges. It is also true that in numbers of degrees (many of the CIA personnel have more than one degree) Harvard, Yale, Columbia and Princeton lead the list, but they are closely followed by Chicago, Illinois, Michigan, University of California, Stanford and MIT. It is interesting, however, to note that taking the approximately one hundred senior officers of the CIA, statistics show that these officers have degrees from sixty-one different universities, representing all parts of the country.

It is, in fact, a highly heterogeneous group of men, representative of the entire United States ... (p. 175).

With employment offices scattered throughout the United States, the CIA and other units within the intelligence community are increasingly likely to recruit a heterogeneous population in terms of region, economic status, religion, and education.

Nonetheless, the question remains whether the intelligence community and possible subcommunities associated with the various agencies recruit selectively in terms of basic attitudes and predispositions. Given the extensive screening procedures, investigative background studies, security clearance procedures, and initial "indoctrination" sessions, the intelligence community has ample opportunity to be extremely selective in its recruits. Moreover, it is reasonable to assume that those who approach the various agencies are already predisposed to support the norms, mores, interests, and objectives of the intelligence community and its constituent elements.

When considering these contributing factors as a composite, the intelligence community-qua-community appears to be one with a high degree of solidarity and significance. The membership, which is relatively isolated from extracommunity sources of influence and socialization, finds its emotive and material rewards and sanctions largely controlled by authorities within the intelligence community. The effect of an elaborate and intensive socialization process on the members who are voluntary adherents to the basic norms and interests of the community is likely to be reinforcing and complementary to the other factors. In sum, the intelligence community represents the basic characteristics and determining factors of a professional community, including an apparently highly developed sense of solidarity and significance.

CONCLUSIONS AND IMPLICATIONS

This study has concentrated on two basic purposes: (1) to ascertain the existence or nonexistence of an intelligence community; and (2) to refine the concept of professional community. The focus on the latter was in terms of delineating the contributing factors and conditions that would encourage the development of community sentiment. The functions of the members of the community (intelligence production in this case) and the attendant prerequisites (secrecy, confidentiality, isolation) apparently provide the critical, but not necessarily sufficient, conditions. Related factors, such as the socialization processes associated with a collectivity, the degree of dispersion of control over the rewards and sanctions within the collectivity, and the type of clientele (attitudinal characteristics) available for membership, seem to be essential determinants.

Moreover, the factors are interrelated and the multidimensionality of secrecy is reflected throughout the U.S. intelligence community, its characteristics, and contributing factors. For instance, secrecy is not only one of the dominant internal norms but also institutionalized through an elaborate system of legal authorities. In addition, the isolation and anonymity of the membership represents another aspect of the secrecy phenomenon as does the confidentiality ascribed to its operations, activities and structures.

An appreciation of this community sentiment intertwined with secrecy was evident in the final report of the Senate select committee on intelligence (1976):

> The intelligence agencies are a sector of American government set apart. Employees' loyalties to their organizations have been conditioned by the closed, compartmented and secretive circumstances of their agencies' formation and operation. In some respects, the intelligence profession resembles monastic life with some of the disciplines and personal sacrifices reminiscent of medieval orders. Intelligence work is a life of service, but one in which the norms of American national life are sometimes distressingly distorted (Book I, p. 7).

The existence of community sentiment, however, does not preclude internal competition, conflict, rivalry, and jealousy, whether in the medical profession that Goode (1957) analyzed or in an intelligence community. Of course, such internal differences are evident among intelligence agencies and members. The notion of a professional community instead connotes a sense of exclusivity vis-a-vis nonmembers and a commonality of values and attitudes within the community, not absolute harmony or unanimity.

An obvious implication of this analysis is for further research in the ingredients of the intelligence community, especially detailing the norms and interests. A substantial body of material exists in the congressional investigations and reports on the intelligence activities as well as in the writings of former associates. However, explicit data about community is either sketchy, lacks authority, or must be inferred. Despite the revelations about covert activities of the intelligence agencies, Horowitz (1976, p. 87) concludes that, "They remain as covert as ever—not about what they do but about who they are." That may be an overstatement, but further examination of an intelligence community awaits more reliable quantitative and qualitative data on membership characteristics, attitudinal matrices, socialization patterns and processes, etc.

A second implication of the analysis of professional community is to extend the framework to other likely candidates—the military, academia, police, and other collectivities that appear to manifest professional community characteristics. Only by such an extension can the fruitful cross-fertilization of comparative analysis be effective. It is that type of analysis that can further refine the necessary ingredients and determine the causal factors.

A series of implications result from the premise that an intelligence community-qua-community exists. Broadly construed, the implications relate to the behavior of the community and democratic controls over it.

Regarding community behavior, the interests of the community might out weigh those of other entities with which the member is associated. The decision of a CIA scientist not to destroy toxic agents in violation of a presidential directive indicates that community interests might supersede the decisions and orders of the national leadership. Other instances in which the interests of the intelligence community prevailed over those of the nation involved the Warren Commission investigation into the assassination of President Kennedy. According to the review by the Senate select committee on intelligence (1976), FBI officials in Dallas intentionally destroyed a threatening note (against the Dallas police and FBI) from Lee Harvey Oswald, delivered approximately seven to ten days before the assassination of the President. The Warren Commission was not informed of the contents or even the existence of the note. The Warren Commission's possible revelation of this and other investigative failings of the FBI induced the following conclusion from the Senate select committee on intelligence (1976):

> If the Warren Commission reported that the Bureau's handling of the assassination investigation or the Oswald security case was deficient in some manner, the FBI would have been open to embarrassment and criticism. Given this possibility, and FBI

Director Hoover's known hostility to criticism or embarrassment of the Bureau, it is not at all surprising that from its inception, the Commission was perceived as an adversary by both Hoover and senior FBI officials (Book V, p. 47).

Another element in the same episode (i.e., the investigation by the Warren Commission) was the withholding of information regarding CIA assassination plots against Fidel Castro, despite Warren Commission membership of Allen Dulles, former director of the CIA.

A final example provides another dimension of the dominance of intelligence community interests and is based on a congressional hearing on mail covers and mail openings (U.S. Congress, House, Committee on Post Office and Civil Service, 1975). The subcommittee inquiry revealed that William Cotter, the chief postal inspector and a former employee of the CIA, permitted the CIA to conduct mail openings, although it was uncertain whether the CIA had such authority. Subcommittee Chairman Charles Wilson observed the divided loyalties of Mr. Cotter, in later questioning of the postmaster general (1975):

> Mr. WILSON. We had the feeling, listening to Mr. Cotter yesterday—I along with some of the other members—that he was still working with the CIA when he was with the Postal Service; that his first responsibility seemed to be to the CIA. And he referred to Mr. Helms as the boss rather than to you as the boss (p. 85).

Again, the interests and needs of other entities might well be secondary to those of the intelligence community.

A second implication is that secrecy and confidentiality, critical to the functioning of the intelligence community, produce unexpected consequences. One latent function is that criminal prosecutions of agency personnel might not proceed without jeopardizing national secrets, as was argued in the plea bargaining arrangement of former CIA Director Richard Helms, who had been charged with failing to testify fully and accurately to a Senate committee on CIA activities in Chile. Such developments are harmful to the democratic process, while other related phenomena may even be dysfunctional to the intelligence community. For instance, an intelligence operative arrested for criminal conduct might avoid prosecution by threatening, explicitly or implicitly, to expose other agents or operations. Recognition of this consequence was reflected in a 1954 agreement between the CIA and the Justice Department that allowed the CIA discretion as to which violators or violations to report to the attorney general and which to suppress on security grounds. That agreement, eventually abrogated 20 years later, permitted the CIA to have drug smuggling charges against an employee dismissed (Percy, 1975). Without recourse to the courts, the intelligence community is either susceptible to the implied threat of operatives, resulting in the suppression of prosecution, or must resort to extralegal channels. In a military situation, the consequences of the confrontation between the demand for intelligence secrecy and the threat of exposure are even more drastic than a denial of prosecution. In 1969, a suspected Vietnamese double (or triple) agent was executed, allegedly by U.S. Army Special Forces personnel. The expected court-martial, however, was dismissed when the CIA ordered its staff not to testify (Treaster, 1969).

Another implication relates to the substantial absence of democratic values and procedures in the intelligence community, reinforced by both the demands of secrecy and the isolation of the membership from extracommunity activities, especially overt political ones. Given this condition in the intelligence community, the basic question is whether it can be controlled by noncommunity authorities, whether it can be made accountable to the elected representatives of government.

Some critics (Wills, 1976) insist that certain intelligence agencies (in particular the CIA, the prototypical intelligence agency) cannot be democratically controlled and must be terminated. But this reasoning seems to ignore the underlying community sentiment and characteristics attendant to the intelligence function, characteristics that are not monopolized by the CIA but that are held, if less intensely, in other member organizations. It further neglects to consider that the existence of the intelligence function and the sine qua non of secrecy and confidentiality will continue, even if particular agencies or units are removed and the duties transferred to other entities. According to the analysis advanced in this paper, it is the function (of intelligence) and its prerequisites that are the major determining variables in the formation of community sentiment (in the intelligence community). The institutional developments and characteristics of particular agencies are partial byproducts of this sentiment and function and not the reverse, as some critics contend.

Furthermore, Wills (1976) and others have viewed the CIA as the "action arm of the Imperial Presidency." This perception, however, is not supported by the considerable evidence that, despite examples of White House manipulation of intelligence agencies, intelligence community units have frequently behaved independently. For instance, presidents have had to circumvent intelligence community components that had proven unresponsive to presidential demands (e.g., creation of the White House "plumbers") and intelligence operations were often undertaken without clear or explicit direction from the President or relevant agency heads—e.g., FBI burglaries, CIA mail openings, and some foreign assassination plots that lacked explicit authorization from even the director of the CIA (Senate select committee on intelligence, 1975). The notion of an intelligence community, therefore, is in opposition to that of an "Imperial Presidency" dominating the agencies and centralizing power. Instead, it is more in line with the concept of "executive-centered" government (Lowi & Ripley, 1973, p. 8), contending that there are multiple independent centers of power and influence, associated with various policy arenas and existing in different levels of the executive. In fact, it might be argued that the covert nature of intelligence policy making reinforces the position of the intelligence community at the expense of the President. The secrecy surrounding such decisions and the command of resources by the community prevent the President from utilizing the competitive sources he might otherwise rely upon. Secrecy restricts the President's appeal to a larger audience (Halperin, 1976), moreover, seriously limiting his normal bargaining advantages over sectors of the bureaucracy.

Related to the phenomenon of community in this case has been a substantial amount of independence and autonomy. This condition has been exacerbated by the absence of usual democratic supervision and by the infusion of sophisticated technological developments (Kaiser & Becker, 1976), the expertise of which is often lacking among the congressional and presidential officials. Given the existence of an intelligence community, the most plausible means for controlling it would be to penetrate the isolation and secrecy through increased oversight and supervision by responsible officials. A related avenue would be to reduce the statutory exemptions granted to various components of the intelligence community in reporting obligations and to specify through legislation guidelines for particular activities, operations, and practices (Kaiser & Becker, 1976).

Some specific recommendations, several of which have been

implemented, provide expanded extracommunity control or supervision and intrude upon the isolation of the community:

- Establishment of an independent office of inspector general for intelligence, statutorily created with explicit and frequent reporting obligations to Congress and directed by an officer who is confirmed by the Senate;
- Expanded Senate confirmation requirements for higher echelon intelligence officers (presently, only the FBI director and the CIA director and deputy director are confirmable appointments);
- A statutorily separated intelligence community staff, independently funded and representative of all sectors of the intelligence community (such requirements exist currently in appropriation and authorization acts but these are limited to the life of the legislation, i.e., one fiscal year);
- Statutory charters for all intelligence units that more effectively and precisely define the scope of authority and permissible activities than presently is done by the variety of laws, executive orders, and administrative directives governing the community;
- Effective monitoring of the Foreign Intelligence Surveillance Act (P.L. 95–511), which includes warrant procedures for most domestic surveillance for foreign intelligence purposes and reporting requirements to the House and Senate Select Committees on Intelligence;
- Clarified and improved reporting obligations contained in the 1974 Foreign Assistance Act, which are now applicable only to covert nonintelligence operations of the CIA abroad;
- Adoption of the "legislative veto" (a device for Congress or a committee to disapprove or defer executive action) for certain proposed intelligence operations;
- Improved General Accounting Office accessibility to intelligence community data, including budget expenditures, proprietary organizations, and internal audit unit reports in order to ensure standardized auditing and review of intelligence units;
- Continuation of existing House and Senate Select Committees on Intelligence, instituted in the last two congresses, accompanied by shared jurisdiction over most intelligence units with other committees;
- Limitations on proprietary operations and reductions in unvouchered (and unaccountable) funds; and

- A legislatively enacted information classification system to replace the one determined by the President's executive order and implemented with substantial administration discretion.

Individually and collectively, these recommendations improve the monitoring and control of the intelligence community by outside entities. The main apprehension is that such units may become co-opted in the process of overseeing this highly secretive community, although the multiplicity of the mechanisms should reduce that likelihood. The underlying premise is that there is an intelligence community-qua-community, based on the intelligence function and the concomitant of secrecy. Since that function and its attendant requisites will remain—quixotic proposals to terminate intelligence or particular agencies to the contrary notwithstanding—the above recommendations appear to be the type of approach necessary to provide democratic controls, and, at the same time, reduce the intensity and exclusivity of this professional community sentiment.

References

Agee, P. *Inside the company: The CIA diary.* London: Penguin, 1975.
Bensman, J. Status communities in urban society: The musical community. In Stub, H. R. (ed.). *Status communities in modern society.* Hinsdale, Ill.: Dryden Press, 1972.
Clark, D. B. The concept of community: A re-examination. *Sociological Review* (New Series), 1973, *21*, 397–416.
Colby, W. *Report to the President* (regarding allegations of CIA involvement in domestic intelligence). Washington, D.C.: Central Intelligence Agency, 1974.
Copeland, M. *Without cloak and dagger: The truth about the new espionage.* New York: Simon and Schuster, 1974.
Cox, A. M. *The myths of national security: The perils of secret government.* New York: Beacon Press, 1975.
Donner, F. The theory and practice of American political intelligence. *New York Review of Books,* April 22, 1971, 27–38.
Dulles, A. *The craft of intelligence.* New York: Harper and Row, 1963.
Goode, W. J. Community within a community: The professions. *American Sociological Review,* 1957, *22*, 194–200.
Halperin, M. Covert operations: Effects of secrecy on decision-making. In Borosage, R., & Marks, J. (eds.). *The CIA file.* New York: Grossman, 1976.
Horowitz, I. L. Science, security, and politics. *Society,* July/August 1976, *13*, 83–87.
Hougan, J. A surfeit of spies. *Harper's Magazine,* 1974, *249*, 51–67.
Hunter, A. *Symbolic communities.* Chicago: University of Chicago Press, 1974.
Kaiser, F. M., & Becker, L. G. Surveillance technology policy and implications: An overview. In U.S. Congress, Senate, Committee on the Judiciary, Subcommittee on Constitutional Rights. *Surveillance technology—1976.* Washington, D.C.: U.S. Government Printing Office, 1976.
Kirkpatrick, L. *The U.S. intelligence community: Foreign policy and domestic activities.* New York: Hill and Wang, 1973.
Lowi, T., & Ripley, R. *Legislative politics U.S.A.* Boston: Little, Brown, 1973.
Marchetti, V., & Marks, J. D. *The CIA and the cult of intelligence.* New York: Dell, 1974.
Martindale, D. *American social structure.* New York: Appleton-Century-Crofts, 1960.

McDougal, M. S., Lasswell, H. D., & Reisman, W. M. The intelligence function and world public order. *Temple Law Quarterly*, 1973, *46*, 365–448.

McGarvey, P. J. *The CIA: The myth and the madness.* Baltimore: Penguin, 1972.

Percy, C. H. The law applies to the CIA, too. *Congressional Record* (daily ed.), Sept. 30, 1975, *121*, S17121–S17122.

Ransom, H. H. *The intelligence establishment.* Cambridge, Mass.: Harvard University Press, 1970.

Ross, T. B. Spying in the United States. *Society*, March/April, 1975, *12*, 64–71.

Sigal, L. V. Official secrecy and informal communication in congressional-bureaucratic relations. *Political Science Quarterly*, 1975, *90*, 71–92.

Stern, L. CIA shaken by timing of firing. Washington *Post,* Nov. 4, 1975, A14.

Stub, H. R. (ed.). *Status communities in modern society: Alternatives to class analysis.* Hinsdale, Ill.: Dryden Press, 1972.

Treaster, J. B. Behind the intelligence curtain. New York *Times,* Oct. 1, 1969, page 2.

Turner, W. *Hoover's FBI.* New York: Dell, 1970.

Ungar, S. J. *FBI.* Boston: Little, Brown, 1976.

U.S. Congress, House, Committee on Post Office and Civil Service, Subcommittee on Postal Facilities, Mail, and Labor Management. *Control of mail surveillance and mail cover programs* (hearings, 94th Congress, 1st session). Washington, D.C.: U.S. Government Printing Office, 1975.

U.S. Congress, House, Select Committee on Intelligence. *U.S. Intelligence Agencies and activities: Domestic intelligence programs* (hearings, 94th Congress, 1st session). Washington, D.C.: U.S. Government Printing Office, 1975.

U.S. Congress, Senate, Select Committee to Study Governmental Operations with respect to Intelligence Activities. *Alleged assassination plots involving foreign leaders* (interim report, no. 94-465, 94th Congress, 1st session). Washington, D.C.: U.S. Government Printing Office, 1975.

U.S. Congress, Senate Select Committee to Study Governmental Operations with respect to Intelligence Activities. *Final Report* (Senate report no. 94-755, 94th Congress, 2d session. Book I: Foreign and military intelligence; Book II: Intelligence and rights of Americans; Book III: Supplementary detailed staff reports on intelligence activities and rights of Americans; Book IV: Supplementary detailed staff reports on foreign and military intelligence; Book V: The investigation of the assassination of President John F. Kennedy: The performance of the intelligence agencies; Book VI: Supplementary reports on intelligence activities). Washington, D.C.: U.S. Government Printing Office, 1976.

U.S. President's Commission on CIA Activities Within the United States. *Report to the President.* Washington, D.C.: U.S. Government Printing Office, 1975.

Wilensky, H. L. *Organizational intelligence: Knowledge and policy in government and industry.* New York: Basic Books, 1967.

Wills, G. The CIA from beginning to end. *New York Review of Books,* Jan. 22, 1976, *22,* 23–33.

Wisc, D. Cloak and dagger operations. *Society,* March/April 1975, *12,* 26–33.

Wise, D., & Ross, T. B. *The espionage establishment.* New York: Random House, 1967.

13

Toward a Sociology of Secrecy and Security Systems[1]

Ritchie P. Lowry
Boston College

Daniel Ellsberg's disclosure of The Pentagon Papers (Sheehan et al., 1971), media support of his actions, subsequent government attempts to suppress the information, and the continuing national debate concerning secrecy are events that dramatically belie a tenuous American myth of the last several decades. The myth grew out of World War II and cold war experiences and depicted America as a bastion for open, democratic societies arrayed against threats from closed, totalitarian societies of the right and the left. Furthermore, most Americans have firmly believed that ours has become a more progressively open society (a kind of natural evolutionary theory of democracy) primarily as a result of the development of means for instant mass communication, a better educated citizenry, and the like. What is probably far closer to the truth is the fact that America has tended toward the norms of a closed society, as secrecy is now standard operating procedure for government agencies, businesses, labor unions, churches, colleges and universities, and private associations and organizations. Indeed, concern for security has become one of the predominant themes for modern American organizational life.

This disparity between myth and reality in the world's most important democracy has gone all but unnoticed by many so-

[1] My special thanks to Everett C. Hughes for some of the inspiration and ideas in this article.

cial scientists and analysts. Apart from occasional studies of special secret societies (the Ku Klux Klan, religious sects) or organizations where secrecy plays an important role (the Roman Catholic Church, the military), and Shils's (1956) examination of the need for privacy in democracies, it is almost impossible to find major research or theorizing about the origins, nature, workings, and consequences of secrecy within social systems. This article provides a starting point for such work. In particular, it utilizes information collected while I worked from 1964 until 1966 for the Special Operations Research Office (SORO), the Army think tank that sponsored the abortive Project CAMELOT (Horowitz, 1967; Sjoberg, 1967). Too, these examples are now most relevant to the problems highlighted by the Pentagon Papers affair—the question of the adequacy of knowledge produced for political decision-makers within security-conscious, secret think tanks.

Defined as the possession of special hidden, and unacknowledged information, secrecy has always been a characteristic of human organizations. Such possession can be merely a function of one's particular social role or position of leadership (Michels, 1949). In contrast, secrecy as an elaborate social system of rules, rituals, codes, and penalties is particularly characteristic in modern organizations. Precisely accounting for this development is not easy, since the causes are multiple. However, it appears that the spread of secrecy has been partly a function of processes of bureaucratization and, ironically, democratization. With the breakdown of traditional sources of authority in medieval society and the subsequent rise of bureaucracy as the predominant mode of organizational life, manipulation and persuasion arose as instruments of power within organizational contexts. As Janowitz (1957) has pointed out, this transition from tradition to "democratic" manipulation has even marked such conservative and authoritarian contexts as the military.

The ability to lead and get the work of an organization done is no longer necessarily a matter of one's previous or present status or prestige. It has become more a matter of one's ability to persuade others to accept various decisions and plans. Manipulation and persuasion depend upon knowledge and information. Thus, what one knows and does not know determines who has power and how that power can be utilized. The plethora of think tanks arose after World War II not simply because knowledge had been previously inadequate or unavailable but also because leaders came to realize that exotic knowledge was a new source of power (Lyons & Morton, 1965). For example, SORO and similar agencies were formed by the army in the 1950s because that service was jealous of the Air Force's RAND Corporation (Smith, 1966). Though there is now ample evidence, even for sponsors of these organizations, that the knowledge produced by many, if not most, of the think tanks is extremely inadequate, there seems to be no serious move to restrict their role or number. After Project CAMELOT, SORO survived by the simple expedient of a name change to the Center for Research in Social Systems (CRESS). It was obvious that the army still realized the larger political significance of such organizations.

The adequacy, correctness, or appropriateness of knowledge and information, therefore, is not the central concern in the maintenance of knowledge factories—only the fact that some sort of information is available in some form to special interests or leaders. In theory, secrecy maximizes the power potential of the knowledge. What is told to whom, when, where, and how determines the ability of leaders to influence attitudes and opinions, in turn affecting behavior. Secrecy theoretically guarantees maximum control over how, when, where, and to whom specific information is released. Thus, more and greater secrecy is seen as indispensable to the proper and efficient functioning of the organization and its leaders. However, here, too, there is a gap between theory and reality. Rumor is endemic in secret contexts and becomes a primary means for informal social control. Rumors about hiring or firing, new projects, changes in budget requirements, long-range plans, and the like can at the very least inhibit unwanted acts and at the most encourage desired behavior. Leaders utilize rumor for these purposes, thus maintaining the dual standard in modern society whereby top government officials selectively leak secret information with immunity to serve their own ends while private citizens or minor bureaucrats are prosecuted under the law for such behavior.

Security and secrecy systems also contain other seeds of their own destruction. Since information is power, there is a strong impulse for leaders to leak special and privileged information to favored sources for purposes of self-enhancement. Therefore, an increasing number of members of an organization play the game of obtaining information in any way possible in the desperate search for organizational power and authority. In this manner they also contribute to the spread of rumor and the deterioration of the security system as a whole. Functionaries cannot perform even the most elementary tasks without minimum basic knowledge; therefore, there is an impetus within secret contexts that encourages individuals to attack the security system.

Furthermore, since secrecy is really an element of power, more and more individuals within organizational contexts become involved in and concerned with the security process. Lower-level personnel frequently classify information at higher standards of security than higher-level personnel, in conflict with the rational organizational structure; and security processes breed upon themselves as more people try to have a hand in the game of power. In 1965, SORO personnel completed a bibliography of all documents produced by the organization —a simple listing of titles and authors essentially for reference and public relations purposes. Before the bibliography was completed it was "classified" as For Official Use Only (FOUO) by SORO leaders to play it "safe." After six months of work, a finished copy was sent through army channels for "declassification." It soon returned reclassified CONFIDENTIAL (a higher level of security) by an unidentified Pentagon bureaucrat. At about the same time, a Soron (as the employees of SORO were forlornly called) was invited to do a critique of Latin American foreign policy for a national magazine. The magazine agreed not to publish any organizational identification (Army, SORO, American University), but officials of SORO insisted upon appropriate clearance from the army. The completed article was sent to the Army Research Office, which cleared it for security purposes. However, a bureaucrat in ARO showed it to a friend in the State Department for "sensitivity reasons." State formally classified the article since it was critical for foreign policy.

These dynamics of secrecy, therefore, work in such a manner as actually to minimize the power potential of knowledge in at least several ways. First, it is possible for those in insignificant positions of authority to deny others in more important positions of authority immediate access to important information. Second, one agency or organization can be denied information generated by and for another agency. What often results is a security system that begins to defeat itself, debase the information available, and create a situation worse than the use of no security whatsoever. As Supreme Court Justice Potter Stewart put it in his 1971 ruling on the Pentagon Papers case (*New York Times* v. *United States*): " ... when everything is classified, then nothing is classified, and the system becomes one to be disregarded by the cynical or the careless and to be manipulated by those intent on self-protection and self-promotion" (*Time*, 1971). Thus, secrecy that was originally designed to protect the organization, the society, or the nation works increasingly to protect special or individual interests, and it does not accomplish this task very well. At the same time, more individuals come to disregard secrecy requirements and procedures or deliberately subvert or misuse them. Rumor supplants rational, open means of communication and interaction. Spies and counterspies are employed to ferret out needed information or to be sure that privileged information is not disclosed. In such a context it is no longer possible to separate facts from lies, truth from fiction, research from gossip, or useful information from useless trivia.

There are other dysfunctions of secrecy as well—disparities between theoretical purposes and actual consequences. Coser (1963) has pointed out that most public policy and military secrecy is based on the belief that if one deprives competitors or enemies of important information, it is possible to keep them off balance to the point where violent conflict is less possible, compromise and bargaining are more probable, and one's chances for success are maximized. He indicates, by referring to Georg Simmel's work on conflict, that a precise knowledge of the comparative strengths of two parties is the most effective deterrent to violent, overt, disruptive conflict. In a context of maximum secrecy, this knowledge can only be gained by actually fighting out the conflict. In other words, secrecy enhances the probability of conflict, attenuates the possibilities for peaceful competition or compromise, and thereby, minimizes one's chances of success and threatens one's position of security.

If security systems based on secrecy, then, are counterproductive, if they function to undermine manifest purposes and goals, why do they not rapidly destroy themselves? In point of fact, in the long run they partially do, as the Ellsberg incident so well exemplifies. However, as is true of any social system, contexts based on secrecy may take on latent functions, for which they were not designed or proposed, as a way of maintaining and perpetuating themselves. My experience in doing research for the federal government on military problems suggests that three of the most important latent functions of secrecy in that context are the production and protection of relatively useless and unreliable knowledge, the consequent guarantee of individual and organizational job security, and a resulting extension of secrecy into areas involving sensitivity (Lowry, 1967b). The dynamics whereby these processes develop are too complex to be traced in detail in this article, but the fundamental processes involved can be briefly examined and illustrated.

At the time of the CAMELOT fiasco in SORO, the major function of such agencies and research proposals was cogently characterized by a slogan of unknown authorship that paraphrased Winston Churchill's famous World War II statement: "SORO should be renamed Military Operations Research Office; thus SORONS could be changed to MORONS, reflecting the fact that never have so many done so little for so much." A SORO researcher summarized the problem by suggesting that SORO was in the business of producing social science fiction and concealing that fact from all but a small group within the organization. In a speech before the AAAS in December, 1967, a nationally-known think tanker provided an expert rationalization for such a purpose. In responding to academic critics who questioned his data and figures and charged him with pseudoscientific and false quantification, he responded:

> I admit it. (The scientists) are in the business of writing dictionaries. Everything must be accurate. If they can't find a figure, they leave it out. But I am in the business of influencing decisions. I don't care whether my figures are accurate. If I can't find a figure, I make one up.

Such a pseudoscientific attitude can rapidly become antiscientific. One SORO assistant director who constantly criticized the work of a Latin American specialist, typically commented, "The trouble with your studies is that all you do is state hypotheses and prove or disprove them." SORO's in-house military adviser, placed in the organization by the Pentagon to insure relevant productivity, critiqued a theoretical paper on the connection between revolutionary movements and changes in the social structure with, "It's not operational." What this meant was that there was not a major in Viet Nam who could use or needed the ideas developed.

The necessity to produce knowledge and information that is practical and useful in immediate crisis contexts erodes the need for traditional scientific techniques and procedures. What results is a system that produces little of lasting merit, depth, or consequence. Indeed, in many cases the misinformation can be dangerously misleading if used as a basis for national policy

(Green, 1966; Rappoport, 1965). One lengthy SORO study, for example, involved considerable cost and concluded that "influence attempts (propaganda) are most successful when the objectives of both the initiator and recipient are most similar." In other words, after much time and expense the study concluded that persuasion attempts requiring the least amount of persuading are the most likely to succeed.

In addition, when SORO research was performed that produced important findings or suggestions it was often misused for political purposes. At a formal briefing for Pentagon officers in November 1965, an administrative official for SORO reported that a recently completed analysis proved "that Latin American officers who receive training in France, in contrast to (those receiving training in) America, are more fascistic." In reality, the study had dealt with only 70 Venezuelan officers, had not mentioned France, and carried one table comparing those officers receiving some training overseas with those receiving training only in Venezuela. These data suggested that those with overseas training were more likely to be engaged in coups or become politically active later in their careers. Nothing in the study indicated, however, whether such activity tended to be rightist or leftist in political content. Indeed, the study did raise, or should have raised, serious questions about the U.S. military program for training foreign officers. In contrast, it was used by an official of SORO to support the Pentagon myth that American training for foreign military personnel enhanced democratic propensities, encouraged antileftist sentiments, and contributed to stability in Latin American politics, a belief that still prevails in Washington. At about the same time, a SORO researcher returned from an extended trip to Vietnam and gave a classified (SECRET) briefing on his "studies." It was a low-grade intelligence travelogue. Slides were accompanied with the following types of comments:

> This is a picture of General _____ and Colonel _____ at the village of _____ in the District of _____ and Province of _____. There were many Catholics here. The general assured me that they were loyal to Vietnam and believe in peace because they are Catholics. The Buddhists believe in honoring their country . . .

So anxious are employees of research organizations to feel a part of ongoing studies that they rarely question the basic purpose or direction, much less the quality, of tasks to which they are assigned. In one army-sponsored think tank, a number of skilled professionals spent some time working on the logistics problems that might be involved in the Army's getting tens of thousands of latrines into Cambodia (ironically anticipating Richard Nixon's invasion of that country some years later). No one in the project questioned the necessity of latrines in a jungle warfare context. In another instance, researchers spent a number of months trying to find out why American military AWOL rates were lower in Vietnam than in previous wars and contexts. Again, no researcher raised the obvious question of whether or not there was any place for an American, Caucasian AWOLer to go in an Asian, jungle context. Furthermore, the assumption had been made that American morale in Vietnam was excellent and that the army might be able to use AWOL rates as an indicator of military morale in future situations.

The almost obsessive concern for research productivity as a meaningful measure of job security and personal identity in the secret think tank context can be illustrated best by comparison to traditional academic roles. Academia offers multiple rewards and opportunities. Professors have students; class sizes, student response, and student performance can become meaningful measures of one's role. Furthermore, opportunities are available for community and institutional service. In the think tank context, only productivity in the form of knowledge creation matters. However, productivity is restricted and manipulated by the wishes of sponsors, the biases of administrative superiors, the necessities of security systems, and the like. Thus, productivity ultimately means one's attachment to a project that has a fair guarantee of generally long life, not the formal publication of reports or the presentation of papers. Anything that threatens the life of a project, therefore, becomes a personal threat to the researchers and involves serious problems of personal identity. The ultimate irony is that meaningful productivity in the classic sense—open publication of final, definitive results—can itself become a threat to the continuance of the project. If such publication is bad, the project may be canceled; if good, the project may be terminated as successfully completed. As a consequence, researchers will do everything possible to minimize these risks and forestall the completion of work. For example, fundamental questions of the value or worth of the research are simply avoided or ignored.

Secrecy plays an especially crucial role in this process, though it acts as a double-edged sword. On the one hand, secrecy severely limits the ability of researchers to demonstrate their competence and contributions to their colleagues, the general public, and even their administrative superiors and sponsors. For this reason, the traditional academic who moves to a secret think tank context runs the very great occupational risk of loss of intellectual visibility and subsequent career decline. Why, then, do researchers not resist the restrictions of security systems? Because secrecy, on the other hand, also provides a screen behind which shoddy, meaningless, and trivial work (and in extreme cases, charlatanism) can continue with minimum criticism and questioning. At SORO, the greatest expenditure of researcher time and costs were involved in thinking about and planning potential projects, preparing reports on what had been thought about and planned in the past, and speculating about short- and long-range organizational goals—rather than in conducting research. I once did an analysis of a "typical" 50-hour week of my research time as principal investigator of TASK ROLE (head of studies of changing military roles) and acting chairman of the Basic Studies Division:

16 hours— Written reports to SORO administrators, military sponsors, and others on work planned and in progress (Lowry, 1965).
13 hours— Verbal briefings to SORO personnel, military sponsors, and others on work planned and in progress.
12 hours— Preparing and completing in-house reports on personnel, budget, and the like.
5 hours— Miscellaneous administrative tasks (answering mail, handling personnel problems, etc.).
4 hours— Conducting research.

Personal observation of researchers assigned to me and of other SORO activities indicated that this was not at all unusual. After the public exposé of CAMELOT, almost all SORO researchers were "taken off research" and assigned the task of preparing an organizational work program for the following fiscal year (1966). One work unit, typical of much of the program, read as follows:

Estimated Completion Date: 2nd Quarter Fiscal 1966
Professional Man Years in Fiscal 1966: 5

To develop a research plan that would specify those research studies necessary to increase understanding of and to identify, analyze and measure inter-relationships of significant variables in the early phases of nationally disruptive social unrest and violent social change ... The military and theoretical requirements for research in this area will be considered, previous research accomplishments reviewed, gaps in existing knowledge identified, and assessments made as to the feasibility of undertaking various optional research studies. Upon completion of these activities, specific research tasks will be developed for conduct.

In other words, five qualified professionals were to spend approximately $170,000 and six months to write some research proposals dealing with revolutionary processes. Another work unit proposed an expenditure of $35,000 for a professional to act as an adviser to "assist the Army on problems involving the application or adaptation of scientific information and knowledge about individual and social factors associated with special warfare and related military operations." Another work unit entailed the preparation of a list of "propositions" about processes of social unrest at a cost of approximately $25,000 for the fiscal year.

Security and sensitivity demands simply compounded this propensity toward make-work. Multiple briefings and reports had to be given and prepared because of a variety of secrecy classifications; one for top-level Pentagon sponsors (cleared through SECRET or TOP SECRET); one for middle-level bureaucrats (cleared through CONFIDENTIAL or SECRET); one for colleagues and professionals (if the substance even warranted); one for release to media sources and politicians (no security clearance, version had to be "sanitized" for political purposes). It was apparent that one could make a comfortable career of writing and delivering reports of reports. If others questioned one's activities, it was easy to respond: "I can't talk about that; it's classified."

The ludicrous extremes to which such a system can be carried were demonstrated by the experience of two SORO researchers who spent six months of intensive work planning and organizing a proposed study of the worth and meaning of military civic action programs utilizing Taiwan as the laboratory. Extensive contacts were developed with Taiwanese officials and scholars, the State Department, and appropriate U.S. military commands. An elaborate participant-observation technique was planned for analyzing Taiwanese military civic action programs at the village level in Taiwan. Elaborate precautions were taken in both the study design and the way in which the project was formulated to handle the potentially explosive political problems. That is, the U.S. army and Nationalist Chinese officials believed that the study would "prove" the value of military civic action, though the eventual study might very well disclose undesirable consequences of such programs from a political and social standpoint. The detailed final proposal was forwarded to army sponsors for approval. Weeks passed with no formal response. The researchers became concerned that the sensitivity of the proposal (the delicate relationship of the U.S. with Taiwan and the possible disclosure of disadvantages in military civic action programs) had killed the project. They began an informal investigation of the status of their proposal and discovered that not only had their project not been killed but that it had been rewritten and turned over to another agency. Furious that their work should be used and stolen in such a clandestine fashion, they demanded a formal explanation. A representative of the Pentagon was sent to SORO to deliver the following verbal reply:

> "The Army rewrote and reassigned the Taiwan study since a project did not really exist yet. No planning, formal proposal writing, or other preliminary actions can take place until permission is obtained from appropriate sources (the State Department, Department of Defense, etc.) to do the study."

No further explanation was given to the researchers. They were never told whether or not the individuals to whom the project had been reassigned were more competent to complete the study, nor were they told how approval for research planning could take place without planning being involved. Both vowed never again to "waste their time" in such efforts and to content themselves with "informally planning to think about plans and report only on (their) thoughts".

Finally, one of the major problems of elaborate secrecy systems within such contexts is the propensity for them to become a latent device for controlling politically sensitive information and individuals. The distinction between secret information and sensitive information, or the need for privacy (Westin, 1967), is not at all clear, but the issue deserves more attention than it has received. Typically, classified information is knowledge that must be protected from unauthorized disclosure, since such disclosure would constitute a severe, immediate, and real threat to national security. The levels of formal security classification (TOP SECRET, SECRET, and CONFIDEN-

TIAL) and a number of informal classifications (FOR OFFICIAL USE ONLY, RESTRICTED DISTRIBUTION) theoretically reflect the degree of threat inherent in the unauthorized disclosure of the knowledge. Such a system appears to have rational, though hard to delimit, boundaries. Most people, for example, would agree that the wide disclosure of troop movement in a hot war context would constitute a threat to men's lives, to the success of military tactics and strategy, and therefore, to the national security. In contrast, information about PX scandals or battlefield brutalities would seem to be merely embarrassing and threatening only to particular individuals.

A closer look, however, at security systems must lead to two additional conclusions. First, as the previous references to Coser indicated, there is good reason to question the fundamental assumption behind classifying any information or knowledge. Disclosure of troop movements might lead an enemy to a more realistic assessment of risks and, thus, to a lessening of the possibility of violent confrontation and the resulting threat to national security. Second, security systems are cressive. Rather than being self-limiting they tend to be expansive. There is an inclination on the part of bureaucrats and leaders to play it safe and classify information at the highest possible level of security. In contemporary organizational life, especially the federal government, security of the system is often equated with security of a particular organization, department, or leader. Furthermore, any knowledge about any phenomenon can be potentially threatening to some individual or organization. If that individual or organization is an important part of the system, there will be a tendency to classify most information at the highest possible levels. That is, there is a propensity to expand the limits of the definition of classifiable information to include all "sensitive" knowledge.

I received one of the clearest explanations and rationalizations of this process in correspondence I had with a State Department official in 1967. Having resigned from SORO in 1966, I wrote State concerning many of the problems involved in government-sponsored public policy research, including the issue of overclassification of research reports. I received the following reply:

> The problem of classification of research reports has long been a difficult one within government. Each agency is responsible for classification of its own work and there are no government-wide

rules in this respect. Some concerns over this problem has recently been evidenced in the Congress ... *The fact that the material upon which a research report is based is public knowledge does not make it any less sensitive.* In exploring policy alternatives and new ideas, the government must often employ the same degree of confidentiality common in the industrial world." (Italics added for emphasis.)

The italicized reference was to a publication edited by me while at SORO and consisting of reports from a number of scholars on problems in studying changing military roles in other cultural contexts (Lowry, 1967a). A conference had been held in 1965 to which scholars from a variety of social science disciplines had been invited to present their opinions, doubts, concerns, and recommendations about the army-sponsored research program. The conference was open and involved no classified information. Yet after I had left SORO, a copy of the final conference report was mailed to me in 1967 classified FOR OFFICIAL USE ONLY. I immediately returned my copies with the indication that since I no longer hold a security clearance, I technically should not have the report in my possession—nor for that matter should any of the original participants. I never did receive an explanation for the classification, though sensitivity seemed to be the issue. Many participants had been sharply critical of the army research program and had freely made comments about foreign countries and leaders ("that leader is dictatorial ... ").

The tendency for security matters to become more concerned with sensitivity than with merely potentially threatening knowledge, however, goes far beyond the classification of all kinds of information. In late 1965, several incidents at SORO indicated that many in the federal government and the Pentagon wished to use social research agencies as latent spies on the academic world. It had long been common practice at agencies such as SORO for officials to collect secret information on their own employees, presumably to be utilized at some later time when reemployment and similar decisions were necessary. In November 1965, an assistant director wrote a confidential memo "for the record" based on gossip about what one researcher's wife had said at a cocktail party. Luckily for the researcher, a secretary stopped the memo before it was filed. Although she told other officials about the incident, no further action was taken. Several weeks later, an official policy of opening all business and personal mail delivered to SORO was promulgated by an administrative official. The reason given was the necessity to log mail for security.

In December 1965, a SORO researcher was asked by the army to investigate all consultants (outside scholars and experts, mostly in the academic community, who were paid fees for various kinds of usually open contributions to SORO research) for "sensitivity" but not for security purposes. The researcher refused, giving as his reasons explanations that are relevant to this discussion:

1. Such investigation is a misuse of security procedures.
2. No one can adequately define sensitivity.
3. Such an action would be undemocratic and grossly inappropriate. It is not the function of research agencies to act as spies on colleagues.
4. Such a precedent would be dangerous. A man could be cleared for sensitivity reasons and later be shown classified information because he thought he had been cleared for security purposes. This would be a clear violation of standard security procedure.

An additional problem of sensitivity classification is that it can profoundly change the basic research meaning or intent of analyses. A Pentagon censor returned a researcher's paper in early 1965 with a reference to a Latin American leader as "a dictator" struck out. The marginal notation in red pencil read: "This man is a friend; we can't call him a dictator." When the researcher responded that the paper contained an operational definition of dictatorship that described this man's style of leadership, he was told to find another definition. A paper entitled "Subversive Manipulation of Crowds and Mobs" to be read before a riot-control class at Fort Bragg was retitled by an army censor "The Role of Crowds in Civil Disturbances." Another paper to be used for the same purposes had an extensive reference to the Los Angeles civil disturbances as a special type of riot red-penciled as "too sensitive". Where sensitivity is involved, all levels of command tend to become sources of advice, regardless of their expertise. A copy of a proposed SORO journal, entitled *Conflict,* was sent to an assistant secretary of the army. The copy was returned with notations on all pages. These included the direction that only SORO personnel should be permitted to publish in the journal. The secretary indicated that the title of the journal was wrong and a term like *Disagreement* should be used instead since the latter was a better social scientific concept (There is a disagreement in Vietnam?). Also included was the notation that numerous references to "revolution" were too sensitive; "rising expectations" or "social change" were suggested as safe alternatives. In such a context, it is impossible for researchers to develop meaningful, reasoned analyses; it is not surprising that some willingly invent figures, data, and concepts to support special biases or myths.

In December 1965, a secretary to a SORO director received a telephone call from an officer in the Social Science Research Division of the Army Research Office, soliciting information about a nationally known sociologist who had been quoted in a Chicago paper as having witnessed American troops committing atrocities in Vietnam. The officer wanted to know if the sociologist had any ties to SORO and if anyone knew anything about him. The incident first came to my attention indirectly. After reporting to work one morning, I began to receive many inquiries from SORO secretaries, officials, and other personnel: "Who is Professor _____?; "Do we do any work with _____?; "What do you know about _____?" Not knowing what was involved, I simply replied that the man was a personal friend who did excellent work in the sociology of the military but who, unfortunately, had never had any formal connection with my research projects. When I asked why the interest, no one gave me a clear response. In the middle of the day, I was called into an administrative superior's office. Present were two colonels, my administrative superior, and another SORO administrator. What followed was a Kafkaesque interrogation:

Col. 1: "Look at this newspaper report from _____." (I was handed a Xeroxed copy of the article.) "It says that this friend of yours accuses U.S. soldiers of committing atrocities; chopping the heads and hands off prisoners, pushing them out of helicopters." (The article report was actually quite mild and reasoned in the light of later atrocity disclosures.) "U.S. soldiers don't do that kind of thing. The Pentagon wants us to investigate this. What connection do we have with Professor _____?"
Me: "What do you mean by connection?"
Col. 1: "The word seems obvious to me."
Me: (I explained my personal connection with the professor.) "As far as I know, Professor _____ has never been paid any money for any of my activities. However, he did attend the conference on military roles as an observer and participated informally. He is also a member of an informal group of national scholars which I and

others have joined to study military problems. The organization is _____."

Col. 2: "What kind of an organization is that?"

Me: "Just what I said, a professional organization."

Col. 1: "Will you state in writing that SORO has never had any formal connection with _____?"

Me: "I will state that to the best of my knowledge he has never received any SORO money from us."

Col. 2: "Why do you keep equivocating?"

Me: "I don't know what you mean. I can't vouch for the whole organization. Nor do I know if those scholars who are on subcontract to us have consulted _____."

Col. 1: "Then you had better call the subcontractees and find out what they know about _____."

Me: "I will not. I am not going to spy on a colleague. Furthermore, I am not going to indirectly accuse someone of ideas without knowing all the facts. I recommend that the army and SORO drop this whole affair. The academic community may be so upset that further contacts will be impossible."

Col. 1: "That is completely irresponsible."

Col. 2: "I don't give a damn what the academic community thinks."

Col. 1: "In my long career with the army I have never seen Americans commit atrocities ... "

Me: "If you want to discuss the merits of what is described in the newspaper report, that is something else again. However, let's argue the problems raised in the article in some other context than trying to spy on Professor _____. As a matter of fact, the article might make the basis of a worthwhile study ... "

Col. 2: "That is the most incredible nonsense I have ever heard."

Admin. 1: "SORO can't study atrocities."

Me: "Why not? It might tell us something about the nature of this war and other problems. By the way, suppose Professor _____ had had some connection with SORO, what then?"

Col. 1: "That's irresponsible. Imagine what the newspaper would do with a story like that."

Admin. 2: "We couldn't have one of our people saying things like that."

The implications of this exchange were obvious. The army was interested in maintaining lists of safe versus sensitive social scientists, and research organizations like SORO were looked upon as good resources for the preparation of such lists.

Two special notes of caution are necessary with reference to this preliminary analysis of secrecy in one particular context. First, elaborate security and secrecy systems develop within various organizational settings for different reasons. In the case of military think tanks, secrecy originates because of an assumed necessity to protect national security. However, it rapidly takes on the primary function of providing a way in which researchers and administrators can manage the peculiar tensions, inconsistencies, and feelings of alienation associated with their special roles and jobs. These unusual conditions, especially characteristic of the transient and unstable Washington, D.C., environment, may not be present in other contexts where secrecy may operate to accomplish different purposes, both manifest and latent. However, at least in this one context the problem of secrecy lies both within and without the security system per se. That is, responses to this problem must include not just modifications of the secrecy systems but also more meaningful roles and statuses for researchers. Comparative analyses of secrecy systems in other contexts will disclose differences and similarities to this analysis.

Second, though the major thesis of this paper is that security systems are inherently unstable and function to undermine themselves, secrecy can perform planned boundary-maintaining functions, especially for institutional leaders. The leaking of sensitive information followed by the formal prosecution of those responsible provides leadership with a way of controlling political behavior. In this sense, the Ellsbergs serve as examples of what is and is not acceptable. A historical analysis might disclose, for example, that security trials occur primarily in periods when political views are undergoing rapid transformation and new opinions become threatening to incumbent leadership. Such a political use of secret information can be deplored for moral reasons, but it cannot be called dysfunctional for the maintenance of the system *qua* vested interest and ruling authority. On the contrary, this use of secrecy enhances the continuation of prevailing policy with minimum criticism. Nevertheless, this use can become dysfunctional if it makes system change impossible, provides a means for sustaining worthless information within the system, and undermines the credibility of scientific and intellectual criticism of prevailing policy. The continuation of bad policy may cause the eventual destruction of the system.

In summary, I have suggested that sociologists should turn their attentions to secrecy and security systems in modern organizational life. Such systems lend themselves to particularly provocative forms of analysis, as well as constituting one of the most serious problems in contemporary society. Utilizing information collected from my experiences working in a Pentagon-sponsored social science think tank, I have theorized that security systems within that type of context function both to undermine the purposes for which they were originally intended and, consequently, to take on additional functions that were unintended and undesired. What is now required are analyses in other contexts (for example, in business, education, and religion) to determine if the same dynamics are operative in most instances. If so, two possible remedies suggest themselves. First, serious question should be raised about the maintenance of secrecy systems in any form. As recent testimony by government censors has indicated, perhaps as much as 99 per cent of all presently classified information should be immediately declassified. Second, if some system of security is required, it is obvious that restricted and severe limits should be imposed. For example, the classification of social science knowledge is too critical a matter to leave to dozens of isolated bureaucrats within a vague chain of command. In 1965, a Pentagon bureau functioned as a censor under the euphemistically misleading name of the Office of Freedom of Information, The Director of Public Information. Perhaps research should carry some estimate by producers of the possible implications of free exposure (to whom, under what conditions, possible benefits, and the like). Designing new systems as a way of reversing the trend toward security consciousness in contemporary organizations would not be difficult. What is first needed, however, is a major reassessment of the functional assumptions upon which prevailing systems have been based.

References

Coser, L. A., The dysfunctions of military secrecy. *Social Problems,* 1963, 11 (Summer); 13–22.

Dyson, F. J., Death of a project. *Science,* 1965, 149 (July 9); 141–144.

Green, P., *Deadly logic: The theory of nuclear deterrence.* Columbus: Ohio State University Press, 1966.

Hitch, C. J., *Decision-making for defense.* Berkeley: University of California Press, 1965.

Horowitz, I. L., *The rise and fall of Project Camelot.* Cambridge, Mass.: The MIT Press, 1967.

Janowitz, M., Military elites and the study of war. *Journal of Conflict Resolution,* 1957, 1 (March); 9–18.

Lowry, R. P., Research note—changing military roles: Challenge to rural sociologists. *Rural Sociology,* 1965, 30 (June); 219–225.

Lowry, R. P. Problems of Studying Military Roles in Other Cultures: A Working Conference. Edited with an Introduction and Epilogue by R. P. Lowry. Washington, D.C.: SORO, The American University, 1967. (a)

Lowry, R. P. Status inconsistency and research productivity: The Washington (D.C.) context. Paper presented at the New England Section of the American Catholic Sociological Society, Providence College. (February 11); 1967.(b)

Lyons, G. M., *The uneasy partnership: Social science and the federal government in the twentieth century.* New York: Russell Sage Foundation, 1969.

Lyons, G. M., & Morton, L. *Schools for strategy: Education and research in national security affairs.* New York: Praeger, 1965.

Michels, R. *Political parties: A sociological study of the oligarchic tendencies of modern democracy.* New York: Free Press, 1949.

Mollenhoff, C. R. *Washington cover-up.* Garden City, N.Y.: Doubleday, 1962.

Rappoport, A. Chicken a la Kahn. *The Virginia Quarterly Review,* 1965, 41 (Summer); 370–389.

Sheehan, N., Smith, H., Kenworthy, E. W., and Butterfield, F. *The Pentagon Papers.* New York: Bantam Books, 1971.

Shils, E. A. *The torment of secrecy.* New York: Free Press, 1956.

Sjoberg, G. Project Camelot: Selected reactions and personal reflections. In G. Sjoberg (ed.), *Ethics politics, and social research.* Cambridge, Mass.: Schenkman Publishing Company, 1967.

Smith, B. L. R. *The RAND Corporation: Cast study of a nonprofit advisory corporation.* Cambridge, Mass.: Harvard University Press, 1966.

Snow, C. P. The price of democracy. New York *Times,* July 12, 1971, page C27.

Time magazine. Three points of view from the court. *Time* magazine, July 12, 1971, page 11.

Westin, A. F. *Privacy and freedom.* New York: Atheneum, 1967.

Unit 6

A Comparative Perspective

14

Secrecy as a Social and Political Process

Stanton K. Tefft
Wake Forest University

THE CONCEPT OF SECRECY

Many of us share the common misconception that secrecy is primarily used by corporations or governments and then only as a device to cover up illegal acts. Of course, governments as well as businesses do employ secrecy for these purposes. But when we take a broader view of the social role of secrecy, we will find that secrecy is a social strategy employed by individuals involved in social relationships from the most simple ones to the most complex. Furthermore, secrecy does not always conceal unlawful, much less, immoral acts. To be sure secrecy is an inherent part of the politics of large as well as small polities. Secrecy has also served the economic interests of the medieval craft guild as well as the modern multinational corporation. Less apparent is the role that secrecy plays in the relations between kinsmen, lovers, friends, families, and ethnic groups—or between stigmatized groups and the wider community.

Indeed, far from having a monopoly on the employment of secrecy for social ends, the human being shares this dubious honor with other primates. Chimps conceal information about the source of preferred food from other troop members (Tanner & Zihlman, 1976). At least one gorilla is known to have "lied" to escape punishment (Patterson, 1978).

The term "secrecy" is usually applied to all types of knowledge or information known to a restricted group of people (Fowler & Fowler, 1964). However, by implication, such a defintion suggests that individuals cannot keep secrets from one another—an obviously false notion. Most definitions of secrecy suggest a conscious and deliberate attempt by individuals to conceal information (Kelvin, 1973; Wilsnack, 1979), but sometimes information is restricted without conscious effort by individuals or groups. Often individuals simply cannot successfully communicate many private thoughts (O'Brien, 1977). Some activities remain private simply because outsiders have no interest in them. In some cases, "secrets" are maintained only because outsiders do not have the intelligence capabilities to discover them; for example, modern private and public bureaucracies by nature of their complex structure foster many forms of nondeliberate concealment, resistant to all but the most persistent outside investigations (O'Connell, Chapter 10 in this book). Secrecy should then be distinguished from such forms of uncalculated concealment.

The concept of secrecy can also be distinguished from the concept of privacy. Various authors separate secrecy from privacy by suggesting that secrecy involves obligatory concealment while privacy involves voluntary concealment (Shils, 1966; Bates, 1964). On the other hand, some writers argue that secrecy always involves concealment as a means for goal achievement, while privacy involves concealment that brings intrinsic satisfaction (Rule, 1974). But, of course, privacy can be obligatory, and secrecy can bring intrinsic satisfaction (e.g., families in financial difficulties may oblige members to keep this information private; members of a secret society may feel a sense of superiority over outsiders not privy to their secrets).

Secrecy, then, might be better defined as the mandatory or voluntary, but calculated, concealment of information, activities, or relationships. From the community's perspective the secrets may involve activities, plans or relationships that are legal, illegal, or ethically neutral. In any case, secrecy exists only in those situations in which "interaction, communication and perception is physically practicable ... " (Shils, 1966).

Further distinctions should be made among intimate secrecy (privacy), private-life secrecy, and public-life secrecy.[1] Intimate secrecy, or privacy, involves the concealment of information or acts that, if revealed, would be considered moral, or, at

[1] I have modified Laslett and Warren's classification slightly by classifying privacy as intimate secrecy. (See chapter 1 in this book.)

least, ethically neutral by most outsiders (e.g., marital sex relations). By contrast private-life secrecy involves concealment of personal acts or relationships that outsiders consider immoral or illegal (e.g., lesbianism). These two forms of secrecy do not ordinarily involve political or economic secrets, rather knowledge about intimate or personal matters concealed by one to two individuals or, at most, only a few persons.

Public-life secrecy involves concealments among social groups or agencies directly involved in the political, economic, religious, and social life of the community. Thus, public-life secrecy refers to secrecy involving associations, conspiratorial groups, Mafia-type organizations, guilds, corporations, and governments. Here again, secrecy may further involve the concealment of moral or immoral, legal or illegal acts, relationships, or strategies.

THE SECRECY PROCESS

Secrecy operates as an adaptive device. It enables individuals, dyads (two-person groups), intimacy groups (including families and kin groups), associations, and governing bodies to attain certain ends. In this sense, at least, secrecy is instrumental and rational behavior (Pétursson, 1977; Wilsnack, 1979). Through regulated control and disclosure of information, individuals as well as groups may exert some control over their environments by making it difficult for outsiders, whether competitors, rivals, or enemies, to predict their actions and take counteraction against them. Of course, secrecy can bring intrinsic satisfaction to the individual (i.e., ego enhancement, by giving individuals a sense of power and superiority over outsiders); but for the most part these psychological benefits are incidental to the original social and political purpose.

Secrecy, then, is a strategy for "behavioral adaptation." By behavioral adaptation I refer as Bennett does "to the coping mechanisms that humans display in obtaining their wants or adjusting their lives and purposes (Bennett, 1976a, p. 246; 1976b)." Secrecy is one of the social resources available to individuals that they can employ in manipulating or reacting to their environment. For secret knowledge always gives its possessors some degree of power over others.

Secrecy sets into motion certain similar social processes regardless of the level of social interaction involved (e.g., individual in relation to individual, family in relation to nonfamily members, criminal society in relation to government, state in relation to other states) or the goals or purposes involved. Simmel (1906) was one of the first to point out that secrecy is a social form clearly distinguishable from its particular contents. What Simmel calls the social forms of secrecy we view as a series of interrelated processes set into operation once secrecy is employed. These interrelated processes suggest a conceptual model useful in a cross-cultural comparison of secrecy, for it enables us to differentiate the unique historical, cultural, or situational factors (the "content" in Simmel's terminology) from the more universal factors when comparing secrecy operations in a variety of cultural and social situations.

The employment of secrecy as an adaptive device involves five interrelated secrecy processes: security (including surveillance, deception, and counterespionage); entrusted disclosure (including certain forms of persuasion); espionage; evaluation; and post-hoc security (Wilsnack, 1979).[2]

In this paper we will review the basic functions of secrecy, the process by which secrets are discovered (espionage), the devices employed to protect secrets (security), the circumstances under which some secrets are revealed (entrusted disclosure), the techniques for evaluating information about secrets, and the reactive mechanisms that operate when unauthorized disclosure of secrets takes place (post-hoc security)

THE NEED FOR SECRECY

The prevailing rationale of secret keepers, whether the secrets concern legal or illegal acts, or relationships, is that outsiders surely have some motive to discover the secrets; and, that, without security, could indeed discover them.

Fear of discovery ("visibility") may arouse the emotion of shame, which in turn may activate strategies of concealment (Schneider, 1977). While this is often the case when individuals hide disvalued qualities, activities, or relationships, more pragmatic concerns rather than shame also motivate secrecy. For example, the spy conceals his activities for fear of arrest and punishment rather than from feelings of shame.

Concerns over privacy and its protection vary from society to

[2] I have modified Wilsnack's original processual analysis, but I am indebted to him for many ideas about the secrecy process incorporated in the text of this unit. Rigney (1975) discusses the idea of post-hoc security. I am indebted to him for this idea.

society. Some tribal societies put great emphasis upon individual and family privacy. The Kpelle of Liberia, for example, highly esteem people who are reticent about expressing their deepest feelings and strongly criticize those who won't perserve secrets (Murphy, 1976). But intimate secrets do not always involve personal acts or relationships. Some knowledge is kept secret if its disclosure would subject family members to unwanted community demands or economic obligations. For example, wealthy Tarahumara families (in Mexico) conceal their wealth in order to avoid economic demands made upon them by destitute tribal members or to avoid government taxes (Passin, 1942). For similar reasons, Gola elders (in Liberia) keep their family histories secret from outsiders in order not to jeopardize rights to certain property or political positions. Disclosure of such information might enable outsiders to challenge land titles or political rights (Murphy, 1976).

In modern society, value is placed on secrecy as a device whereby the "private self" can be kept separate from the "public self" (Bates, 1964). There has emerged the notion of personal life styles as a kind of private property which individuals can reveal or not reveal as they see fit (Shils, 1975). In France, for example, the strong value placed on personal autonomy and independence together with a predominant fear of criticism, ridicule, gossip, and other conformative pressures reinforce the other motives for privacy (Victor, Chapter 4 in this book).[3]

The veils of secrecy preventing outside intrusion on acts and relationships within the modern family provide an opportunity for invisible subversion of many social norms. Some of these secret acts will obviously be violations of the law, such as child or wife beating in the United States; while others may only violate the norms of appropriate behavior, such as deviant heterosexual techniques.

Secrecy becomes even more vital to individuals whose "deviant " acts or relationships take place within more public arenas. Some gays, for example, find it expedient to hide their sexual deviancy from members of the straight (heterosexual) community to avoid legal and economic sanctions (Ponse, 1976).

People organize groups to pursue special interests. These are

[3]Obviously some societies do not put a high value on privacy at all but emphasize the importance of public over private activities. In classical Athens, for example, public political life was considered more fulfilling than private life; indeed, privacy was viewed as a privation rather than something to be defended (Bryant, 1978).

associations. While even open associations maintain some secrets, secret associations or secret societies, by contrast, are groups whose continued existence relies totally on the continuous concealment of ideas, objects, activities, plans, objectives, and membership from outsiders (Hazelrigg, 1969; Gist, 1936, 1938, 1940; Wedgwood, 1930; Bhuntani, 1962). In a few cases the existence of the association itself may be kept secret (Simmel, 1950). Some secret associations pursue goals that are hostile to the central values and institutions of the political community. Such secret associations are alienative ones. Other secret organizations support or, at least, are in close accord with the dominant values of the community. These are conformative secret orders (Lyman, 1970).

Secrecy enables alienative associations to avoid political persecution or destruction. Revolutionary or subversive organizations are more well-known examples of groups that must employ forms of secrecy as a means of survival against the police forces of the governments they hope to overthrow. One such early subversive organization, the Arab Karmathians, aimed at overthrowing the Sunni Caliphs and replacing them with Ismailis, by undermining the religious authority of the existing political leaders (Keightley, 1964). Their successors, the Assassins, turned to terrorism in 11th century Persia and Syria as a means to achieve the same ends (Annan, 1967b; Daraul, 1961, pp. 28–29).

In early China, secret societies defended peasant interests. Many of these Chinese secret associations, originating either from religious sects or mutual aid associations, not only countered the power of government by defending the local peasantry against looting soldiers, bandits and excessive taxation, but also provided leadership in the struggle against the Mongols and, after the Manchu conquest, organized insurrections against Manchu rule (Comber, 1959; Bianco, 1972, pp. 204–15; Chesneaux, 1971; Davis, 1971). In his crusade to overthrow the Manchu dynasty, even Sun Yat-sen, the Chinese revolutionary, was able to get support from secret societies among the overseas Chinese (Lyman, 1970).

But many conformative secret orders employ secrecy as a device to maintain an exclusive monopoly on esoteric knowledge: the Greek Pythagorean brotherhood, the Mithra cult in Persia, the seventeenth-century Rosicrucians and the eighteenth-century Masons provided members, dissatisfied with conventional sources of wisdom, an alternative source of inspiration and hope (Daraul, 1961; Smart, 1967; Roberts, 1972). In these cases, secrecy increased the value of such exclusive knowledge and thereby enhanced the prestige of those who possessed such secrets.

Membership in conformative secret societies may also give mystical reinforcement to the secular authority of political leaders or to groups claiming social distinction. Either leaders are the only ones eligible for membership in the inner councils of the society and thus privy to secrets not shared by the lower grades or they are only ones allowed membership in a particular order (Gunther, 1927; Koch, 1974; Little, 1948; Ford, 1941). Secret societies of the Indians of the Pacific Northwest were open only to those who had an hereditary right to membership (Drucker, 1965; Boas, 1970). Similar requisites of both hereditary prerogative and wealth had to be met for admission into the Ogboni of the Yoruba (Morton-Williams, 1960), and the Banks Island secret associations (Webster, 1908).

Secret society leadership also enables tribal heads to maintain their political dominance within the community. For example, Kpelle (Liberia) elders use their position of leadership in tribal secret societies, and their special control over access to special knowledge that this position gives them, to assert and maintain their dominance over youth (Murphy, 1976). And Brandt (Chapter 5 in this book) demonstrates that Taos Pueblo leaders (the "Old People"), by controlling access to the secret knowledge of the kiva groups through their leadership of these religious cults, prevent members of opposing factions from gaining authority in the Pueblo.

Powerful secret orders in the employ of governments provide political leaders with an organizational weapon for punishing, repressing, or destroying political enemies. There are as many modern examples of ruling class use of secret societies for purposes of political control. During the period of Chinese history when the Kuomintang was in power (1912–1949), agents of various secret associations were used by the government to suppress dissenters among the workers at home and to terrorize political enemies in the overseas Chinese communities (Chesneaux, 1972; Deacon, 1974). In eighteenth-century Ireland the Orange Order was formed to defend Protestant interests against secret Roman Catholic terrorist groups (Senior, 1973; White, 1973; McCartney, 1973). By the end of the nineteenth century the Orange lodges numbered about 90, with a total membership of several thousand (Senior, 1966). In Czarist

Russia, after the assassination of Alexander II, a Sacred Brotherhood was organized to fight revolutionary terrorism with counterterrorism.

Even the governments of newly independent, third-world states have co-opted traditional secret organizations for state functions. In Liberia, for example, the tribal Poro and the Sande secret organizations serve the interests of the ruling aristocracy, while on the Ivory Coast the ruling political party uses local Poro lodges for political recruitment (Liebenow, 1964; Wallerstein, 1964). In modern Sierra Leone the secret women's society, the Bundu, gives powerful political support to the political aspirations of some of the female members (Hoffer, 1972).

Secrecy plays a role even in so-called open organizations whose major goals are overt rather than covert. Economic competition has always provided a rationale for secrecy, especially when certain exclusive knowledge possessed by one competitor gives that party a power advantage over any economic rivals.

Craft organizations and guilds guarded trade secrets for much the same reasons as modern corporations. Muslim craft guilds of the eleventh and twelfth centuries preserved trade secrets (Massignon, 1932). For similar reasons Roman and Byzantine members of trade guilds were allowed membership in only one guild (Boak, 1932). The English and Scottish Masons of the fourteenth and fifteenth centuries formed craft guilds as a means of preserving trade secrets by giving some unity to their itinerant membership (Roberts, 1972; Whalen, 1966). In like fashion, modern professional associations and craft unions restrict membership in part, at least, to limit the access of outsiders to technical knowledge (Moore & Tumin, 1949).

However, secrecy plays an even more predominant role within and among modern businesses. For example, the fierce competition between modern Newfoundland deep-sea trawler fishing captains for large catches necessitates each keeping economic secrets from the other. Secrecy enables a captain to retain a temporary monopoly on a successful fishing site and thus bring more profits to his crew and himself; by so doing he retains the valuable loyalty of a highly trained crew (Andersen, Chapter 9 in this book).

However, since large private bureaucracies dominate the life of modern capitalist society, they are the major reason for so much secrecy in the economic life of modern state systems. Corporations keep secrets from competitors (external secrecy) to maintain a competitive advantage. By so doing, they can realize the corporation goal of profit maximization as well as stability. Secrecy, moreover, enables such private economic bureaucracies to shield illegal acts such as bribes, price fixing, and political gifts from both the government and the public.

On the other hand, both corporation hierarchies as well as specialized department or divisional structures give rise to internal secrecy. Top management may conceal information about overall corporation planning from the lower management levels in order to retain their authority and avoid criticism from the middle management employees. Corporation management may further encourage corporation officials to conceal information about their salaries from each other in order to prevent jealousy over such differential rewards (Moore, 1962). Both the technical staff and middle-range managers may conceal blunders as well as information about product safety defects and inefficient operations from the top management to protect themselves from criticism or censure; but the top management may deliberately keep themselves ignorant of subordinates' illegal or unethical activities in order to avoid accountability in the event that such activities are uncovered and publicized by outsiders (e.g., the press, the legislative branch) (Rigney, 1975; O'Connell, Chapter 10 in this book). Ironically enough, management pressure for profit maximization may be the principal factor that has pressured divisional managers to sanction dubious if not illegal production or marketing practices. Even corporation departments may keep secrets from each other if this protects them from top management criticism or enables them to achieve their own specific goals free of interference by other departments.

More familiar to us is the role that government secrecy plays in both the internal and external politics of states. Modern states, whether totalitarian or democratic, justify secrecy as necessary for efficient government, to protect national security, and as a means to discover and control domestic groups which threaten state security.

Whatever the necessary functions of government secrecy may be, it is obvious that secrecy also provides a cloak behind which forbidden acts, legal violations, evasion of responsibility, inefficiency, and corruption are well concealed (Simmel, 1950). The executive branch of modern states often uses the requirements for state secrecy as a device to hide such illegality and corruption (Reese, 1977). Closed sessions by legislative bodies may hide the influence of powerful interest groups on lawmakers' legislative decisions.

In general, Rigney (1975) is quite correct when he suggests

that "forms of secrecy that characterize private organizations are not markedly different from those that characterize governmental organization." As among the specialized divisions of a corporation, so do government agencies compete fiercely for money. They keep hidden secret information which would damage their budget claims (Wilensky, 1967; Rigney, 1975). The hierarchical organization of government bureaucracies prevents the downward flow of damaging information that would threaten the position of agency heads who must maintain the mystique of superior administrative leadership, and the upward flow of information that would subject experts to criticism or reveal the mismanagement and violation of formal and informal rules at the lower levels (Wilensky, 1967; Rigney, 1975).

Each state also conducts its political transactions with similar political units in terms of its own self-interests. The usual mistrust and rivalry that marks such interstate relationships makes secrecy an inevitable factor in such intercommunity affairs. The major concern of the government, in this instance, is with the protection of military, political, or economic information useful to the rival or enemy community. Such "state secrets" must be protected from the espionage of enemy states.

SECURITY SYSTEMS

No matter for what objective or motive, calculated concealment by secret sharers necessitates the establishment of a security system, whether simple or elaborate, sophisticated or unsophisticated.

No matter who shares secrets and no matter how close and trusted their relationship may be, there is always the "temptation of betrayal." Group members who develop bonds of mutual loyalty pose less security risks for organizations than those groups in which morale is low, and dissension and conflict prevail. Security systems may require tests of loyalty for new members, total obedience to the secret group at the expense of other social ties, only gradual revelation of secrets to members, and the imposition of strict norms of silence and taciturnity (Simmel, 1950).

Members of kin or friendship groups are less likely to divulge secrets to outsiders for economic or political motives. But secret associations must deal with the ever-present danger of member disloyalty for these reasons.

To assure member loyalty, criminal gangs such as the Chauffers of Italy and the Thugs of India only initiated their own children or adopted children (Annan, 1967a; Heckethorn, 1965). The I-Kuan-Tao society of China recruited entire families (Deliusin, 1972). More modern secret orders have organized juvenile and female auxiliaries to draw members' families under effective control of the male parent organization (Gist, 1940). In this way kinship loyalties reinforce secret society loyalties.

In some cases, however, members of secret associations must disavow kinship loyalties in order that they may give undivided loyalty to the society itself. In these cases the society investigates the character and background of the potential member before admitting them (Davis, 1971; Daraul, 1961).

Not all secret organizations can initiate only close kinsmen or engage in elaborate screening. Thus, before initiates are entrusted with crucial secrets they must go through a period of trial. Unreliable initiates will never advance to the stage where the best-guarded secrets will be transmitted to them (Simmel, 1950; Gist, 1938a). Through this process secrets are revealed only by degrees. For example, the Haiti Bizango society subjected initiates to tests as well as secret surveillance (Laguerre, Chapter 6 in this book).

Periodic meetings, initiation rituals or religious ceremonies serve to reaffirm the unity of the group, the loyalty of its members, and the purposes for which it was formed. For example, Chinese secret association rituals not only dramatized the ideology and history of the organizations, but also, through the drama of ritual death and rebirth, impressed upon the initiate the idea that he was entering a world quite apart from that outside the society, a world which had prior claims on his loyalties (Davis, 1971).

Any dissention within a secret society would, of course, be dangerous, for such conflict could easily create resentments that might ultimately lead to a breakdown in internal security. One way of preventing this is illustrated by a technique used within the above-mentioned Assassin organization: Members were required to refrain from overt expressions of doubt about the organization's beliefs; an initiate was expected to communicate any such doubts to his teacher alone. This rule helped preserve unity by preventing ideological debates between members as well as enabling teachers better to indoctrinate the initiates (Keightley, 1864).

In a similar fashion modern corporations show great concern

about employer loyalty. Since intercorporate employee mobility is great, short-term employees may prove security risks in that, lacking strong ties to their current company, they may leak secrets to rival companies as a means of increasing their job chances with the competitor (Rourke, 1961). Thus surveillance of employees continues even after they have been hired (aftercare).

But top management also often uses internal espionage against company unions or worker staff committees in order to garner advance information about the feelings and attitudes of employees, or advance warning about strike issues (Smith, 1970).

Government bureaucracies use much the same security techniques as many private organizations. These include secrecy classifications, screening and security clearances for potential employees, indoctrination, oaths of loyalty (sometimes), severe penalties for unauthorized disclosure, and continued surveillance of employees once hired ("aftercare") (Rigney, 1975). Within the executive branch only the most trusted officials may be privy to the totality of some secret plans or activities, while others know only small details rather than the whole picture. Still others gain access to certain details on a need-to-know basis (Rigney, 1975).

Various forms of deception may be used to protect strategic secrets from outsiders. The lie is one technique wherein blatant falsehoods are disseminated to cover up true purposes and activities. The secret sharers may also divluge certain "free" secrets (regulated disclosures), such as information about certain rituals, giving the impression to outsiders that such innocent activities are the primary purpose for which the group was organized. The success of such deceptions rely on the persuasive capabilities of the secret sharers, that is, their ability to convince outsiders that the transmitted information is believable (Wilsnack, 1979).

The deceptions used to protect private-life secrets are much the same in both tribal and urban society: lies, "covers," and cover stories are used. For example, Mechinaku Indian lovers of central Brazil pretend they are pursuing innocent activities to cover up their secret extramarital trysts in the jungle (Gregor, Chapter 3 in this book). In like fashion, lesbians, when operating in the straight world, pretend to be heterosexuals ("passing") (Ponse, 1976). In modern urban society, the greater possibility for anonymity makes such deception much easier than in the tribal community.

Secret societies require even stricter secrecy than stigmatized groups. However, even secret organizations use various strategies to disguise their true goals or activities. Some secret societies seek to avoid political persecution by identifying themselves with acceptable social goals. Thus some Chinese clandestine orders, subject to suppressive measures by the government authorities, began to call themselves Chinese Masons as a means to escape the ban on all secret associations (Lyman, 1964). Other Chinese secret associations, during periods when the Chinese state was especially powerful, disguised themselves as friendship clubs or mutual aid societies.

Of course, some organizations disguise their illegal activities by making public certain "free secrets" as a means to delude the public into believing that their activities are both legal and harmless. The modern Ku Klux Klan, for example, publicized certain initiation rituals as a device, no doubt, to convince the public that their organization had chiefly religious ends, hoping to cover up its more illicit and violent goals (Schaefer, Chapter 7 in this book).

Modern governments, however, whether democratic or totalitarian, have even greater capabilities than secret societies to disseminate false information about their activities, intentions, or goals. Often the media are useful allies in a government's attempt to deceive its citizens. While, in democratic states the media has often been a strong advocate of public disclosure by government bodies, the media, also, on other occasions, has, knowingly or unknowingly become tools of government propaganda. During the Yom Kippur War of 1973, for example, the Israeli press, long conditioned to cooperate with the army in national security matters, accepted and published the military's optimistic assessment of the fighting. In reality the Israeli army was suffering heavy casualties and once the public learned the true facts, the government, the press, and the military lost credibility of the public (Goren, 1977).

The complex politics of international relations also require many forms of deception. The espionage activities of modern governments provide one example. The identities of agents in foreign countries are disguised by providing them with the proper covers. Not only do embassies provide such covers but also the foreign subsidiaries of multinational corporations. Companies believed to have concealed CIA personnel on their payrolls are International Telephone and Telegraph Corporation and Pan American World Airways, among others. The CIA, under a cover supplied by the AFL-CIO, infiltrated the Chilean labor movement in an attempt to forestall Allende's election (Halperin et al., 1976). The CIA has also created and financed its own foreign businesses to provide covers for its agents in foreign countries (Rositzke, 1977, p. 212).

ESPIONAGE AND EVALUATION

Espionage involves the acquisition of information held secret by another group or individual. By giving advance knowledge of a rival's or enemy's plans or strategies, espionage enables groups or individuals to counteract activities or undermine the goals of the groups with which they are in conflict or competition. Moreover, some secret information gained in this way can serve to inform the secret group of potential or existing threats to its security systems posed by the espionage of its rival. Such counterespionage corrects defects within its existing security system. In other instances, community espionage merely provides information for a neighbor's gossip mill.

The small-scale tribal surveillance systems create a threat to privacy in precisely the same way that large-scale surveillance systems do in modern states. In tribal communities the daily activities and relationships are subject to minute scrutiny. Neighbors closely observe the coming and going of people. Community stability enables members to accumulate mental dossiers covering many intimate details about a community member's life history. For example, Kalahari Bushmen camps (Southwest Africa) provide little opportunity for privacy, since socializing and most sleeping takes place outside the huts at the camp fire. Lee suggests that in the camp "everyone knows everyone else's business (Lee, 1977, p. 378)."

In modern states we find quite the reverse, with small-scale surveillance systems constituting less of a threat to privacy than the large-scale surveillance systems of governmental and private bureaucracies. The mass media and, to a lesser extent, the behavioral researcher pose further threats (Shils, 1975; Rule, 1974). Neighborhood "espionage" has lost the prominent role it enjoyed in tribal life. Modern families lack the deep community roots of the past; friendships are not localized, but dispersed. A mobile population is less subject to local scrutiny (Shils, 1975; Shils, 1966; Rule, 1974).

Nonetheless, modern surveillance systems pose a greater threat to privacy than earlier ones. Computers have enabled private as well as governmental bureaucracies to accumulate and store a vast array of information on citizens' private lives and habits. Individuals have no assurance that such agencies or corporations will not reveal such information to third parties who might use it to further their own political ends (Shils, 1966; Rule, 1974). A further danger is the vulnerability of such computer storage systems to unauthorized access by outsiders (Miller, 1971).

This increase in public surveillance by the modern state has accompanied the growing responsibilities of the state for economic and social welfare of its citizens. As a result of these wide-ranging tasks, the state needs a vast amount of information, research data and documentation about social needs and demands.[4] The collection of such data by state agencies had made it more difficult for citizens to maintain their traditional rights to privacy. In contrast, eighteenth- and nineteenth-century European governments had less responsibility for individual citizens and, in turn, required less detailed information on lives, habits, or needs of their people (Mellors, 1978). Thus, government surveillance was much less intense.

Modern states conduct espionage against many types of secret societies, even the so-called conformative types. Secret societies provoke much government curiosity as well as suspicion. Secrecy, indeed, breeds the suspicion by outsiders that activities that must be hidden are likely illegal or immoral. Moreover, the secret society being a power separate and independent of state government is often considered a threat by political leaders unless they can establish control over it or discover its true plans and have knowledge of its activities.

Much of the espionage is carried out by government agents who join the secret organization in order to keep the police informed about its activities and plans. In some cases such agents act as agent provocateurs, encouraging violent acts or even helping in initiating them to bring discredit on the organization or to enable the authorities to arrest and put in jail the membership for illegal activities. Such agents may also sow dissension and conflict within the organization to weaken it.

In recent years American police agents have often served as agent provocateurs within dissident groups (e.g., FBI agents

[4]In Great Britian the official records systems include: registers of births, marriages and deaths; passports; immigration records; criminal and court records; police files; television and shotgun licenses; driving licenses; Goods vehicle operators list; medical records; dental records; school, college and university records; census data, social security contribution records; income tax records; as well as local government and armed forces records (Mellors, 1978). In the United States there are similar records available. Such records can, and sometimes do, provide government investigations with a vast array of information of the private life and habits of citizens.

within the Ku Klux Klan or the Communist Party (Marx, 1974; Rositzke, 1977).[5] But the use of such agents by governments has a long history. For example, the seventeenth-century British governments under Charles II and James II employed agent provocateurs against antiroyalist groups (Walker, 1932). In like fashion in the nineteenth century, the czarist government sent secret agents to London to join expatriate revolutionary organizations in order to compromise them, so that they would get into trouble with the British authorities and be expelled from Britain (Deacon, 1972).

Surveillance of their activities by state intelligence services or the secret police compels many secret organizations to conduct counterespionage. The Camorra, for example, a Mafia-type society that was a power in eighteenth-century Naples, infiltrated the police force with spies so their leaders could learn beforehand what the police planned against them (Heckethorn, 1965), and the Nian, a Chinese secret society, recruited into their organization low-ranking officers of the imperial army, for similar reasons (Chesneaux, 1973). Some Chinese secret societies, such as the Triads, infiltrated government departments, local magistrates, and even rival secret orders (Davis, 1971). Irish and Russian revolutionaries used similar tactics against their respective governments (Bell, 1971; Deacon, 1969).

Industrial espionage has a long history too. In the past a great deal of foreign industrial espionage has been conducted by private individuals using various legitimate positions or occupations as covers, which enable them to gain access to the secrets. In the eighteenth century French Jesuits stole the secret process of porcelain manufacture from the Chinese; but the British, in turn, stole it from the French through the work of an English agent employed at a French porcelain factory (Smith, 1970). A Britisher, who obtained work in various Swedish ironworks, brought back the secret of the iron-splitting process (Deacon, 1969). And in a similar fashion, another Britisher stole the secrets of Italian silk mill production (Smith, 1970).

Modern industrial espionage is not basically different from these earlier forms, although the agents may be specially trained for their work. Such spies often join an organization as secretaries, clerks, laboratory assistants, and technicians to get

---

[5]Planting or recruiting agents within terrorist groups may prove difficult since such terrorist organizations either operate from secure geographic bases (like the Palestine Liberation Organization) or have no fixed headquarters or visible ties with society (e.g., the Japanese "Red Army").

at specific information for their employer, usually a rival company.

Successful modern industrial espionage produces all sorts of useful information that a rival company may use to advantage: the know-how and details of secret processes and formulas, plans and drawings, specimens, prototypes of machines or apparatus, as well as commercial information involving marketing and sales plans, promotional designs, and so forth (Smith, 1970).

Early states were as interested in the military or political benefits of foreign espionage as modern governments. For example, the Aztecs employed agents who, disguised as traders and speaking the language of the region to which they journeyed, collected vital information for the Aztec rulers (Soustelle, 1962). The use of professional merchants as spies was also a quite common practice of governments in the civilizations of the Middle East, Southern Europe, and Southeast Asia (Berdan, 1975). Carthaginian, Egyptian, Hittite, Assyrian, Greek, Persian, Babylonian, Byzantine, and Roman rulers employed spies for foreign espionage. These were usually individuals who in their official or occupational roles, traveled widely in foreign lands. In some cases they were natives of the territory (Dvörnik, 1974).

It appears that Prussia under Frederick the Great and Bismarck was the first modern European power to use espionage on any vast scale. The Prussians used so-called trash men disguised as peddlers, journeymen, and waiters to infiltrate Austrian, and French military establishments (Cookridge, 1974). Other European powers soon followed their example (Friedrich, 1972; Deacon, 1969, 1972). On the eve of World War I complex espionage and counterespionage networks covered Europe (Ransom, 1968, 1970).

Foreign espionage by modern states serves much the same function today as in earlier times. However, modern intelligence units have become more involved in economic as well as new forms of political and military espionage. For example, the Soviet State Committee for Science and Technology (the Soviet agency dealing with foreign business) has intelligence agents in its employ who covertly try to obtain technical secrets from Western business executives. In addition, Soviet secret police organizations check on Russian emigré groups as well as place Russian diplomatic and commercial personnel under secret observation (Sampson, 1973; Gerson, 1976). The intelligence agencies of Western democracies conduct similar industrial espionage and diplomatic surveillance.

Counterintelligence agencies are responsible for investigating foreign espionage. In the United States, agencies involved in such investigations include the FBI, the army's Counter Intelligence Corps (CIC), and special investigative units within the Postal Service, Federal Communications Commission, Civil Service Commission, and the Treasury, Commerce, and Interior departments. The British Special Branch of Scotland Yard and MI-5 perform similar roles as does the Soviet MVD (Ministry of Internal Affairs) plus other unknown counterintelligence units (Barghoorn, 1971).[6] The work of counterintelligence or counterespionage agents involves a wide variety of tasks, including checking on reported disaffection cases (employees with grudges against a government organization or personnel with big financial problems), suspected leaks, routine surveillance of embassies or diplomatic residences, and suspicious incidents such as missing documents that might indicate espionage (Copeland, 1974). Counterespionage also aims at recruiting agents within enemy espionage organizations. Such organizations are vulnerable to penetration at various levels including the headquarters staff itself (Rositzke, 1977).

The great concern for state security within totalitarian systems obliterates the distinction between internal and external intelligence. Foreign intelligence is combined with domestic counterespionage. Such distinctions between internal and external intelligence operations also become hazy in democratic societies during periods of major international crisis, war, or periods of political paranoia generated by hyperpatriotism and xenophobia. During these periods, intelligence agencies are quite capable of utilizing the same espionage techniques employed in foreign espionage against their own citizens.

Historical evidence seems to support the view that intelligence services, whatever their nature, are usually co-opted by political leaders for internal surveillance in addition to their role in foreign espionage. The Assyrian kings employed a group called *angaros,* not only for royal messengers but also as secret police to spy on political opponents (Dvörnik, 1974). In the second century A.D. intelligence agents (*frumentarii*) served the Roman emperors by spying on political rivals and officials. They also played a leading role in persecution of Christians. Later in their cover role as couriers, the *frumen-*

---

[6]The Ministry of Internal Affairs (MVD) and the Committee of State Security (KGB) have been preceded in the course of Soviet intelligence history by the Cheka, CPU, OGPU, KNVP, NKGR, MVD, MGB, and MOOP.

tarii engaged in the surveillance of ordinary Roman citizens (Dvörnik, 1974). It is interesting to note that *frumentarii* were originally a special military intelligence detachment of the Roman legions who were co-opted by Roman authorities for other functions. In effect they remained soldiers "trained in military intelligence, (but) borrowed by the central and provincial authorities for special purposes which they could accomplish more effectively than the ordinary police or the regular army (Dvörnik, 1974).

In the Soviet Union, the CPU and OGPU, offspring of Lenin's first secret police organization, the VCheka, were concerned not only with counteracting foreign espionage within the USSR and conduting Soviet espionage abroad (including spying on Russian emigré colonies and Soviet diplomatic and commerical representatives) but also destroying underground opposition movements and political parties and keeping watch on all commercial and industrial establishments within the USSR to make sure they did not disobey the economic laws and regulations or fail to meet required production quotas. Even today the Soviet KGB (Committee for State Security) is more concerned that its Western European and American counterparts in investigating ideological subversion, political crimes, and economic crimes. The role it plays in investigating such crimes is the basis of its powerful position in the Soviet political, legal, and administrative structures (Gerson, 1976; Lane, 1971).

Espionage may provide unreliable information. Intelligence agents may lie, exaggerate, misperceive, or assess improperly the significance of the facts they collect. Enemy counterespionage may be responsible for the dissemination of false information. Agents often betray their employers for political or economic motives. Under these circumstances a constant evaluation of intelligence information is necessary. But accurate assessment, in turn, rests on more secret information being obtained from a rival. Thus, espionage seems to generate the need for more espionage (Marx, 1974; Wilensky, 1967; Wilsnack, 1979).

POST-HOC SECURITY

Regardless of the effectiveness of the security measures, sooner or later unregulated disclosure takes place. Protection, as Simmel (1950) suggests is never complete; at best, it is only partially successful. The tension between those who hold secrets in common and the unknowning outsiders makes this inevitable. Such disclosure may or may not prove detrimental to the secret sharers, both insiders and outsiders may exaggerate the value or the importance of the concealed facts. The unregulated disclosure of subjectively valued secrets will usually not be as damaging as the revelation of secrets that enable the outsiders to discredit, destroy, or manipulate more effectively the secret order or group (Simmel, 1950; Pétursson, 1977).

However, if secrets are uncovered, a group may employ post-hoc security measures or post-hoc deceptions, either to soften the effects of disclosure or to prevent further disclosure (Rigney, 1975). For example, most secret associations react to breaches of security by improvement of security techniques, going further underground and hiding the very existence of the society, further deception through propaganda aimed at creating an image of the society as one supportive of status quo values and institutions, public lies covering the true nature of organizational goals, conversion of secret agents to their cause, and use of such agents to spread misinformation to their enemies.

Corporations react much as secret associations when some well-guarded secrets become public. For example, ITT used a variety of post-hoc security devices when its intrigues in Chile were revealed. ITT officials disclaimed that certain damaging documents had the significance attributed to them by government investigators. They also put out cover stories to disguise the true intent of certain illegal plans and proposals. Company officials further claimed they could not recall certain events that had occurred several years earlier. ITT management, when confronted with damaging documents by Senate investigators, reinterpreted them in such a way as to give them an innocent significance (Rigney, 1975).

Major government security failures may lead to executive pressure for more extensive internal surveillance of government officials. The leakage of dark secrets may force government officials to use post-hoc security strategies in face of legislative investigations, including prevarication, misrepresentation, and the "You did not ask me the right question, so I did not give you the right answer" game. Stonewalling is another favorite tactic. Here executive officers delay in responding to congressional committee requests for information or in testifying before such committees, the press of other business always justifying their delay (Dorsen & Gillers, 1974).

CONCLUSION

Secrecy, then, is an inherent part of many social and political relationships and transactions. It always will be because it enables individuals and groups to achieve certain goals. But the secrecy process often promotes maladaptation as well as adaptation. In the long run, this rational social process often proves to be irrational.

For example, secrecy that reduces the accountability of private economic organizations whose actions and policies have profound and widespread effects on public affairs and interests proves maladaptive to the society. The secrets maintained by large national and international corporations do give such economic organizations powerful economic and political advantages over not only their smaller rivals but also other interest groups trying to influence governmental policy. The fact that the more powerful corporations share many secrets with government agencies makes them privy to much valuable economic information not available to smaller and less influential rivals, information vital to profitable business investment of capital (Nadel, 1975). Further, these special ties with government give the heads of such corporations highly profitable knowledge about stocks and taxes not available to outsiders (Nadel, 1975). Secrecy also enables multinational corporations to shift huge sums of money freely in and out of countries, often to the detriment of the countries in which they have made hugh profits (Sampson, 1973).

The public too may be injured, directly or indirectly by corporation concealments. Corporation scientists may hide the fact that new products may have undesirable effects on the environment or are defective, thereby constituting a health hazard to the consumers. Complex accounting practices may enable corporation executives to justify price increases when these were not really necessary, given the corporation's actual profits (O'Connell, Chapter 10 in this book). And often business secrecy enables these large-scale private concerns to hide illegal or highly dubious business practices.

Corporations may withold data from both the government and the public that is vital in future economic planning (e.g., oil companies refused to give the government their reserve and production data (O'Connell, Chapter 10 in this book).

Both public and private bureaucracy seems to generate forms of internal secrecy that make for inefficiency and conflict. Poor performances by employees are concealed from top administrators. Compartmentalization promotes divisional secrecy that undermines the overall coordination and planning within corporations, government agencies, or government as a whole. Much time is wasted in giving trivial data top secret classifications. In an atmosphere of secrecy, rumors replace more rational and open means of internal communication.

We must keep in mind, however, that secrecy has promoted inefficiency in small-scale industries as well as large; for example, competition between Newfoundland fishing trawler skippers necessitates mutual deception about catch size, even among captains working for the same processing companies. Such secrecy promotes inefficiency in the integration and use of expensive capital equipment and manpower (Andersen, Chapter 9 in this book).

Political leaders choose between alternative courses of action to solve problems or meet crisis situations. But when governmental decisions are made in secret by a restricted body of political leaders, this secrecy increases the chances that more desirable alternatives will be ignored; or that when decisions are made, they will be less effectively carried out. The decisions made by modern leaders are based on much complex and technical information, information not necessary in the decision-making of tradition rulers. Executive secrecy may close off the valuable expertise of excluded officials, experts, or agencies. Subject to no outside evaluation, these secret decision-makers may make policies that are based on wrong or distorted information. They may ignore other alternatives that might prove to be more effective. Executive secrecy, therefore, makes constructive criticism by knowledgeable outsiders impossible (Curzon, 1977; Wilensky, 1967, Nadel, 1975; Halperin & Stone, 1974; Christoph, 1975a, 1975b; Griffith, 1974).

In addition, government secrecy, like corporation secrecy, may enable political leaders or government agencies to cover up mistakes and violate laws in the interests of political and economic expediency. Secrecy also enables political leaders to conceal the fact that their political decisions were made to further personal interests or those of political allies at the expense of the public interest (Curzon, 1977; Rourke, 1975, 1977).

The pervasive concern that modern states display over national security has generated large-scale intelligence organizations that conduct internal as well as external espionage to protect state secrets. Through their foreign operations, they often have undermined foreign policy initiatives of the governments they supposedly protect. The internal security required by such vast intelligence bureaucracies to protect themselves from enemy infiltration as well as betrayal by their own employees produced many of the same dysfunctions that characterize other government and private bureaucracies. For instance, internal security often prevents the flow of vital information within the organization, undermining the formulation of successful policies and operations (Wilensky, 1967).

Another inherent danger characteristic of intelligence agencies is that, immersed in a world deception and secrecy, they come to form a closed society with few links to the real world. They create their own moral and legal codes, codes quite different from those of the nation whose interests they defend. Such intelligence morality may justify all sorts of illegal or, at best, questionable activities (Schlesinger, 1977).

In the long run, then, we must evaluate the consequences of secrecy in terms of its impact on the social processes promoting societal adaptation and change. The social process involves a constant reassessment of existing coping strategies, based in part on traditional precedents and perspectives and in part on a consideration of the nature of the threat to existing strategies. Secrecy proves to be maladaptive for society when it prevents a consideration of alternative strategies and a realistic evaluation of the opportunity costs of such strategies, that is, assessments of the emotional, social, and economic costs of changing from old strategies to new ones. Secrecy may also prove to be maladaptive when it restricts knowledge about the short- and long-term consequences for the community in continuing existing strategies.

The success of government in maintaining the loyalty of its citizens as well as eliciting their support for its programs and policies rests, to a large degree, on social trust. The spread of deception throughout societal institutions by imitation of or in retaliation for government secrecy promotes the kind of citizen cynicism that undermines the normal political process (Bok, 1978).

The loss of public trust threatens a policy in the same way as the loss of vital material resources. The erosion of public confidence in government makes it difficult, if not impossible, for political leaders to mobilize effectively the populace to respond to adaptive crises faced by the society (e.g., war, loss of vital resources, pollution). Thus, the costs of political secrecy seem greater than its benefits, if judged by its ultimate maladaptive consequences for the state and its citizens.

References

Annan, D. Thuggee. In *Secret Societies* (edited by N. MacKenzie). New York: Collier Books, 1967.(a)

Annan, D. The Assassins and the Knights Templar. In *Secret Societies* (edited by N. MacKenzie). New York: Collier Books, 1967.(b)

Barghoorn, F. C. The security police. In *Interest Groups in Soviet Politics* (edited by N. G. Skilling and F. Griffith). Princeton, N.J.: Princeton University Press, 1971.

Bates, A. P. Privacy—A useful concept? *Social Forces,* 1964, *42,* 429–434.

Bell, J. B. *The Secret army.* New York: John Day, 1971.

Bennett, J. W. *The ecological transition: Cultural anthropology and human adaptation.* New York: Pergamon Press, 1967.(a)

Bennett, J. W. Anticipation, adaptation and the concept of culture in anthropology. *Science,* 1967, *192,* 847–852. (b)

Berdan, F. M. J. *Trade, tribute and market in the Aztec Empire.* Ph.D. dissertation. University of Texas: Austin, 1975.

Bhuntani, S. *Secret society system among the American Indians and the Africans.* Master of Arts Thesis. Chapel Hill: University of North Carolina, 1962.

Bianco, L. Secret societies and peasant self-defense, 1921–1923. In *Popular Movements and Secret Societies in China, 1840–1950.* (edited by J. Chesneaux). Stanford, Calif.: Stanford University Press, 1972.

Boak, A. E. R. Guilds: Late Roman and Byzantium. In *Encyclopaedia of the Social Sciences* (edited by E. R. Seligman). New York: Macmillan, 1932.

Boas, F. *The social organization and the secret societies of the Kwakiutl Indians.* New York: Johnson Reprint Corporation, 1970.

Bok, S. *Lying.* New York: Pantheon, 1978.

Bryant, C. G. A. Privacy, privatisation, and self-determination. In *Privacy* (edited by J. B. Young). New York: Wiley, 1978.

Chesneaux, J. *Secret societies in China.* London: Heinemann, 1971.

Chesneaux, J. Secret societies in China's historical evolution. In *Popular Movements and Secret Societies in China 1840–1950* (edited by J. Chesneaux). Stanford, Calif.: Stanford University Press, 1972.

Chesneaux, J. *Peasant revolts in China, 1840–1949.* New York: Norton, 1973.

Christoph, J. B. A comparative view: Administrative secrecy in Britain. *Public Administrative Review,* 1975, *25,* 23–32. (a)

Christoph, J. B. High civil servants and the politics of consensualism in Great Britain. In *Mandarins: The Political Role of the High Civil Servants* (edited by M. Pogan). New York: Wiley, 1975. (b)

Comber, L. F. *Chinese secret societies of Malaya* (Monographs of the Association for Asian Studies, No. 6). Locust Valley, N.Y.: J. J. Augustin, 1959.

Cookridge, E. S. *Gehlen: Spy of the century.* New York: Random House, 1974.

Copeland, M. *Without cloak or dagger.* New York: Simon and Schuster, 1974.

Curzon, D. The Generic secrets of government decision making. In *Government secrecy in democracies* (edited by I. Galnoor). New York: Harper and Row, 1977.

Daraul, A. *A history of secret societies.* New York: Citadel Press, 1961.

Davis. F. *Primitive revolutionaries of China.* Honolulu: University Press of Hawaii, 1971.

Deacon, R. *A history of the British secret service.* New York: Taplinger, 1969.

Deacon, R. *A history of the Russian secret service.* New York: Taplinger, 1972.

Deacon, R. *The Chinese secret service.* New York: Ballantine Books, 1974.

Deliusin, L. The I-Kuan-Tao Society. In *Popular movements and secret societies in China, 1840–1950* (edited by J. Chesneaux). Stanford, Calif.: Stanford University Press, 1972.

Dorsen, N. and Fillers, S. (editors). *None of your Business.* New York: Viking, 1974.

Drucker, P. *Cultures of the North Pacific Coast.* San Francisco: Chandler Publishing, 1965.

Dvörnik, F. *Origins of intelligence services.* New Brunswick, N.J.: Rutgers University Press, 1974.

Ford, C. *Smoke from their fires.* New Haven, Conn.: Yale University Press, 1941.

Fowler, H. and Fowler, F. (editors). *The Concise Oxford Dictionary.* Oxford: Claredon Press, Fifth ed., 1964.

Friedrich, C. L. *The pathology of politics.* New York: Harper and Row, 1972.

Gerson, L. D. *The secret police in Lenin's Russia.* Philadelphia: Temple University Press, 1976.

Gist, N. P. Culture patterning in secret society ceremonials. *Social Froces,* 1936, *14,* 497–505.

Gist, N. P. Structure and process in secret societies. *Social Forces,* 1938, 16, 349–57. (a)

Gist, N. P. Dogma and doctrine in secret societies. *Society and Social Research,* 1938, *23,* 121–30. (b)

Gist, N. P. *Secret societies: A cultural study of fraternalism in the United States* (The University of Missouri Studies 15), 1940.

Goren, D. *Secrecy, the right to know and the news.* Unpublished manuscript, 1977.

Griffith, J. A. G. Government secrecy in the United Kingdom. In *None of Your Business* (edited by N. Dorsen and S. Gilers). New York: Viking, 1974.

Gunther, E. *Klallam ethnography.* University of Washington Publications in Anthropology, 1927, *I*, 171–314.

Halperin, M. H. et al. *The lawless state.* New York: Penguin, 1976.

Halperin, M. H. and Stone, J. J. Secrecy and covert intelligence collection and operations. In *None of Your Business* (edited by N. Dorsen and S. Gillers), 105–135. New York: Viking, 1974.

Hazelrigg, L. E. Reexamination of Simmel's *The Secret and the secret society:* Nine propositions. *Social Forces,* 1969, *47,* 323.

Heckethorn, C. *The secret societies of all ages and countries,* New Hyde Park, N.Y.: Universal Books, Vols. I&II, 1965.

Hoffer, C. P. Mende and Sherbro women in high office. *Canadian Journal of African Studies,* 1972, *6,* 151–165.

Keightley, T. *Secret societies of the Middle Ages.* London: Nattali, 1964.

Kelvin, P. A socio-psychological examination of privacy. *Journal of Social and Clinical Psychology,* 1973, *12,* 248–261.

Koch, K. F. Sociogenic and psychogenic models in anthropology: The function of Jale initiation. *Man,* 1974, *9,* 367–372.

Lane, D. *Politics and society in the USSR.* New York: Random House, 1971.

Lee, R. B. The !Kung San: A hunting and gathering community. In *The study of cultural anthropology* (edited by D. E. Hunter and P. Whitten). New York: Harper and Row, 1977.

Liebenow, J. G. Liberia. In *Political parties and national integration in tropical Africa* (edited by J. S. Coleman and C. G. Rosberg). Berkeley: University of California Press, 1964.

Little, K. L. The Poro Society as an arbiter of culture. *African Studies,* 1948, *7,* 2–15.

Lyman, Stanford M. Chinese Secret Societies in the Occident: Notes and Suggestions for Research in the Sociology of Secrecy. *The Canadian Review of Sociology and Anthropology,* 1964, 1, 79–102.

Lyman, Stanford M. *The Asian in the West* (Social Science and Humanities Publication No. 4), Western Studies Center. Desert Research Institute. University of Nevada, Reno and Las Vegas, Nevada, 1970.

McCartney, D. The church and secret societies. In *Secret Societies in Ireland.* (edited by D. Williams). New York: Barnes and Noble, 1973.

Marx, G. Thoughts on a neglected category of social movement participant: The agent provacateur and the informant. *American Journal of Sociology,* 1974, *80,* 402–420.

Massignon, L. Guilds: Islamic. In *Encyclopaedia of the Social Sciences* (edited by E. R. Seligman). New York: Macmillan, 1932.

Mellors, C. Government and the individual—Their secrecy and his privacy. In *Privacy* (Edited by J. B. Young). New York: Wiley, 1978.

Miller, A. R. *The assault on privacy.* Ann Arbor: University of Michigan Press, 1971.
Moore, W. E. *The conduct of the corporation.* New York: Random House, 1962.
Moore, W. E. & Tumin, M. Some social functions of ignorance. *American Sociological Review,* 1949, *14,* 787–795.
Morton-Williams, P. The Yoruba Ogboni cult in Oyo. *Africa,* 1960, *30,* 362–372.
Murphy, W. P. *A semantic and logical analysis of Kpelle proverb metaphors of secrecy.* Ph.D. dissertation: Stanford University, 1976.
Nadel, M. V. Corporate secrecy and political accountability. *Public Administration Review,* 1975, *35,* 14–23.
O'Brien, D. M. *Privacy: purposes and paradoxes.* In press, 1977.
Passin, H. Tarahumara prevarication: A problem in field method. *American Anthropologist,* 1942, *44,* 235–247.
Patterson, F. Conversations with a gorilla. *National Geographic,* 1978, *154,* 438–367.
Pétursson, P. *The function of secrecy in rational behavior* (Research Policy Program), Unpublished manuscript. University of Lund, Sweden, 1977.
Ponse, B. Secrecy in the Lesbian world. *Urban Life,* 1976, *5,* 313–337.
Ransom, H. H. Intelligence, political and military. In *International Encyclopaedia of the Social Sciences* (edited by D. L. Sills). New York: Free Press-Macmillan, 1968.
Ransom, H. H. *The intelligence establishment.* Cambridge, Mass.: Harvard University Press, 1970.
Reese, J. The Federal Republic of Germany. In *Government secrecy in democracies* (edited by I. Galnoor). New York: Harper and Row, 1977.
Rigney, D. C. *Organizational secrecy. An investigation of hidden realities.* Ph.D. dissertation. The University of Texas, Austin, 1975.
Rositzke, H. *The C.I.A.'s secret operations.* New York: Readers Digest Press, 1977.
Roberts, J. M. *The mythology of the secret societies.* New York: Scribners, 1972.
Rourke, F. E. *Secrecy and publicity.* Baltimore: John Hopkins Press, 1961.
Rourke, F. E. Administrative secrecy: A comparative perspective. *Public Administrative Review,* 1975, *35,* 1–2.
Rourke, F. E. The United States. In *Government secrecy in democracies* (edited by I. Galnoor). New York: Harper and Row, 1977.
Rule, J. B. *Private lives and public surveillance.* New York: Shocken Books, 1974.
Sampson, A. *The sovereign state of ITT.* New York: Stein and Day, 1973.
Schlesinger, A. M., Jr. Introduction. *The C.I.A.'s Secret Operations* (by H. Rositzke). New York: Readers Digest Press, 1977.

Schneider, C. D. *Shame, exposure and privacy.* Boston: Beacon Press, 1977.
Senior, H. *Orangeism in Ireland and Britain: 1795–1836.* London: Routledge and Kegan Paul, 1966.
Senior, H. The early Orange Order 1795–1870. In *Secret Societies in Ireland* (edited by T. D. Williams). New York: Barnes and Noble, 1973.
Shils, E. Privacy: Its constitution and vicissitudes. *Law and Contemporary Problems,* 1966, *31,* 281–306.
Shils, E. *Center for periphery: Essays in macrosociology.* Chicago: University of Chicago Press, 1975.
Simmel, G. The society of secrecy and the secret society (translated by A. W. Small). *American Journal of Sociology,* 1906, *11,* 441–498.
Simmel, G. *The sociology of Georg Simmel* (edited and translated by K. H. Wolff). New York: Free Press, 1950.
Smart, N. The mysteries. In *Secret societies* (edited by N. MacKenzie). New York: Collier Books, 1967.
Smith, P. S. *Industrial intelligence and espionage.* London: Business Books, 1970.
Soustell, J. *The daily life of the Aztecs.* New York: Macmillan, 1962.
Tanner, N. and Zihlman, A. Discussion paper: The evolution of human communication: What primates can tell us. *New York Academy of Sciences,* 1976, *280,* 467–480.
Walker, J. The secret service Under Charles II and James II. *Transactions of the Royal Historical Society,* 1932, *115,* 211–235.
Wallerstein, I. Voluntary associations. In *Political parties and national integration in tropical Africa* (edited by J. S. Coleman and C. G. Rosberg, Jr.). Berkeley: University of California Press, 1964.
Webster, H. *Primitive secret societies: A study of early politics and religion.* New York: Macmillan, 1908.
Wedgwood, C. H. The nature and functions of secret societies. *Oceania,* 1930, *1,* 124–141.
Whalen, W. J. *Handbook of secret organizations.* Milwaukee: Bruce Publishing, 1966.
White, T. de V. The Freemasons. In *Secret societies in Ireland* (edited by T. D. Williams). New York: Barnes and Noble, 1973.
Wilensky, H. L. *Organizational intelligence.* New York: Basic Books, 1967.
Wilsnack, R. Information Control: A Conceptual Framework for Sociological Analysis. *Urban Life,* 1979 (In Press).

Index

Accounting procedures, and regulation of business, 234–235
Advertising, governmental restrictions on, 239
Alienative secret orders, 324
Anaconda Co., 234
Audibility, Mehinaku, 83–85

Bacon, Mary, 170
Baker, Howard, 231
Bizango, *see* Voodoo secret society
Blau, Peter, 44, 45
Bryant v. *Zimmerman,* 164
Bureaucracy
 conflict in, 60–63
 secrecy in, 44–45
Business secrecy, 56–57, 229–231
 and internal and external regulation, 234–239
 policy considerations, 239–242

Canal, Carlos M., 238
Center for Research in Social Systems (CRESS), 299
Central Intelligence Agency (CIA), as complex adaptive system, 48–49, 331–332
 See also Intelligence community
Ceremonial organization, Pueblo society, 135–137
Churchill, Winston, 302
Clarke, Edward Young, 163
Coadventureship and vertical integration, trawler fishing, 217–224
Competition, secrecy, and power, 231–234
Complex adaptive system theory, disclosure, and secrecy, 47–49
Concealment, in trawler fishing transactions, 206–207
Conflict theory, disclosure, and secrecy, 49–63
Conformative secret ordres, 324–325
Conspiratorial military group, 178–179
 and dilemmas of secrecy, 182–184
 and equality, 184–187

348 · INDEX

ideology, 193–194
and interest groups, 192–193
leadership, 190–192
organization, 189–190
recruitment, 187–189
strategies and tactics, 194–195
Cooperative transactions, trawler fishing, 211–213
Copeland, Miles, 276
on CIA, 184–185
Coup, in military conspiracy, 195
Cox, Arthur, on CIA, 283
Credit, and regulation of business, 237–239
Cross-cutting societies, Pueblo, 135–137
Cultural values, and regulation of business, 236
Cultural, guilt vs. shame, 112

Deviance, and secrecy, 46
Disclosure and secrecy
and complex adaptive system theory, 47–49
and conflict theory, 49–53
and exchange theory, 42–45
and functional theory, 45–47
and social theory, 35–38
and symbolic interactionism, 38–42
Displacement, and military conspiracy, 194
Distrust perspective, and police planning for political convention, 252–254
Dulles, Allen, on CIA, 279, 281–282, 285–286

Ellsberg, Daniel, 297
Environmental uncertainty, and police planning for political convention, 256–260
Equality, in conspiratorial military group, 184–187

Espionage, 57–60, 332–337
historical evidence, 337–338
See also Intelligence community
Evening rallies, Voodoo secret society, 153–155
Exchange theory, disclosure, and secrecy, 42–45
Exposure, Mehinaku
and accessibility to social engagement, 87–90
observability, audibility, and gossip, 82–87
and seclusion, 95–97
and study of small societies, 97–98

Family, social conflict, 51
See also Privacy and secrecy
Federal Bureau of Investigation, see Intelligence community
Fishing, see Trawler fishing
Ford, Gerald, 234
France, attitudes toward privacy in village, 103–113
Functional theory, disclosure, and secrecy, 45–47

Gays, 40, 323, 330
See also Privacy and secrecy
Goffman, Erving, 41–42, 173
Gossip, Mehinaku, 85–87
Government
and business secrecy, 56–57
espionage by, 57–60
regulation of business, 234–239
See also Intelligence community
Greenspan, Alan, 234–235
Group, *see* Conspiratorial military group
Gulf Oil Corp., 235, 236–237

Haiti, *see* Voodoo scret society
Handshake, Voodoo secret society, 154

Helms, Richard, on CIA, 280
Hersey, John, 234
Homans, George, 42, 43
Hoover, J. Edgar, 61

Identity, communal, intelligence community, 281–282
Ideology, conspiratorial military group, 193–194
Independence, and privacy in French village, 106
Initiation
  Pueblo society, 137–138
  Voodoo secret society, 151–152
Intelligence community, 273–275
  characteristics, 277–282
  as complex adaptive system, 48–49, 331–332
  contributing factors and conditions, 282–286
  defined, 275–277
Interest groups, and conspiratorial military groups, 192–193
Intimacy and privacy
  in French village, 109–111
  theory and research, 100–103
Iron law of oligarchy, 186
Isolation, Mehinaku, 90–95

Ku Klux Klan
  history, 162–170
  managing secrecy, 170–172
  roles of secrecy, 172–174

Leadership
  conspiratorial military group, 190–192
  kiva, Pueblo society, 138–140
Long, Russell, 241

Magruder, Jeb Stuart, 231
Management
  of secrecy, 170–172
  transactions with skipper, trawler fishing, 209–211
Maroons
  in Haiti, 148–149
  to Voodoo secret society from community of, 155–157
Mehinaku Indians (Brazil), 81–82
  exposure through accessibility to social engagement, 87–90
  exposure through observability, audibility, and gossip, 82–87
  seclusion, 90–95
Military group, *see* conspiratorial military group
Military school system, and politicization, 179–182

NAACP v. *State of Alabama*, 164
New York Times v. *United States*, 300–301
Norms, intelligence community, 277–279

Observability, Mehinaku, 82–83
Organization
  ceremonial, Pueblo society, 135–137
  conspiratorial military group, 189–190
  paramilitary, in police planning for political convention, 260–268
  political, Pueblo society, 140–142
Overseas Private Investment Corp. (OPIC), 234

Paperwork, and regulation of business, 236–237

Paramilitary organization, in police planning for political convention, 260–268
Parsons, Talcott, 45
Passport, Voodoo secret society, 152–153
Pentagon Papers, 297, 300–301
Police planning for political convention, 251–252, 254–256
 distrust perspective, 252–254
 environmental uncertainty, 256–260
 implications, 268–269
 paramilitary organization, 260–268
Policy considerations, and business secrecy, 239–242
Political organization, Pueblo society, 140–142
Politicization, and military school system, 179–182
Power, secrecy, and competition, 231–234
Privacy
 in French village, 103–113
 and intimacy, 100–103
 vs. secrecy, 25–26, 232
Privacy and secrecy
 dimensions, 26–28
 and public order, 28
 structural distribution, 31–32
Private-life secrecy, 29–31
Project CAMELOT, 298, 299
Public-life secrecy, 29–31
Public order, privacy, and secrecy, 28
Pueblo society
 ceremonial organization, 135–137
 consequences of secrecy, 130–135
 initiation, 137–138
 kiva leadership, 53, 138–140
 political organization and process, 140–142
 secrecy in, 123–129
 strategies maintaining secrecy, 129

Quinn, Vincent, 239

Rallies, Voodoo secret society, 153–155
Recruitment, conspiratorial military group, 187–189
Regulation of business, 234–239
Regulatory agencies, 237
Republican National Convention, *see* Police planning for political convention
Rowe, Gary, 170

St. Germain, Fernand, 238
School system, military, and politicization, 179–182
SCM Corp., 236
Seclusion, Mehinaku, 90–95
 and exposure, 95–97
Secrecy
 in business, 229–231
 concept of, 319–321
 consequences of, 130–135
 dilemmas of, 182–184
 management of, 170–172
 need for, 322–328
 power, competition, and, 231–234
 vs. privacy, 25–26, 232
 private-life, public-life, 29–31
 process, 321–322
 in Pueblo society, 123–129
 roles of, 172–174
 and security systems, 297–314
 strategies maintaining, 129
 See also Business secrecy; Disclosure and secrecy; Privacy and secrecy
Secret society, *see* Alienative secret orders; Conformative secret orders; Ku Klux Klan; Pueblo society; Voodoo secret society
Securities and Exchange Commission, 235, 237

Security, post-hoc, 337–338
Security systems, 328–332
  and secrecy, 297–314
Shame and privacy in French
  village, 111–112
Shils, E. B., on dimensions of
  privacy and secrecy, 29–31
Simmel, Georg
  on characteristics of secret
    societies, 170–171
  on secret, 26
  on secret group, 28
Simmons, William Joseph, 163
Skipper-management
  transactions, trawler fishing,
  209–211
Skipper-skipper transactions,
  trawler fishing, 207–209
Skully, Jane, 236–237
Small societies, and exposure,
  97–98
Social engagement, accessibility,
  Mehinaku, 87–90
Social theory, disclosure, and
  secrecy, 35–38
Special Operations Research
  Office (SORO), 298, 299, 302,
  309–312
Stennis, John C., 230
Stewart, Potter, 300
Stimson, Henry L., 161
Strategies and tactics,
  conspiratorial military
  groups, 194–195
Structural distribution, privacy
  and secrecy, 31–32
Stubbornness and privacy in
  French village, 105–106
Supplantment, in military
  conspiracy, 194–195
Suspiciousness (*méfiance*), and
  privacy in French village,
  105, 106
Symbolic interactionism,
  disclosure, and secrecy,
  38–42

Taos Pueblo, *see* Pueblo society
Think tanks, and security
  systems, 298
Trawler fishing, 205–207
  bad breaks in, 215–216
  coadventureship and vertical
    integration, 217–224
  concealment in transactions,
    206–207
  cooperative transactions,
    211–213
  skipper-management
    transactions, 209–211
  skipper-skipper transactions,
    207–209
  uncertainty in, 216–217
  and unequal distribution of
    values, 214–215
Tribal secret societies, 54, 56
Tyler, Elizabeth, 163

Uncertainty, in trawler fishing,
  216–217

Values
  and regulation of business,
    236
  unequal distribution, in
    trawler fishing, 214–215
Vertical integration and
  coadventureship, trawler
  fishing, 217–224
Voodoo secret society, 147–149
  evening rallies, 153–155
  functioning of, 150–153
  from maroon communities to,
    155–157

Weber, Max, 229
Wills, Garry, 276

Xerox Corp., 236